HOW TO DEBATE

A Textbook for Beginners

BY

HARRISON BOYD SUMMERS
Professor of Speech, Ohio State University

FOREST LIVINGS WHAN
Professor of Speech, Kansas State University

THOMAS ANDREW ROUSSE
Late Professor of Speech, University of Texas

Third Edition

THE H. W. WILSON COMPANY
NEW YORK   1963

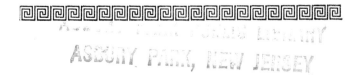

Dedicated to the memory of
THOMAS A. ROUSSE
who died while this revision
was in progress

TO THE INSTRUCTOR

As the title indicates, How To DEBATE is intended as a text-book for the beginning debater. It attempts to present in non-technical language those elements of debate theory and technique which we believe have the greatest practical value for the beginner in the field of formal and informal debate.

In the preparation of this book we have kept two basic aims in mind. First, a serious attempt has been made to discuss debate in such a way that the beginner will understand and appreciate the simple needs involved in the selling of an idea—whether the situation should call for a formal or an informal debate speech. Formal logic, the use of syllogisms, inductive or deductive, and rhetorical theory have not been discussed as such. We have attempted, however, to stress the fundamental methods of reasoning which the student uses in everyday life and with which he is already familiar. Perhaps this oversensitiveness to the nomenclature of formal logic is not justified. We feel, however, that expressions such as "the disjunctive syllogism" or "enthymeme" tend to confuse, and even bewilder, the beginning student of debate. For the beginner, at least, some things are more important; the processes and technical language of formal logic well can wait until the debater has mastered the first and simple rules of argumentation.

Second, a very definite effort has been made to present the subject of debate in a practical manner. Whenever possible the debater has been told what to do and definite procedural steps have been indicated. In this edition, much of the illustrative material has been selected from actual debates or from speeches and articles wherein the speakers and writers were attempting to sell an idea. It is our hope that although the material is not extensive it will prove valuable to the beginning debater. In the illustrations contained in the book, he will have examples of debate speeches to back up the theories.

Finally, it will be noted that the term *discussion* has been used very sparingly in this textbook. Herein is contained our philosophy of the oft-discussed distinction between *discussion* and *debate*. Generally speaking, discussion may be defined as an attempt to arrive at a solution through the cooperative thinking of a group. Debate, on the other hand, attempts to persuade an audience into accepting (or rejecting) a belief. Obviously, both discussion and debate use logic, reasoning, and argumentation. The distinction, however, between these two methods of procedure are real and should be understood by the beginning debater. For example, discussion, through argumentation, attempts to *find the solution,* while debate, having a solution, attempts to sell it to a group. Again, discussion begins with a problem and it attempts through cooperative thinking to find an answer, or more accurately, a solution to that problem. When a solution has been proposed, based upon a pro and con analysis of the problem, an agreement by the group is usually reached on the solution. Debate, on the other hand, would take a proposed solution, presumably one that is not acceptable to all of the people, and attempt to secure acceptance of this proposition. Stated differently, a debate ensues when there is disagreement on a given solution to a given problem. The debater would *sell* his solution to a group. Thus it is possible to have debate *in* a discussion, particularly where disagreement is encountered in the sub-points of a given problem. These sub-points are proposed as concepts and have to be accepted or rejected as such as we attempt to find the solution to the problem under discussion. In short, *debate begins where discussion ends!*

This Third Edition of How To Debate is actually the third revision of a text first published in 1934 under the title *Contest Debating.* The present title was adopted when the original work was extensively revised in 1940.

Throughout the revisions the general plan of the work has remained constant, although attempts to clarify and simplify some of the theory have been made. New illustrative materials have been supplied in each edition. In this edition the materials are reasonably current and are drawn from subjects that may be chosen as debate topics in the near future.

H. B. Summers
F. L. Whan

July 1963

CONTENTS

PART I—DEBATING

WHY DEBATE?

Why debate?

For more than eighty-five years, contest debating has had a place in our system of education. Although the first high school contest is not recorded, intercollegiate debating goes back seventy-one years to a debate between Harvard and Yale, held at Cambridge on January 14, 1892. Since that early contest, debating spread rapidly to every college and to nearly every high school in America. It is estimated that this year more than 72,000 college and a quarter of a million high school young men and women will take part in inter-school debate contests arranged and sponsored by schools, state high school associations, and colleges.

Leading thinkers in the field of education have always encouraged debate. For what reason? From long experience, educators have found that debate is a valuable means of developing the individual student and of training him to meet the problems of life. The student who gives debate his best efforts gains much in return. He learns to use a library, and to find the exact information he needs in the shortest possible time. He learns to be thorough and accurate. He learns to analyze; to distinguish between the vital and the unimportant. He learns the need of proving his statements; of supporting every statement with valid evidence and sound reasoning—and he learns to demand the same sort of proof for the statements of others. He learns to present ideas in a clear and effective manner, and in a way which wins others to his way of thinking. He learns to think under pressure, to "use his head" in a time of need, to make the decisions quickly and accurately. In a word, the essential point in any debating situation is that of convincing the listener that your side of the proposition is desirable. This is true in all types of debate—whether it is a "formal" contest or an informal attempt to *sell* an idea to one or more people. When one participates in contest debating, therefore, he has an opportunity to develop the necessary speaking and persuasive skills so necessary to true leadership.

Of course, the degree in which these benefits are realized depends upon the individual. But that they are inherent in good debating seems beyond question. The proportion of college debaters who win outstanding success in life is much greater than that of college graduates in general. While complete figures are not available, a number of studies suggest debating's value. A 1941 study of Bell Telephone employees found that the highest paid had either debated or served on the school paper. A 1947 poll of debate champions of thirty years found them unanimously in agreement that high school debate is worth while; they unanimously recommended it to modern students and unanimously agreed they would debate again if they could go back to school. A 1950 study of *Who's Who in America* showed that debaters were five times as likely to get into *Who's Who* as were other college graduates. And a 1960 report revealed that twenty-two of twenty-three top executives in International Harvester Company named debate as their most valuable college experience. Such findings are partly due, of course, to the fact that debating attracts the student of unusual ability; but the fact remains that the student who debates receives training of a type that makes for success in life.

Dr. Alexander Meiklejohn, former president of Amherst College and later in charge of the Experimental College at the University of Wisconsin, sums up the case for debate as a factor in education when he says:

As I look back upon my own experience . . . when I try to single out from the long line of students some one group which shall stand forth as intellectually the best—best in college work and best in promise of future intellectual achievement . . . I cannot draw the line around my own favorite students in philosophy, nor the leaders in mathematics, nor those successful in biology; nor could I fairly award the palm to the Phi Beta Kappa men who have excelled in all their subjects.

It seems to me that stronger than any other group, tougher in intellectual fiber, keener in intellectual interest, better equipped to battle with coming problems, are the college debaters—the boys who, apart from their regular studies, band themselves together for intellectual controversy with each other and with their friends in other colleges.[1]

While the value of the training given by debate is beyond question, the activity has a more immediate appeal. It is a battle of wits with worthy opponents; a fight for intellectual supremacy in which victory rests with the warrior who "uses his head" and thinks problems through most effectively. It is a game which calls for special skills and abilities in thinking and in presenting your thought to others. And it is an activity in which you are given an opportunity to exercise the powers of leadership; in which you influence and direct the beliefs of audiences, and bring them to your own point of view concerning vital public questions.

If you are interested in debate, let that interest carry you further; let it lead to active participation. Debating is well worth your time and your energies for the training it gives. But beyond that, you will find debate intensely interesting. You will enjoy the game for its own sake.

[1] From *The Liberal Arts College.* Quoted by permission of Dr. Meiklejohn and of Marshall Jones Co., Inc., publishers.

MODERN DEBATING

When lawyers in the courtroom argue the guilt or innocence of a prisoner on trial, they are engaging in a form of debate. When two political opponents meet in a television series, they are engaged in debate. When our representatives in Congress discuss the merits of some proposed law, they likewise are engaging in debate. And when Mr. Brown and Mr. Smith meet on the street corner and argue with their friends about the merits of a proposed new high school building, or the government debt, or which team will win the World Series, they too are engaging in debate. The individual participant, in other words, is trying to convince a group that his "side" is right and should be accepted. In doing this, the debater argues *from a belief* and attempts to win his audience for his contention. The debater, in short, believes that he knows the answer, and, unlike a person in a discussion (who attempts to *find* the answer to a problem) his job, his desire, is to have this solution adopted. *Debate, therefore, may be defined as an attempt by the participants to persuade the audience to accept (or reject) the resolution under consideration.*[2]

Contest debating. Most of the debates of everyday life are very informal affairs. In our schools and colleges, however, we have developed a more formal type of debate—a contest in which the argument is carried on under a definite set of rules, and which may be referred to as *contest debating*. The rules which govern a contest debate are quite simple; they may be summed up in the seven principles given below:

1. The question for debate is stated in the form of a resolution.

---

[2] See To the Instructor, page 5, for a more detailed distinction between *discussion* and *debate*.

2. Speakers are divided into two teams: an affirmative team which upholds the resolution, and a negative team which opposes it.

3. The number of debaters on each side is the same, and the time allotted each side approximately the same.

4. Each speaker gives an opening or "constructive" speech, and usually a closing speech known as a rebuttal.

5. The two sides alternate in presenting their arguments, with the affirmative opening and closing the debate.

6. A chairman presides over the meeting, and the ordinary rules of parliamentary procedure apply.

7. A winner may be chosen in any of a number of ways, usually by the vote of one or more "judges."

Until thirty or thirty-five years ago, every high school or college debate was a contest for a *decision*. Today, in many high school debates and in an even greater number of college contests, the formal judges' decision is omitted; the chief purpose of the debaters is to win the audience as a whole to some desired point of view. In other debates, the practice of having a decision is retained. But even in these decision contests, the efforts of the speakers are directed toward persuading the audience as well as winning the decision of the judges. After all, the judges *are* members of the audience and must be so considered at all times. No matter which form is used, high school and college debate is still a *contest* between opposing teams; and both the decision and the non-decision types are *contest debates*.

DEVELOPMENT OF CONTEST DEBATING

Contest debating has been carried on in colleges and universities for many years; just how many, it is difficult to estimate. We know that in medieval times, students at the University of Paris were required to present *disputations*—argumentative speeches on philosophical questions, written and delivered in Latin—and that similar discussions were required in leading

universities in England. We know, too, that more than three
centuries ago, students in Oxford and Cambridge took part in
debates—informal, two-sided *contests over propositions or reso-
lutions* selected in advance. And we know that as early as 1800,
students of Oxford University who were members of the Oxford
Union were engaging in a form of debate that met all the requirements of a *modern contest debate*, with a *resolution or
proposition* selected in advance, speakers assigned to support or
to oppose the proposition, the same number of speakers on each
side, and a debate carried on under definite rules. By 1830 or
1840, literary societies modeled after the Oxford Union had been
organized in practically every American university, with formal
contest debates the most important element in their weekly
programs.

Literary society debating. These early literary society debates were very simple affairs. Subjects discussed were quite
different from those used today. "Was there a rainbow before
the deluge?" "Which is the more useful, wood or iron?" and
"Which is the more destructive, fire or water?" are typical of
the questions used. As a rule, four or five speakers were assigned
to each side. Each of these speakers presented a single carefully
memorized constructive speech—a speech prepared in advance,
and delivered exactly as it was prepared without the slightest
effort to adapt or adjust the argument to the speeches presented
by those on the opposite side. Libraries were rare, and those
which did exist contained almost nothing in the way of proof
materials as used by present-day debaters; so the argument presented was based chiefly upon a statement of the speaker's own
opinions. Under the circumstances, the decision of the judges
had to be based almost entirely upon delivery, so that a debate
in the literary society period was little more than an oratorical
contest in which all of the speakers talked on the same general
subject.

The law school influence. As debating became more common in American colleges and universities, important changes
began to be made. Many of the debaters were students in law

schools; and it was only natural that many of the practices of the law courts were gradually introduced into debate. To begin with, a *burden of proof* [3] was placed upon the affirmative, corresponding to the burden upon the prosecution, in a case at law, of proving the defendant guilty. Next, the idea of *proof* was introduced in debate; since the only evidence accepted as valid in the law court was *testimony* of witnesses and the *opinions* of legal experts, *statements of authority* were used to support contentions in contest debates. Third, since in suits at law the opposing attorneys attempted not only to build up their own arguments but also to tear down those presented by their opponents, the use of *rebuttal* or the attacking of opposing arguments became an important element in debate. In the debates held in the period around 1900, each team was given a single *rebuttal speech* in addition to the three constructive speeches allotted the side; and later, a rebuttal speech was given by each of the debaters. From the time that separate rebuttal speeches were introduced, it became a rule of debate that no new or constructive issues could be presented during the rebuttal period.[4]

Two other changes introduced during the "law school" period of debating reflect the influence of legislative discussion rather than of the law court. Questions dealing with the political, social, or economic problems of the day replaced the simpler propositions of the literary school era. And the form in which the proposition for debate was stated was changed

[3] See page 29.

[4] This rule does not follow exactly the procedure of the law court. In legal actions, no new *evidence* may be offered in the summing-up speeches; in formal debate, new evidence may be offered during rebuttal speeches to support or to tear down an issue already introduced by either side, but no new *contention* may be advanced. Stated differently, the affirmative, for instance, because it has the burden of proof, must present its entire constructive case during the *main speeches* of the debate and *defend* the case in the *rebuttal speeches*. New *evidence* to support the issues presented in the first or second main speech of the affirmative would be permissible. But the introduction of *new* issues in the rebuttal speeches would (and should) be considered unethical, because the negative side has a right to assume that new *issues* will not be inserted into the debate *after* the affirmative has finished its constructive argument. Good contest debating calls for adherence to this simple rule and good sportsmanship makes observation of the rule imperative, regardless of the fact that some judges may not know the rule or fail to observe its violation.

from that of a question, to that of a *resolution*: "Resolved,
that . . . ."

Recent changes. Within the past thirty or forty years, still
other changes have taken place in the procedure of contest
debate. The number of speakers has been reduced; at the present time, two-speaker teams are the rule, although in some
sections three speakers are still used on each side. The formal
"oratory" of the early debate speech has largely disappeared in
favor of a conversational, extemporaneous style of speaking.
New types of debate evidence have come into general use; while
opinions of authorities are still used to some extent, debaters
chiefly depend upon factual materials—examples, statistics, and
the like—to prove their contentions. Greater emphasis has
been placed upon rebuttal; in many debates, much of the constructive time will be devoted to refutation in addition to the
time provided for the regular rebuttal speeches. In most sections of the country, the three-judge decision has been replaced
by the decision of a single "expert" judge, chosen for his knowledge of debating and debate techniques; in many debates,
especially in colleges, the decision feature has been eliminated.
And whether a decision is given or not, the chief aim of good
debating has come to be the presentation of arguments which
will win the audience to a desired point of view.

Present-Day Debating

The specific rules governing contest debates in our schools
and colleges vary somewhat in different sections of the country.[5]
Variations are to be found in the number of speakers, the length
of speeches, the number of judges, and the methods of arriving
at a decision. In other respects, however, high school and college debating has become fairly well standardized. The following description of a typical debate may help the beginner in
gaining a knowledge of the more important customs and formalities of contest debating.

[5] See Appendix 5 for an example of rules and regulations for the formal type of
interschool debate contest.

Prior to the time of the debate, representatives of the two teams agree on the time and place of the contest, the question to be discussed, and the side to be upheld by each team. If a decision is to be given they also agree on the method of judging, and probably on the individuals who are to be invited to serve as judges.

The debate may be presented in a school auditorium before a student audience, or before some group not connected with either school represented—a civic club, a labor organization, an evening gathering in some church. The subject debated should be some important public question—one which would be of direct interest to the audience, and still within the ability of student speakers to discuss intelligently. Probably the question will deal with some bill currently before Congress or before the state legislature, or with some general problem such as tax-supported hospital care, abolition of nuclear tests, or federal aid to education. Sometimes the question may deal with a purely local problem—the need for a new school building or for additional recreational facilities. Present-day high school or college debating usually centers about a resolution selected by the schools in a league or in a state association. All schools in the league or association debate the same proposition, using it throughout the school year.

The chairman and the four debaters are seated on the platform, the affirmative speakers having a table at the chairman's right, and the negative speakers at his left. In opening the debate, the chairman briefly introduces the subject to be discussed, and states the exact proposition for debate. Each speaker is introduced by the chairman when it is his turn to take the floor. At the close of the debate, the chairman makes a few concluding remarks, and if the debate is of the decision type, announces the vote of the judges.

Speakers representing the two sides alternate in presenting their arguments. The debate is opened by the first affirmative speaker, who is followed by the first speaker for the negative. The first negative rebuttal speaker is introduced following the final constructive speech for that side, and the two sides again alternate so that the affirmative closes the debate. Each of the four speakers is allowed ten or twelve minutes in which to present his constructive argument, and an additional five minutes for the rebuttal speech. A timekeeper, seated in the audience, notifies speakers of the expiration of their allotted time.

The constructive argument of each team will probably be based upon from three to five main points or arguments, each of which gives a reason for accepting or rejecting the proposition for debate. Each of these main points is supported by some form of proof material—examples, illustrations, statistics, comparisons, or statements of authorities. The main speeches should be carefully organized, with each main point clearly introduced and concluded, so that the audience will have no difficulty in following the argument. Each speech after the opening argument of the affirmative is adjusted to fit the opposing arguments already given, and refutation is introduced to weaken one or more of the opposing points.

Following the constructive speeches, each debater presents a rebuttal speech. In the rebuttals, debaters are not permitted to introduce new issues; each speaker must limit himself to the tearing down of points advanced by his opponents or to meeting the attacks of his opponents on the case of his own side. Rebuttal speeches are organized no less thoroughly than the constructive arguments; attention is centered on the points of greatest importance, and each point in refutation is carefully introduced and concluded.

The procedure outlined above is that used in practically all high school debates, and in the majority of the contest debates in colleges and universities. Departures from the conventional style are sometimes used, especially when the debate is held before some off-the-campus adult group, for the purpose of creating greater interest on the part of listeners. But these special forms are used only by experienced debaters; the beginner should give his entire attention to the methods of conventional contest debating.

Requirements of Good Debating

On the basis of present-day standards, good debating must satisfy all of the following requirements:

First, each debater must show an intelligent understanding of the question, and knowledge of all of the important facts concerning it.

Second, there must be evidence of careful planning. The arguments presented must be integrated into a unified, constructive case, presenting the points or issues which offer the strongest reasons for accepting the desired point of view concerning the question.

Third, both constructive speeches and rebuttals must be carefully organized so that each point stands out clearly and the case as a whole is easy to follow.

Fourth, every issue advanced must be amply supported with evidence or "proof," sufficient to establish the point as true in the mind of an unprejudiced listener. Rebuttal arguments must be supported with proof materials no less than those advanced in the constructive argument.

Fifth, every important constructive point advanced by the opposing speakers, and every attack of consequence upon the main points in the debater's own case, must be considered in rebuttal. Good debating *demands refutation ability* on the part of the debater. He must learn to summarize the opposing contentions in a clear, fair manner, and then submit his answers to these contentions, properly supported with convincing evidence. Furthermore, the refutation must be effective in its presentation, and wherever possible, every major opposing contention should be attacked.

Sixth, the ideas presented must be expressed in effective language. Good English is necessary in any type of speech; but over and above the demands of good grammar and good English style, the debate argument must be presented in language which conveys the speaker's thought most effectively.

Seventh, the debater must be a good public speaker, talking directly to his listeners in an informal, conversational style, but with earnestness and vigor of expression which compels attention.

Above all, every good debater must remember one important fact. The *ultimate purpose of debate is to win the listener,* to bring those in the audience to the debater's desired point of view concerning the question, in spite of the efforts of the opposing speakers. Successful debating is that which accomplishes this purpose, and makes members of the audience believe the things which the speaker wants believed. It is true that in some debates the number in the audience is very small, sometimes only the judges and a few others. However, the number present does not change the basic purpose of the debater. His purpose is to win belief of as many of those present as he can, and to keep the members of the audience from accepting the proposal of opposing speakers. The decision of the judges is, after all, a minor matter; throughout the whole period of preparation and presentation of the debate argument, the debater's attention must be centered upon this one vital purpose—the purpose of *persuading the audience.*

DEBATE TERMINOLOGY

Before concluding this section on the general nature of modern debating, some attention should be given to various terms used in connection with debate. Those which are listed below are widely used in this text. Familiarity with their meanings will be necessary for an understanding of the discussion of different phases of debate which appears in the following pages.

Debate refers to any two-sided discussion of a controversial question. As used in this text, however, the term refers to *contest debate,* or the form conducted under definite rules in schools and colleges.

The *question* or *proposition* is the subject which is debated. In contest debating, it is stated formally as a *resolution,* and in the case of questions of *policy* it always asks for a change from the status quo. It begins with the words, "Resolved, that . . . ."

The *affirmative* team is the team which supports or upholds the proposition; the *negative* team opposes it. Similarly, an *affirmative argument* is one in favor of the proposition, and a *negative argument* one which opposes it.

A *case* is the general plan of attack of a debate team, the combined arguments of the speakers on one side.

A *contention* is a statement offered to support the debater's position in the debate, usually giving a *reason* for accepting the point of view he holds with respect to the proposition. A contention is a statement of opinion, rather than of fact; to be accepted, it must be *proved*. The term *issue* is used as a synonym with *contention*.

A *main point* or *major contention* is one of the major reasons given for accepting or refusing to accept the proposition for debate. A *sub-point* or *minor contention* is a reason for believing or accepting a main point.

An *argument* is a section of a speech in which any single point or contention is developed and supported with proof. The expression is also used to refer to an entire speech in a debate, and sometimes, to all of the speeches on one side taken collectively, as "the negative argument."

A *constructive argument* is one in which one of the major contentions is developed, to support one side of the proposition for debate. The same term is also used to refer to the main speeches for one side taken collectively, or to any one of the main speeches.

Rebuttal is the process of attacking the argument of the opponents. Rebuttal may consist of attacking the opposing constructive arguments, or of supporting one's own constructive arguments after they have been attacked by the opposition. The term *refutation* is used in this text as synonymous with *rebuttal*.

A *rebuttal speech* is one of the short speeches in the latter part of the debate, as opposed to the constructive main speeches, wherein the debater may not introduce *new issues* for his side. However, he may use *new evidence* to support (or attack) the issues presented in the constructive speeches.

A *rebuttal point* is a contention presented in the course of rebuttal or refutation—it may be presented either during the constructive speeches or in the rebuttal speeches. The rebuttal point is usually expressed as a statement directly denying or contradicting some point advanced by an opponent.

Proof is the process of *supporting a point* with reasoning and evidence. Or, the term may refer to the *materials*—both reasoning and evidence—which are used to support the statement.

Reasoning is the process of *giving reasons* for believing a proposition or statement. Some process of reasoning is necessary to show the relationship between the statement to be proved and individual items of evidence which support it.

Evidence is a term used to refer to various *factual materials and opinions* which are cited to support a contention or statement to be proved. The more important forms of evidence used in debate are instances, statistics, comparisons, illustrations, and statements of opinion by authorities. In this text, these various materials are also referred to as *proof materials;* the terms *evidence* and *proof materials* will be used as synonyms.

Other terms used in the pages which follow will have the meanings usually given them in ordinary conversation. The expressions defined above have been mentioned because their meanings as related to debate are sometimes different from the meanings given in other specialized fields.

PART II—PROOF

WHAT IS PROOF?

Every debater has one basic purpose in presenting his arguments—he wants his listeners to accept some desired *belief*. To get them to believe as he wishes, he supports his position with *proof*—reasons and factual materials which he hopes will cause the listeners to accept his point of view. Since belief is the basic aim of debate, and proof the means of securing belief, proof is the most important element in debating, whether in the formal contests of schools and colleges or in the informal discussions of later life. Debating is good or bad according to the effectiveness of the proof presented. And the effectiveness of the proof is a matter of audience acceptance.

The essential parts of proof. Few men will change their minds merely because someone tells them that their opinions are wrong. People demand *reasons* for changing their beliefs, and they usually ask for "facts" or *evidence* to support those reasons. You can tell an acquaintance a thousand times that your television set is better than the model he owns, but unless you can give him definite *reasons* for believing your contention, and back up those reasons with *evidence* that they are true, you have little chance of convincing him that you really have the better television receiver. To *prove* a contention, then, you must do two things: first, use reasoning (or give reasons) to show why your contention is true; and second, offer facts or evidence to support the reasoning. If the listener accepts your *reasoning* as valid, and considers your *evidence* conclusive, he will *believe* your contention. In other words, *reasoning* plus *evidence* equals *proof*.

In the foregoing paragraph, the term *reasoning* has been used in its most literal sense—that of giving reasons. Perhaps this oversimplifies the meaning of the term. Reasoning is a process of giving reasons, to be sure—but at times the procedure is some-what roundabout and indirect. In a broader sense, reasoning might be defined as a process of *showing relationships* between ideas—of drawing conclusions from established facts. If, for example, you see that the sky is overcast and decide that it is going to rain, you have used a process of *reasoning;* you have drawn a conclusion from a set of observed facts. Or if, in a laboratory, you combine certain chemicals and note that a gas having an unpleasant odor is produced, you conclude that the same combination of chemicals will always produce that gas—again, you have used a process of reasoning.

Evidence, on the other hand, is not a process; it is a collection of facts or opinions, of things that are known or that are accepted as true. When you decided that rain was threatening, you argued from evidence—the condition of the atmosphere, the clouds you saw in the sky. Or, in the laboratory, you had equally definite facts from which to draw your conclusions. You knew what chemicals were used, how they were combined, and the general nature of the gas which was formed—at least, the odor of the gas. Again, your conclusion was based on evidence, on things known to be true. In addition to the "facts" (or in their absence) you may use expert opinions as evidence. For instance, you may accept the prediction of the weatherman as to the probability of rain. Because the weather forecaster is considered an authority (or an expert) in predicting the weather, his opinion, as opposed to the non-expert's, would be considered good evidence.

Perhaps an everyday comparison will help you understand the relation between the different elements in the proof process. Suppose that you wish to make a footstool. The boards, nails, and varnish are the materials from which the stool is made; they correspond to the *evidence.* But they must be put together so that each part has its proper relationship to the finished stool—the plan you have in mind for the footstool makes that relationship clear, and corresponds to the *reasoning* element in proof. The process of making the footstool corresponds to the process of *proof.* And the finished footstool corresponds to the *belief* secured.

In debate, the "facts" (*evidence*) are put together (*proof process*) in the manner determined by their relationship (*reasoning*) to the complete structure (*the point to be proved*); and the combination of evidence and reasoning results in *belief*.

Burden of proof. One of the widely accepted principles of contest debating is that a *burden of proof* rests upon every debater. "He who *asserts*, must *prove*." In general, we say that *the* burden of proof rests upon the affirmative, for it is the affirmative which advances and upholds the resolution for debate. But burden of proof is not limited to the affirmative. An equally great burden rests upon every debater, affirmative or negative, who advances any contention whatever in the course of his speech. The fact that a debater *makes* a statement places upon him the obligation of *proving* it. Furthermore, whenever the negative team offers a plan or remedy of its own as a *substitute* for the affirmative plan, the negative assumes the *burden of proof* for its solution.

The degree of proof. Of course, most statements in debate could not be proved in the sense of establishing their absolute certainty. But they can be proved to the satisfaction of a listener. And for the purposes of debate, a statement is *proved* if it is supported by enough *reasoning* and *evidence* to cause an unprejudiced listener to believe that it is true. Obviously, the amount of proof material and reasoning necessary to gain belief will vary greatly, according to the nature of the statement to be proved and of the audience to be influenced. For example, it would take much less evidence and reasoning to persuade most Americans to believe that democracy is a desirable principle of government than it would to get Khrushchev or the king of Thailand to believe it. With respect to the idea of democracy, the listeners are prejudiced—in the case of the average American, in favor of the idea, but in the case of Khrushchev, against it. It would hardly be reasonable to expect the debater to provide enough proof to support the desirability of democracy to induce an autocrat to accept his idea. Consequently, as regards debate, we say that a thing is *proved* when there is *enough reasoning* *and evidence* given in support of it to induce an *unprejudiced* listener to believe it true.

Some statements, of course, simply cannot be proved to an average listener. No amount of evidence or reasoning would make you believe that the sun rises in the west, or that a railroad rail will float in water. Those ideas are contrary to your *experience*. And men and women refuse to believe statements which are contrary to their own individual experience, or to fundamental beliefs they hold which have been based on experience. They will refuse to accept ideas which are contrary to any strongly held belief, no matter how that belief was acquired. Certainly you could not get an average American audience to believe that the United States should adopt a system of communism, or that our standard of living is lower than that of Italy, or that we should abolish our policy of free public education.

On the contrary, it is easy to make the average audience believe that a statement is true, if that statement is in harmony with some belief he already holds. Very little evidence and reasoning will be required to convince the average American that a government-owned barge line is "inefficiently operated," or that higher taxes on the very rich are "just"—he already has a firm belief that government management is "less efficient than that by business" and that the rich "should be taxed on their ability to pay."

From the discussion above, two principles may be drawn which should be observed by the debater in his selection of contentions to be proved, and in deciding how much proof is to be used:

1. Never advance a contention or an issue or make a statement which directly opposes the experience, or the strongly held beliefs, of the listeners.

2. The amount of proof offered to support each contention should be varied according to the degree in which the contention conforms to existing beliefs of the listeners.

THE REASONING PROCESS

For a thorough understanding of the various forms of proof and the various factors which help persuade a listener to accept a statement as true, the debater would have to give months of study to theories of evidence, to methods of reasoning, to the forms of formal logic, and to the numerous psychological factors affecting belief. Entire books have been written on various single phases of the general field of proof. But for the ordinary purposes of contest debate, no such elaborate study is required. For the beginning debater at least, all that is necessary is a working knowledge of a few of the more important methods of reasoning and of the general types of evidence. Methods of reasoning will be discussed in the pages which follow, and the types of evidence used in debate will be taken up in Section 3.

The reasoning processes used in debate may be divided for practical purposes into two general types: proof by *classifying*, and proof by *eliminating*. Both are widely used in debate. And while the *names* given the two methods may be new to you, the methods themselves are far from new—you use both methods a hundred times a day in your everyday life. Every decision you make—whether to study or go to the movies, what hat to wear, which road to take to go to school—involves the use of one method or the other of reasoning, and frequently of both. You will have no difficulty in recognizing them in the discussions which follow.

PROOF BY CLASSIFYING

The men and women who make up any audience have a great number of basic beliefs and attitudes in common. They unite in upholding certain principles and ideals and institutions, and in opposing certain other principles and institutions. Naturally, the list of strongly held attitudes will not be exactly the same for all audiences, or for all of the individual members of any one audience. The laboring men in an audience, for example, will probably have a set of beliefs concerning labor unions quite different from the beliefs on the subject held by bankers or business executives. But no matter how mixed the audience, there are some beliefs—a great many beliefs—which *all* of the members will hold in common.

To illustrate, the members of any audience can be expected to *favor* those things which are "efficient," or "beneficial," or "democratic," just as they are *opposed* to things which are "wasteful," or "injurious," or "autocratic." They believe in common that anything which "will raise the standard of living" is desirable and good, just as they believe in common that anything which "destroys the liberties of the individual" is bad. All of those things which are "efficient" constitute a *class*—a class which the audience favors. Things which are "beneficial" constitute another class; things which "will raise the standard of living" a third class; things which "will raise taxes" still another class, and so on. And concerning each of these classes, the members of the audience have common attitudes or beliefs— they are strongly in favor of certain classes, and strongly opposed to others.

Of course, there are thousands of such classes of things— classes concerning which all the members of an audience will have common attitudes and beliefs. Some of the classes are very broad and general, including hundreds of different ideas— the things which are "businesslike," or "progressive," or "economical," for example. Others are more specific and more limited—the things which "make it possible to reduce government expenditures by 50 per cent," or which "will greatly increase the efficiency of our educational system," or which "will attract new industries to our city." To the audience some are "good" classes; others are "bad." But about all of the things which combine to make any one class, the members of the audience have common beliefs and opinions.

The fact that these various classes exist gives the debater a means of inducing his listeners to accept and believe a given proposal, or to reject it—whichever he desires. If he can show his listeners that the proposal properly falls within one of the "good" classes, the listeners are likely to favor the proposal. And if he shows that the proposal belongs in one of the "bad" classes, they are likely to oppose it. Of course, if he can show that the proposition belongs in two or three or four of the "good" classes, the listeners will have even more reason to support it.

Suppose, for example, that you are debating the question of establishing an Atlantic Union. If you can make your listeners believe that such an organization would provide a more effective method of *defending the Western Hemisphere*, they probably will favor it. For those things which "defend the Western Hemisphere" make up a "good" class, in the opinion of the average American. The listeners' mental processes will run something like this: "Anything that will protect us is certainly desirable. The speaker has just shown that an Atlantic Union would protect us. So the Atlantic Union must be a desirable institution; I'm in favor of it." All that you have done is to *place the Union in one of the desirable classes;* your listeners have done the rest.

On the same principle, whenever you argue in favor of some new proposal, your task is to show that the thing you uphold falls within one of the "good" or desirable classes—that it is "necessary," or "economical," that it "will lower taxes," or is "in harmony with American institutions." Your statement that the proposal is "necessary," or "economical," or otherwise falls within one of the "good" classes, must be supported by evidence, of course. But once you establish your proposal in one of the many possible classes of desirable things, you have given your listeners a *reason* for supporting the proposal.

In the same way, a negative speaker can make his listeners oppose a proposition by showing that it falls within one or more of the undesirable or "bad" classes. He may show that it is "too expensive," or that it is "communistic," or that it "will bring on a new industrial depression," or that it "violates the rights guaranteed to individuals in the American Constitution." If he shows that the proposal falls within one of these undesirable classes, his listeners will oppose it. By putting it in an objectionable class, the debater has given his listeners a reason for opposing the proposition.

This method of showing that a proposal falls within one or more of the many desirable or objectionable classes is called *proof by classifying*, because all that the debater has to do is to *classify* the proposition—put it in some *class* of things about which listeners already hold strong beliefs. It is an effective method of proof; when the debater puts the proposal in a general class, he gives his listeners a *reason* for accepting it or for opposing it. The more strongly the average listener *feels* about the desirability or undesirability of the class, the stronger is his reason for upholding or opposing the proposition which has been placed within that class. To a large proportion of the people of the United States, to show that a given proposal is "communistic," or even that it is "one of the practices used in Red China," would be to condemn it absolutely, without further discussion.

Of course, the method of classifying is nothing new in your experience; you use it dozens of times every day. You use it in making your own decisions about things to do; and you use it almost as often in persuading your friends to do things you want them to do. Suppose you want to induce one of your schoolmates to take a trip with you to a nearby city; you show him that it will be "fun," or "exciting," or promise him a chance to meet one of your attractive girl friends, and he decides to go. Or if your purpose is to keep him from going, you tell him that the trip will be "expensive," or "dull," or that the train will be hot and uncomfortable, and he decides not to go. All that you have done is to place the idea of making the trip in certain desirable or undesirable classes—and your friend decides as you wish.

The method of classifying is the basis of nearly every debate argument. Note, for example, how Senator Henry Cabot Lodge,

Jr. (R-Mass.), paints a rather fearful picture of what *could* happen under the present system of electing a President. He says:

Still fresh in our minds is the feeling of frustration we experienced on election night last November when it seemed possible that we would enter the year 1949 without an elected President. That would have been an actuality had Governor Dewey carried any two of the states of California, Illinois, or Ohio. With all three of these close-vote states, he would have won; with any two of them he would have deprived President Truman of a majority; that is, his votes and those of Governor Thurmond, who was also in the three-man race, would have totaled more together than Truman's. Thus the election would have gone to the House. A deadlock there could quite conceivably have found the nation without a President at noon on inauguration day—with a rush to the statute books to see what, if anything, the law says about succession in such preposterous cases.[6]

Again, in supporting his proposed remedy, he appeals to the idea of fairness and justice for the voter when he says:

Under such a system the U.S. citizen would at last have a legal voice in his choice of President—not a mere expression of preference as at present. His vote would count for the man he intended to support and never, as now often happens, for the man he opposed. Furthermore, the electoral vote, worked out to the third decimal place if necessary, would exactly reflect the popular vote.

And now compare the use of the *classification* technique by an opponent to Senator Lodge's plan. Congressman Wright Patman (D-Tex.) says, in part:

On first examination the Gossett-Lodge amendment seems an admirable step toward modernization of our Constitution. Further study, however, reveals in it several dangerous and far-reaching implications. One is this: Because the proposed system would credit each person for whom votes were cast for President in each state "with such proportion of the electoral votes thereof as he received of the total votes," the plan would greatly stimulate and encourage the formation, merger, and development of *minority parties*. Our present two-party system would be destroyed.

Let me ask this: Why is it that neither the extreme right—the Fascist groups—nor the extreme left—the Communist group—has offered any objection to this amendment? Can it be that they see

[6] Lodge, H. C. Jr. and Patman, Wright. "Should the United States Abolish the Electoral College?" *Rotarian.* 75:52. July 1949.

it as an opening through which they can slip into our government and undermine its democratic nature? For the first time these radical groups could obtain electoral votes for their candidates for President and Vice President.[7]

The following additional examples illustrate the use of *proof by classification.*

We are opposed to any system involving censorship of television programs by the government in the third place, because such a system would make it possible to control all political broadcasting in the interests of the party in power. And I can think of no greater danger to democracy, no more effective agency for the establishment of an American political dictatorship, than the control of broadcasting for the benefit of a single political party.

There are numerous serious objections to government control of business enterprises, but I shall mention just three. To begin with, government management means political management, by politicians and in the interests of politicians. Second, government management means a serious lowering in the quality of the rank-and-file personnel. And third, government management fails to offer any incentive for efficient operation. I shall spend my time, this evening, in establishing those three points.

Rules for using proof by classifying. Three important rules should be followed in checking the effectiveness of your use of the method of classifying.

1. Choose the classes which arouse the most intense feeling on the part of the listener.

Suppose that you are upholding the proposition that the United States should join the nations of Europe in their Common Market. And suppose that you show that American entry would *strengthen the free nations opposing communism.* But at the same time, your oppenents show that our entry would *lower the American standard of living to that of Europe.* Would your listeners favor or oppose America's joining the Common Market? Probably they will be divided. Those most fearful of a Communist attack on the United States would favor the

[7] *Ibid.,* p 52.

plan; those who wish to maintain our high standard of living at all costs would oppose it. The final attitude of every listener will be determined by *the intensity of his feeling concerning the classes mentioned.* So it is highly important that the classes, within which you place the proposal you support or attack, should be capable of arousing the highest pitch of feeling on the part of your listeners.

This demands careful consideration of your probable audience. No rule can be laid down by which you may know what beliefs your audience, as a group, will hold most vital. The question is one which you must answer for yourself. But the more you know about the people who make up your audience, the more accurate your answer is likely to be.

2. Make sure that the subject you classify is actually the proposition you are trying to prove.

Suppose you are arguing the question of *"the use of armed force* by the Government of the United States to protect the investments of American citizens in foreign countries." In upholding the proposition, you show that protection of American investments is "necessary," that such protection is "approved by the rules of international laws," and that "failure to protect American interests would result in loss of prestige by the United States." Unquestionably, you have shown that *protection* of our interests in other countries has a number of highly desirable features. But the question for debate is not merely whether our foreign interests should be *protected*—it is whether they should be protected *by use of armed force.* Your *classes* have all applied to protection itself, and not to the *method* of protection. So your proof does not actually support the proposition you have been trying to prove, or lead listeners to believe in and accept that proposition. Be sure that the subject you classify is your *actual proposition,* and not something else.

3. Be certain that you offer enough evidence to support every classifying statement you make.

It is not enough for you merely to *tell* your listeners that your proposal falls within a certain class. Whenever you make such a statement, you accept a burden of proof regarding it; you must offer *evidence* to show that the proposition really falls within the class you name. If you cannot offer *enough* evidence to *make your listeners believe* that the proposition really falls within the class you name, that particular classifying statement should not be advanced at all.

If these three rules are rigidly observed, your arguments should be highly effective in securing the belief of your listeners. But failure to follow any one of them will seriously weaken your case.

Proof by Eliminating

The second important method of reasoning used in debate is that based on the principle of *eliminating alternatives*. This method is used in everyday life almost as frequently as the method of *classifying*. Every time you make a choice between two possible courses of action, your decision is based in part at least on the procedure of *eliminating*. In other words, when you attempt to choose between two possible solutions to the problem, you are forced to compare and contrast the two or more possible alternatives. You will (or should) accept one solution and reject the others on the basis of their relative value. To illustrate, suppose you learn that you must take an important examination in one of your classes tomorrow morning, and you know that you need two or three hours of study to get ready for the examination. Two possibilities present themselves: you can either study tonight, before going to sleep, or you can wake up early and do your studying in the morning. But if you know that some factor exists which will prevent you from studying in the morning, necessarily you conclude that you will have to do your studying tonight. That, in brief, is the principle on which the proof method of *eliminating* is based. If every possibility is considered, and every possibility save one is eliminated, the one remaining is necessarily the one which must be followed.

Of course, we seldom find a situation which offers only two possibilities. In the case suggested above, there really was a third possibility which was not mentioned—the possibility of not studying at all. But regardless of the number of possible courses of action, the *method* of *eliminating* would remain the same. All of the possibilities are listed, and all but one are discarded, for one reason or another. And thus, through a process of *eliminating*, you arrive at the alternative that you accept.

As may readily be seen, the method of eliminating is widely used in everyday life. You use it whenever you buy a hat or a pair of shoes or a new suit of clothes; when you select a book or magazine to read; when you choose the combination of courses you will take in school or college. Many of the important decisions of adult life are based on the same method of eliminating—the selection of a house to buy, or of an automobile, or of the candidate to support in an election. Even your choice of a life work will be based in most instances on the reasoning method of eliminating. In most cases, of course, the method of classifying will be used in connection with that of eliminating; you consider the reasons for following the course selected as well as eliminating other possible courses.

Now, let us apply the principle of eliminating to the debate situation. In debate, as in decisions made in the practical affairs of life, you establish one alternative as the course to be followed by eliminating the other possible alternatives. Suppose, for instance, that you are upholding the proposition that the federal government should subsidize the expansion of medical schools in the United States. You might point out to your listeners that there are only three possibilities open to us in training doctors, dentists, and nurses. First, we may continue to depend on private and state financing of medical schools. Second, we may go to the other extreme of placing all medical schools in the hands of the federal government with federal ownership, control, and operation of medical training. Third, we may continue with private and state control and operation, backed by additional subsidies from the federal government to finance expansion.

But after listing these possibilities, you show that the first is unthinkable as the present crisis in medicine shows. Private and state funds cannot provide for needed expansion. Second, you show that government control and operation of educational facilities is extremely dangerous, as the people of Germany, Russia, Italy, and other countries have discovered to their sorrow. Only one alternative remains open to us: our federal government should subsidize the expansion portion of the medical school program, leaving control and operation in the hands of educators. Since the only other alternatives open to us have been eliminated as unworkable and undesirable, federal subsidy for expansion is the policy we must follow.

The debater should notice that the process of eliminating the discarded possibilities depends directly upon the method of *proof by classifying.* The best way and in most instances the *only* way in which you can eliminate the possibilities you do not favor is to show that each of them falls into one or more undesirable *classes.* With these alternatives discarded by use of *classification,* however, the proof method of *eliminating* is used to draw the final conclusion: since no other alternatives are feasible, the one course which remains must be the best course to follow. The method of *eliminating* is the second important type of reasoning used in debate.

Proof by eliminating is most frequently used by affirmative speakers, usually in developing the first main argument in the affirmative case. Usually they assume that only two alternatives are important enough to be considered—the present system, and the new system proposed by the affirmative. Then an attack is launched against the first alternative—the present system—and evils are pointed out which are so great as to demand a change. Then the speaker points out that, since the present system is so undesirable that it must be abandoned, the only possibility remaining is to accept the plan of the affirmative.

Sometimes, however, the need for change from the existing system is so great that there is little possibility that listeners will even consider keeping the present system; they are concerned principally with the problem of choosing the most practical and desirable of several methods of reform which have been suggested. In such a case, the opening affirmative speaker may list a number of possible alternatives—the present system, and all of the major reform systems which have been suggested, including, of course, the particular system which he is upholding. Then each of the alternatives is attacked in turn, and reasons given to show that they should be discarded, until only the plan suggested by the affirmative remains.

The two methods of using proof by eliminating alternatives are illustrated in the selections which follow:

Now, it seems to me that one of two things could be done. First, the railroads might continue as they are until forced to the wall, take bankruptcy, wipe out their debts, and start over. Or second, the national government must take over this industry, so vital to the defense of our nation.

Suppose we accept the first, and the railroads continue until forced to take bankruptcy. What then? The blow that would fall on the financial structures of the United States would drive us into a depression such as this nation has never seen. Even if we ignore the untold tragedy to the 800,000 stockholders, we must consider the various financial institutions which hold $11 billion worth of bonds. Do you realize that thirty-nine of our largest insurance companies have 10 per cent of their assets in railroad bonds, twenty-three over 15 per cent, and nine have 20 per cent? And the New York Life Insurance Company has one third of its assets so invested. If we permit the railroads to be pulled under, the Insull tragedy will seem mere child's play. If they go to the wall they will drag down the basic credit structures of the United States. This plan is unthinkable!

That leaves only the plan Mr. Baird and I are advocating this evening, government ownership and operation of railroads in the United States. The government is the only agency with sufficient financial strength and power to take over what private capital is not able to handle. Private capital cannot manage the railroad industry as it exists today. The United States Government is the only institution that has the strength to take over and operate this industry. The fact that this will work is not a question for discussion tonight, because most of the countries of the world have already taken over the railroads and have shown it could be done successfully. And when it is done, what will it mean to you who are here tonight? It will mean security such as you cannot have under the present system. It

will mean that you are more apt to receive a living wage. And it will
mean your system as a whole will be able to serve the public much
more efficiently . . .

————————

   In discussing the problem of subsidization of athletics, we might
take any one of three possible views. The first would be an attitude
of condemnation of the present system of intercollegiate athletics in
general, as it exists today. This idea would attack athletics, on the
ground that sports have been overemphasized at the expense of the
more important phases of a college education. . . . They tell us that
there has been too much commercialism, too much business connected
with the present system—that our athletes and our athletic programs
have ceased to be sports and have become merely business ventures
for the enriching of college treasuries. . . . These good people, with
the best intentions, mind you, would want to . . . scrap our million-
dollar stadiums and million-dollar gate receipts. . . . Now let us face
the facts. Any proposal which would in any way even threaten the
profits derived from our intercollegiate athletic contests, is impractical
and unworkable. . . . Whether we approve of it or not, commercialism in our athletics is here and it is here to stay. Therefore I
submit to you, Ladies and Gentlemen, that the first possible point of
view—that of condemning the present system and attempting to de-
commercialize it, in favor of simon-pure amateurism—is not practical
at all, and therefore not desirable.
   The second position that one might take is a defense of the
status quo. Let things stand as they are. . . . Athletes are being
subsidized, with either zealous alumni or local businessmen putting
out the money. So why worry? But I say that this system cannot
be defended any more than a proposal for doing away completely with
commercialism in athletics. . . . We have confusion, chaos, a wild
scramble for better games, for opponents that are big drawing cards,
for more gate receipts. . . . All in all, we have a system which I
submit just isn't right.
   A third possible view, and the one for which I stand here tonight,
is that we have out and out cash payment of athletes. College athletics
is a business, organized like every other business, to make profits. We
should come out in the open and admit that it is a business, a form
of big business, and that we are going to run our athletic program on
a big business basis. Let's pay our athletes what they earn. . . . In
this way we can insure closer competition among conference members
and do away with the system of having one school win conference
championships year after year. The whole system would raise the level
of competition, make games closer, and increase gate receipts. . . .
   In summary, may I say this. It is my sincere opinion that commercialism in athletics cannot be eliminated. Our present system,

however, does have certain evils which should be eliminated. The only solution that is workable, is an open and above-board system of cash athletes.

Note the use of contrast and comparison, as a method of *proof by eliminating*, in the following quotation:

Now let me discuss briefly some of the main arguments against our proposed amendment. While a vast majority of our political scientists, legal scholars, and serious students of government agree that our present system is dangerously defective, they do not agree upon proposed remedies. Some favor electing Presidents by a direct vote of the people. A direct-vote method raises all of the issues between the large states and the small states, and such an amendment could never be ratified. Again, it would destroy state sovereignty in the matter of national elections. It would aggravate rather than alleviate sectional differences. It would reduce all states to the lowest common denominator. For example, all states would have to lower their voting age to eighteen to be on a parity with Georgia. Again, in a sectional controversy, New York might vote their dogs, cats, and dead grandmothers, and Texas would retaliate by doing the same thing. Each state would be accusing the other of fraud in piling up big votes and each would probably be correct in such charges. Under our proposal, it is of no concern to Texas how many vote in New York and of no concern to New York how many vote in Texas. New York would still have forty-seven electoral votes, divided, however, in the exact ratio in which they were cast.[8]

Rules for using proof by eliminating. In using the method of eliminating in your argument, two important rules should be observed.

1. Every important alternative should be considered.

If any important possibility is omitted in your discussion, your opponents have only to bring it to the attention of the listeners to overthrow the entire conclusion which you have drawn. It is obvious that to dispose of but *two* alternatives out of *five* which are possible does not establish any one of the remaining three as the only one which may be considered. So, if

[8] Congressman Ed Gossett (D-Tex.). *Amend the Constitution with Respect to Election of President and Vice President*; hearings before the Committee on the Judiciary, House of Representatives, 81st Congress, February 9, 1949. Government Printing Office. Washington, D.C. '49. p 19.

five possibilities exist, and you mention only two or three of
them, your proof is exceedingly weak. Affirmative debaters are
often guilty of this error. They assume that the only alternatives
possible are the present system and the affirmative plan, when
in reality there may be a number of other feasible solutions
which have been entirely ignored.

2. Attacks upon discarded alternatives should be strong enough to dispose of them beyond question.

If you consider every possible alternative of importance, the
only means by which opponents may attack your conclusion is
that of supporting one of the alternatives you have discarded.
The stronger your original attack upon the discarded possibilities,
the more difficulty your opponents will have in trying to uphold
one of them.

A suggestion. Arguments supporting or opposing certain ideas
are constantly encountered in your everyday life. Your friends
argue among themselves, trying to induce each other to accept
the ideas or plans of action in which they are interested; your
teachers use arguments in the classroom; arguments are presented
in newspaper editorials and in many articles in magazines.
During the next few days, try to pay particular attention to
these arguments; see if you can "spot" the type of reasoning
used in each argument. Before long you will be able to pick
out the arguments in which proof by *classifying* is used and
those in which the method is that of *eliminating*. After you
reach the stage when it is easy for you to identify the type of
reasoning used, begin to apply the tests that have been suggested.
See if the arguments often ignore one rule or another; try to
determine which rule is most frequently violated.

When you are able to pick out the weaknesses in the reasoning
used by your friends, begin to give serious attention to your
own arguments. You probably will find that your own reasoning
is unsound a good deal of the time—but if you can identify
your own weaknesses, you will find yourself unconsciously checking and correcting each argument even before you present it.

And when you reach that stage, you are well on the way toward becoming a good debater; if you form the habit of using sound reasoning in your own arguments with your friends, and develop the ability to pick out the weaknesses in the reasoning they use, you have mastered two of the essentials of effective debating.

EVIDENCE

As we have already noted, proof is a combination of two distinct elements: *reasoning* and *evidence*. Some type of reasoning is used to show the relationship between a set of known facts and some statement or contention to be proved—and the *facts* from which the reasoning proceeds are known as *evidence*. Evidence, then, is the foundation of every argument, and the basis upon which the entire proof structure is built.

Types of evidence. As used in debate, evidence falls into four general classes, as follows:
1. Examples or instances
2. Statistics
3. Statements by authorities
4. Illustrations

In our discussion of proof, evidence has been referred to as synonymous with "facts." However, material used as evidence is not always factual, in a literal sense. Statements by authorities are usually statements of opinion, and illustrations may present situations that are wholly imaginary. But to have value as evidence, the opinions expressed by authorities must harmonize with what the listener already knows to be true, and the imaginary situations used as illustrations must be accepted by the listener as true to life. Evidence as used in debate may be defined as including both *factual materials* used as proof, and *materials that are accepted by the listener as true*.

USING EXAMPLES OR INSTANCES

Most of our stock of general knowledge comes from first-hand observation. It we scorch our fingers in a flame, we learn that

fire burns. It we see that a fly has six legs, we conclude that all
other flies have six legs, as well. If we have difficulty in one
mathematics course, we decide that all courses in that field are
difficult. In each case, one individual experience or instance has
been sufficient to produce a definite belief in our minds. And if,
of course, we find that the same general conclusion holds true in
four or five different experiences, we are even more strongly convinced of the truth of that belief.

The fact that men and women form beliefs in this way suggests the first type of evidence which may be used in debate. If
you can give your listener an *example* or *instance* in which a
certain fact holds true, he is likely to believe that the same fact
will hold true in other similar situations. And if you can give
him four or five different examples, in all of which the same fact
holds true, he will be even more likely to accept the belief that,
under certain conditions, the given fact or conclusion will always
hold true.

To illustrate, suppose that in a debate you are trying to convince your listeners that lack of military preparedness is dangerous. To support your conclusion, you cite the *examples* of Poland, of Denmark, of Norway, of Belgium and Holland, and of
France; in each instance you show that lack of adequate preparation caused national disaster. The use of these examples will
probably cause your listeners to accept your conclusion that lack
of military preparedness is dangerous. They know the fact to
have been true in each of the *instances* you cite; and they are
likely, therefore, to believe it is always true. If your listeners are
already inclined to believe the statement you are trying to prove,
two or three examples will probably be enough to convince them;
but if they lean in the opposite direction, a greater number of
examples should be used.

Examine the use of examples in the following illustrations:

First, then, I must show you that our record of past cooperation
is not based on altruism or mutual love. Since the Honourable Pro-
poser has made reference to past history, I am sure that he must
agree with me that *American foreign policy has been consistent in*

only one point; always to protect the vital interests of the United States and to insure American political security and economic prosperity.

The methods used to carry out this foreign policy have been many and varied. In 1778 we tried an *alliance* with France to protect our vital interests. During the Napoleonic Wars we tried *neutrality.* Later we started what used to be thought of as the traditional American foreign policy, *isolation.* In 1812, we turned to active fighting to protect our prosperity and security. When our South American interests and our western coast were being threatened, we enunciated the *Monroe Doctrine.* And so it has gone all through our early history. Later, during World War I, we tried *aloofness,* changed to *neutrality,* and ended up with *active participation.* The same may be said of World War II. In its many varied forms it has been consistent only with protecting the vital interests of the United States, and indeed, the only justification for diplomacy connected with foreign relations is the protection of a nation's own vital interests. *No nation has yet reached the point where it uses its resources and strength solely in the interest of some other country.*

————

You have been told that wage rates are higher where there is compulsory union membership, and lower in states having right-to-work laws. The facts, however, do not bear this out. For example, in manufacturing industries in Nevada with its right-to-work law, wages are higher than in the neighboring state of California which does not have the law. They are higher in Indiana that has no compulsory union law than in Kentucky where compulsory union membership is allowed. In fact, in 1955 the manufacturing wage rate in three right-to-work states equaled or exceeded the rates in New York, Pennsylvania, and New Jersey. Actually, wage rates have nothing to do with compulsory union membership, but depend instead on other circumstances which caused wage disparity between states to exist long before unions or right-to-work laws were in existence. Do not believe that compulsory union membership is necessary for high wages—it simply isn't true.

————

But blast, firestorm, and fall-out are not the only dangers of nuclear war. Bombs exploded under water off our shores would drown millions. For example, a bomb with a boron blanket exploded in water two miles deep would create waves 100 feet high as far as 200 miles away. The *World Almanac* tells us that 50 of our 200 largest cities have their highest point under 100 feet above sea level. Exploded in the Atlantic, a series of bombs would put the highest point of land in New York City under 45 feet of water; Washington, D.C. under 75 feet of water; Jersey City, Bridgeport, Portsmouth, Patterson, St. Petersburg, and Jacksonville under 80 feet of water; and Savannah, Cambridge, Norfolk, Montgomery, Albany, Elizabeth, Miami, and Charleston under 90 feet of water. And of course time-fuses on bombs set secretly by submarine in the Atlantic, the Gulf, and Pacific could simultaneously flood not only 50 of our biggest cities, but the many hundreds of towns and villages on our coastal plains. All would be washed away with greater loss of life and property from these 20 well placed bombs than have been caused by all the floods, hurricanes, and earthquakes in recorded history combined. All of this could be done by an enemy without damaging us by blast, firestorm, or fall-out, and without loss to the enemy of a single pilot, aircraft, or soldier. Atomic war is unthinkable.

You have been told that the Soviet Union is rapidly catching up and will soon surpass the United States in peacetime industrial production—in effect will soon surpass the American standard of living. But what are the facts? A recent exhaustive study by Professor Warren G. Nutter, Chairman of the Department of Economics, University of Virginia, utterly refutes such statements. The 706-page scholarly report is the latest and most careful research available on this subject. Professor Nutter found that between 1913 and 1958 the Russians forged ahead of the United States in only five of the 47 products studied—in sewing machines, bicycles, fish, flour, and rubber footwear. In three other products the Russians held their own. In nineteen other products they lessened the gap somewhat. But in 25 of the 47 vital products the Russians fell further behind the United States than they were back in 1913. For example, in 1958 the United States was further ahead of Russia than we were in 1913 in such products as electric power, crude oil, paper, motor-vehicle tires, railroad cars, butter, meat slaughtering, soap, and cotton fabrics. It is true that by 1958 the Soviets had gained on us slightly in coal production, steel, lumber and canning—but they were still 19 years behind us in steel, 44 years behind in coal and canning, and 59 years behind us in lumber production, according to Professor Nutter's analysis. It simply is not true that the Soviet Union has become a giant among nations industrially, or that it is far outstripping the United States in rate of growth.

Let us look at the last presidential election, when Mr. Kennedy defeated Mr. Nixon, although Kennedy received fewer than half of the votes cast. You remember that fewer than 120 thousand votes separated the two leaders although nearly 69 million votes were cast. But the real evil of our system of electing Presidents is shown by the action

of the Electoral College. One elector from Oklahoma refused to vote
for Nixon although elected on the Nixon ticket in that state. The
electors from Illinois and New Jersey cast all of their votes for Kennedy,
although Kennedy received fewer than half of the votes in each state.
The shift of those two states alone to Mr. Nixon would have deprived
Mr. Kennedy of a majority of the Electoral College votes, and would
have thrown the election under our system into the House of Representatives. In Hawaii the shift of 58 votes out of more than 184
thousand would have given Nixon, rather than Kennedy, all of that
state's electoral votes. And such examples have occurred in every
presidential election in our history. In fact, in three instances Presidents
were elected after drawing fewer votes than their leading opponents.

Rules for using examples. Three rules are important in using
examples or *instances* as proof in debate:

1. Several examples leading to the same general conclusion
   should be used.

The listener *may* accept the conclusion you wish as a result
of a single example, but he is much more *certain* to accept it if
you give him a number of instances. There is safety in numbers.

2. As far as possible, use examples which are already known
   to the listener.

When the listener recognizes an example you give and thinks,
"Yes, I know about that; it's true," the value of that example
in supporting your conclusion is increased tremendously. Notice
the instances given in the first illustration above. They are all
familiar to any adult audience. Taken as a group they give
effective support to the speaker's contention.

3. The examples given should be typical.

A general truth cannot be based upon exceptional cases. Of
course, in using instances as proof, you probably will choose
those examples which are most striking and which present your
own conclusion in the most effective way. But if the basic facts
in the examples you cite do not agree with those found in the
average or *typical* instance, your evidence has little value. Your

listeners probably will know of instances in which your conclusions will not hold true. They will recognize the instances you cite as being exceptional, and will flatly refuse to accept your conclusions as true. The examples used to support a conclusion must be typical, not exceptional.

USING STATISTICS

The second important type of evidence consists of *statistics,* or tabulated numerical figures. They result from the collection of a great number of examples, presented not as individual instances but as a group. When you cite statistics, you do not simply give the listener two or three examples of the thing you are talking about; you give him information about a great number of examples, all of which are alike in some one important way.

To illustrate, suppose you are debating the outlawing of strikes by compulsory federal arbitration, and you want to show the great loss to the nation when labor-management disputes result in strikes. You could offer *examples,* showing the number of days of work lost by John Jones and by Henry Smith and by Bill Robinson. But citing three or four examples out of many thousands of workers may not be enough to convince your listeners. It is much better in such cases to tell the audience of all of the examples of those losing work by citing *statistics,* which total all of the examples into a single figure. Quoting from government records you can show that in 1959 more than 3,700 work stoppages caused more than 1.8 million workers to lose more than 69 million man-days of work. And during the last ten years 33 thousand strikes have cost this nation a total of 359 million man-days of work—all lost merely because of strikes. The problems causing the strikes have all been solved to the satisfaction of labor and management—but not before workers, industry, and the nation lost 359 million man-days of production. Had strikes been outlawed and compulsory arbitration used, the nation would be 359 million man-days of work richer.

The foregoing example should indicate to you the primary advantage in the use of statistics—you can summarize the facts concerning thousands of cases in a single sentence or two.

Sometimes beginning debaters have trouble in telling the difference between statistics and other numerical figures. Not all figures that you encounter are statistics. In the above paragraph the year, 1959, is composed of figures, but is not made up of a number of examples and therefore is not a *statistic*. The price of a hat or the distance from your home to Chicago can be expressed in numbers, but are not statistics. They do not represent numbers of examples that have some important feature in common. The term *statistics* includes only those figures which represent *tabulations of examples or instances*.

Quite often, statistics are presented in the form of *percentages*, simply to make it easier for the listener to grasp their significance. For instance, you can tell your listeners that from 1959 to 1960 murders in the United States increased from 8,580 to 9,140 whereas the number of all types of serious crime increased from 1,630,430 to 1,861,300. But the audience would understand the *relationships* between the increases better if you say that from 1959 to 1960 murder increased 6 per cent whereas all types of serious crime increased 14 per cent. These percentages are still statistics; although they are not given in the form of actual tabulated figures, they represent such figures. Percentages are merely a more simple way of expressing the relationships that exist between the "raw" figures which were tabulated by the government.

Sometimes statistics are used in connection with other types of proof material; but often they are used independently. A comparison of figures for different years, or for different localities, or for different sets of conditions may be very effective in securing belief. Note the way in which statistics are used in the following illustrations.

Now all evidence points to the fact that we must have federal help of some kind if we are to train enough doctors and nurses to meet our medical needs. Figures from the Department of Health, Education and Welfare make the problem clear. Our present system of private and state schools cannot cope with increased medical need, and are constantly falling further behind. In 1950, for example, the United States had one family doctor for each 1,300 Americans. In 1960 we had only one doctor for each 1,700 Americans. By 1970 the Department estimates that at the present rate of population growth and doctor training we will have only one family doctor for each 2,000 Americans. The medical schools are turning out about 7,000 doctors per year, plus an additional 500 osteopaths. But by 1970 we will need at least 11,000 medical graduates per year.

In dentistry the situation is equally bad. For 30 years the supply of dentists has been falling behind population growth. In 1930 there were 59 dentists for each 100,000 people. By 1960 there were only 43. Dental schools under our present system of private and state control are turning out only 3,200 dentists per year. But the Department tells us that by 1970 we will need 6,000 new dentists each year just to keep pace with population growth.

And our supply of nurses under our present system is equally bad. The Department estimates the minimum need today is 300 nurses for each 100,000 Americans. We have only 257. By 1970 at present rates of training we will have only 246 for each 100,000 Americans.

Our present system simply cannot cope with our medical needs.

But some may ask, "Can the American people afford to put more of their annual income into education, regardless of how much the schools need greater budgets?" Certainly we can afford it. Listen to this. According to the Internal Revenue Service, the American tobacco companies sold over 506 *billion* small-sized cigarettes in 1960. This half a million *billion* does not include king-sized cigarettes, does not include 7 billion cigars, nor 27 million pounds of plug tobacco and 3 million pounds of twist chewing tobacco, nor 76 million pounds of packaged smoking tobacco, nor 35 million pounds of snuff. According to *Tobacco News* in 1961 the U. S. Treasury collected in tobacco taxes alone nearly a quarter of a million dollars every hour of the year—day and night, Sundays and holidays included. Tobacco taxes in 1961 totaled over $2 billion or $230,317.72 for every hour of the year. And for cigarettes alone Americans spent more than $7.5 billion. In other words, we burned up nearly $9 million every hour of the year. Certainly, a country that can afford to spend nearly $9 million an hour for cigarettes can afford to spend a small fraction of that amount to save American education.

And where is the need for union-security-clause elections? We held such elections from 1947 to 1951 under the old Taft-Hartley Act, and abolished them as costly waste of time and money. You will remember that 46,000 elections were held under that law with about five and a half million workers casting ballots for or against union-shop agreements in contracts with employers. And you will remember that 91 per cent of the votes favored the union shop and that 97 per cent of the contracts were so written. The elections cost millions of dollars. Has abolishing these costly elections hurt union security? Far from it. Last year four out of five of nearly 250,000 collective-bargaining agreements in the United States provided for some type of union security. In the light of experience, what need is there of spending time and money on elections whose outcome is known in advance?

————

You have been told tonight that local, state, and federal taxes have increased greatly in the last 12 years, and that high taxes act as a drag on business and cut deeply into profits. My opponents would have you believe that business is on the verge of collapse because of the cost of government. Well, it is true that local, state, and federal taxes have climbed since 1950. However, it is not true that higher taxes have hurt business. In that same period sales jumped almost $325 billion according to *U.S. News & World Report*, and in 1962 corporate earnings *after taxes* were 11 per cent greater than they were in 1950—nearly $26 billion in 1962 and less than $23 billion in 1950. Increased taxes have not resulted in business lag.

————

We have been told tonight that the federal budget was only $7.5 billion out of balance last year, and that this was only 2.5 per cent of the total budget. *Only!* Ladies and Gentlemen, do my opponents know how much $7.5 billion really is? Do they know that $7.5 billion would have given every college student in the United States a scholarship of $2,100, and there would have been $3 million left over? Do they realize that $7.5 billion would give every public school teacher in the country, from kindergarten through high school, a salary raise of $5,475, with $1.3 million left over? Do they know that at 4 per cent interest alone, the American taxpayer will pay $300 million in interest on this $7.5 billion—pay it every year—from now on, forever! *Only* a $7.5 billion deficit, indeed. It is thinking such as this that prevails in Washington and causes unbalanced budgets. Again we plead for economy and balanced budgets.

Rules for using statistics. Four important rules must be followed in using statistics as evidence:

1. Avoid the use of too many sets of figures.

In debate, it isn't what you *tell* the listener, but what he *remembers,* that counts. A few sets of figures, carefully presented, will have definite meaning. But the human mind has its limits; it can grasp only a very few ideas at a time. Figures are especially hard to grasp, particularly when they are not made concrete by comparison with everyday things. When many figures are offered in rapid succession, the listener becomes confused and the statistical material fails to "make sense," as far as he is concerned. If any importance is to be attached to the figures you give, not more than two or three sets, at most, may be used in any single argument.

2. Figures usually should be presented in round numbers.

The human mind not only is unable to grasp *many* ideas at a time, but likewise is unable to grasp a *complex* idea, unless that idea is carefully explained. Consequently, figures that are complete to the last digit have little meaning for the average listener. He can see the force of a comparison between 15 and 21, whether the figures refer to sheep, miles, battleships or millions of dollars. But he will have a great deal of difficulty in puzzling out the relationship between $15,083,471.37 and $20,988,363.50, especially when the figures are heard and not seen. There is too much detail when the complete figures are given; the force of the simpler figures is entirely lost. When comparisons of figures are given, use round numbers in place of the detailed figures.

There are times, however, when you wish to give special emphasis to some particular figure—to impress your listeners with the great size of the figure you are mentioning. In such cases, the use of the *exact* figure, complete to the last digit, gives added force. But not more than *one* such complete figure should be included in any one paragraph in your argument, and not more than two or three in an entire speech.

3. Be conservative in interpreting statistics; avoid the tendency to exaggerate.

So many speakers have made absurd claims, using statistics as evidence, that listeners have become wary of accepting figures at all. They remember that "figures won't lie, but liars will figure." And very often, listeners are justified in taking such an attitude, because it is a common failing of debaters to exaggerate and distort the figures they use. Sometimes they "hand-pick" their statistics, citing figures only for those years or for those localities which support their contentions, and carefully ignoring those which contradict. Another common tendency is to exaggerate in using round numbers—changing the figure $13,211,116.75, for example, to "nearly $15 million."

Be accurate and fair in using statistics. Don't take advantage of the truth when you use round numbers. And don't "hand-pick" the figures you use. Include the statistics for unfavorable as well as for favorable years—and make it clear to your listeners that you are being entirely fair in your use of figures, at all times. Once your listeners suspect you of exaggeration or distortion in your use of statistics, they will doubt the accuracy of all the rest of your evidence. It is better to be conservative, and hold the good will and confidence of your audience.

4. To make statistics vivid, use comparisons with things known to and understood by your listeners.

Figures used in statistical proof are usually too large to carry much meaning for the average listener. For example, we know that the total cost of World War II to the United States was over $200 billion. But two hundred or more billion dollars means very little to most of us; we have no idea of the value of so much money. However, the figures take on greater meaning if we realize that this sum is enough money to run all of the colleges and universities in the United States for several hundred years. And the statistics of cost would be more meaningful to us, if we attempt to show that with the same $200 billion we could build comfortable homes for every family in the United States, provide each family with a moderately priced car, ad infinitum. In short, comparing and contrasting statistical material with things the audience already understands and appreciates make the figures far more meaningful to the listener. And if statistics are worth using at all, they are worth making meaningful.

Using Statements by Authorities

The third type of evidence consists of *statements by prominent authorities,* relating to the point at issue. When a person has no first-hand information about a subject, he is usually willing to accept the views of other people who *do* know the subject first hand, and in whose honesty and judgment he has confidence. Consequently, statements by authorities provide an important form of evidence in debate.

From the standpoint of their use in debate, statements by authorities fall into two general classes. First, we have statements as to *facts,* made sometimes by individual witnesses, but usually by government departments, authoritative research organizations, or recognized publications such as encyclopedias and yearbooks. From the standpoint of evidence, these statements of fact comprise a distinct class, since they are almost invariably used as a part of some other form of evidence—*examples, statistics,* and occasionally *illustrations.* Unless the facts concerning the examples or instances used as proof are already known to the listeners, the debater usually gives the *source* of his information or facts; and when statistics are presented, the name of the agency or organization which collected and tabulated the figures is a necessary part of the evidence.

The second type of statements by authorities is used independently, as a separate form of evidence. This consists of statements of *opinions,* taken sometimes from reports of government investigating committees or of private research organizations, but usually taken from statements of individual authorities. If the person whose opinion is offered is a man held in high esteem by the audience, the statement of his opinion may have tremendous weight with listeners. Consider, for instance, the attitude expressed in Washington's "Farewell Address" toward foreign alliances: "It is our true policy to steer clear of permanent alliances with any portion of the foreign world." Washington's opinion, quoted again and again by opponents to the League of Nations in 1920, was largely responsible for the unwillingness of the American people in that year to join the League.

Note the use of the two different classes of statements of authorities in the following illustrations. The first two illustrations make use of the *statements of facts* by authorities; the other illustrations make use of *statements of opinions* by authorities:

Don't be fooled by my opponent's unsupported charge that television network programs consist chiefly of mystery and western programs. Dr. Frank Stanton, president of CBS, reported the real facts in his Benjamin Franklin Lecture at the University of Pennsylvania in December of 1961. Listen to what he had to say: "In the month of November, for example, the three networks provided their affiliates with over a thousand hours of programing. This consisted chiefly of 99½ hours of actual news events and straight news broadcasts, 23¾ hours of documentary news, 19 hours of discussion, 45 hours of education and religion, 77 hours of sports, 63¼ hours of general drama, 8 hours of panel shows, 84 hours of situation comedy, 41½ hours of variety, 84¾ hours of serial drama, and 74¾ hours of children's programs. Of the total, 56 hours were mysteries and 60½ hours were westerns—a combined total of 11 per cent of all the programing." [9] Those are the facts—fewer westerns than newscasts and fewer mysteries than children's programs.

We dare not outlaw atomic research which depends on further nuclear blasts, regardless of the danger of using nuclear findings in war. Our atomic research is already of tremendous value to the human race. Nobel Prize winner Dr. Glenn T. Seaborg, chairman of the Atomic Energy Commission, pointed up this fact in addressing the American Association for the Advancement of Science on December 27, 1961. Dr. Seaborg said, "In 1940 there was no such thing as atomic energy. Today, atomic energy is one of our biggest enterprises. The capital investment of the Atomic Energy Commission is $7.5 billion before depreciation. Its annual budget is $2.5 billion. It is true that approximately 75 per cent of this is devoted to defense activities. Yet, some $600 million per year are also dedicated to peaceful arts—to the development of productive industries for the present and the future, such as power reactors and research on controlled fusion; to the advance of medicine and its application; to the growth of knowledge in many areas of fundamental research; to the export of materials and techniques as a part of our international relations program. In addition, there is the private atomic energy industry, involving non-governmental expenditures of $50 million annually on development, and with a capital

[9] *Representative American Speeches: 1961-1962* (Reference Shelf. v 34, no 4. 1962) p 81.

investment of $400 to $500 million. And we can hardly visualize the ultimate potential of this great private industry." [10] To bring this industry to a standstill, or to abolish it, because we fear wartime nuclear blasts, is unthinkable. We might as well abolish medicine because we fear the findings of its research might be used by criminals in murder. We must find some other solution to warfare. We dare not outlaw nuclear research that depends on atomic blasts.

You have heard that we should abandon West Berlin because it is impossible to defend it in case of war with the Soviets. President Kennedy, who is in a better position to know than are we, does not think so. On July 25, 1961, in his radio-television address to the nation he said, "I hear it said that West Berlin is militarily untenable. And so was Bastogne. And so, in fact, was Stalingrad. Any dangerous spot is tenable if men—brave men—will make it so." [11]

Senator Margaret Chase Smith is on the Senate Committee on Armed Services and on the Senate Aeronautical and Space Science Committee. She has access to information not available to the public. Does she believe, in the light of her special knowledge, that a balance of nuclear power can be counted on to keep the peace? Speaking on this very subject to the United States Senate on September 21, 1961, she said, "Deterrence cannot be regarded as an assured fact. . . . We are dealing with military power on both sides that is infinitely complicated, composed of many critical elements. This power itself floats on a sea of uncertainty, constantly subject to the restless tides of progress and the tidal waves of great change. *To say that we can count on achieving and maintaining balance or stability in these conditions—even if we had the Soviet's cooperation, much less their opposition—is nothing short of wishful thinking—a form of 'nuclear escapism' to dodge the hard, cold facts.*" [12]

And how does President John F. Kennedy, commander-in-chief of our armed forces, feel about disarmament? Speaking to the General Assembly of the United Nations on September 25, 1961, he spoke for disarmament in crystal-clear terms. He said, "For fifteen years this organization has sought the reduction and destruction of arms. Now

[10] *Ibid.* p 115-16.
[11] *Ibid.* p 10.
[12] *Ibid.* p 34.

that goal is no longer a dream—it is a practical matter of life or death. The risks inherent in disarmament pale in comparison to the risks inherent in the unlimited arms race." [13]

Rules for using statements by authorities. There are definite limitations upon the effectiveness of statements of opinion as a form of proof. If a listener has strong views of his own on a given subject, he may be influenced toward a contrary point of view by piling up a cumulation of well-supported *facts*—but he will be influenced but little, if at all, by the *opinions* of men who differ with his own beliefs no matter how widely recognized may be the authorities quoted. Statements of opinion are valuable only when listeners have no fixed beliefs on the matter at issue, or when they are already somewhat inclined to favor the side upheld by the authorities quoted.

Several important rules should be kept in mind in using statements by authorities, whether in the field of opinions or of facts:

1. The authority cited must be recognized by the listener as a man worthy of belief.

Individuals known to the listener and in whom the listener has full confidence, and publications with a reputation for reliability, are the best sources of testimonial evidence. The opinions of a man whom the listener does not know have no value in debate, unless you "build him up" as an authority by telling of his experience and accomplishments in the field on which he speaks. Men whose names are entirely unfamiliar to the listener may be "built up" in this manner by telling of the important positions they hold, or of the books they have written, or of the important investigations they have made. But the listener must recognize the person quoted and accept him as a real authority before the opinions quoted have any value as evidence.

2. The authority must be in close touch with the field about which he speaks.

[13] *Ibid.* p 44.

Naturally, we demand that our authorities should have a first-hand knowledge of the facts about which they speak. Hearsay testimony is not accepted in the law court, and it is of no greater value in debate. The most respected member of the Senate cannot be accepted as an authority on some complicated question of atomic energy unless he is also known to be a specialist in the field or in a position to know because of committee appointments. Colonel Glenn, the astronaut, may be considered an authority on space travel, but his opinions on international politics or on farm relief are no better than those of the average man. First-hand acquaintance with the facts must be demanded of every authority.

3. The authority must be recognized as being free from prejudice on the subject.

A prejudiced witness cannot be accepted as worthy of complete belief, no matter how honest and sincere he may be. If the listener knows that prejudice exists, or even suspects its existence, he will not accept the opinions of that authority, or even his statements as to the facts in the case. The head of the Anti-Saloon League may make interesting statements concerning the failure of our present liquor laws, but his opinions will hardly be taken at face value. The same would be true of a statement opposing government ownership which comes for the president of a great railroad system. Even a statement by the President of the United States would be discounted by most listeners, if the statement dealt with the accomplishments of his party while in power. Of course, if a prejudiced witness makes an admission which favors the side he opposes, that statement would be valuable as evidence. But ordinarily the statements of every authority are entirely in harmony with whatever bias he may have on the subject. So the authorities cited in debate should be chosen, as far as possible, from men who have no reasons to be prejudiced concerning the subject under discussion.

Many individuals meet this test, of course. But the most valuable evidence is that which is taken from reports of government bureaus, from the findings of research agencies, or from statistical publications or yearbooks with a reputation for accuracy and disinterestedness. Such publications will be accepted by almost every listener as free from bias and worthy of belief.

4. The statement quoted must be clear and definite.

Any statement that is so vague that it might mean almost anything will naturally be of little value as evidence. Debaters sometimes offer quotations whose language is so indefinite that listeners cannot be sure whether the authority was speaking about the matter under discussion, or about some entirely different subject. Be sure that every statement you quote is so clear and direct that your listeners will know exactly what opinion the authority holds; if the statement is not straightforward and clear, it is better not to use it at all.

5. Give the opinions of several authorities, rather than of one.

The final test of all evidence is the *willingness of the listener to accept it as providing sufficient reason to believe the statement it supports.* Any listener is more likely to accept as true a statement supported by the opinions of *several* authorities, than one which represents the beliefs of only one man. One man may make an honest mistake, but it is unlikely that three or four men will make exactly the same error. In using testimony as evidence, the greatest strength comes from using the opinions of *at least three or four* good authorities who express the same general views.

Opinions as proof. While the opinions of authorities are a valuable form of evidence, debaters should remember that they are not the *only* type of evidence available, nor even the *best* type in most cases. Many beginning debaters collect ten or twelve statements in support of each point they advance, and expect the audience to listen patiently as they read all of these opinions to their listeners. Statements of authority used in that way have three grave weaknesses. First and most important, listening to statement after statement makes monotonous and dreary work for listeners. Second, opponents are able to nullify this sort of evidence by citing an equally long list of equally good authorities supporting *their* side of the proposition. And third, listeners like to feel that they are doing some of the thinking. They grow tired of being told, in effect, that they should believe something or other because some authority says they must.

Statements by authorities have the greatest effectiveness in debate when they are used in connection with other forms of evidence. If the debater supports his contention with familiar examples and vivid statistics, his listeners can arrive at the desired conclusion through their own efforts—at least they feel that they have had a part in reaching the conclusion. Then, if two or three statements by authorities are added, agreeing with that conclusion, the listener is flattered to learn that the authorities you mention have arrived at the same view he holds himself. Never use the opinions of authorities alone, if other forms of evidence can be found to support your point.

Using Illustrations

Illustrations or *comparisons* provide the final form of evidence to be considered. An illustration is an *imaginary example,* showing *how the idea works* or how it would work in practice. Sometimes the illustration is taken from the same field as the idea it supports; sometimes it is taken from an entirely different field, closer to the everyday experience of the listener. In either case, it should build a *vivid picture* in the listener's mind, showing just how the thing you are discussing can be expected to work. If the picture is *striking* enough to make the listener remember it, it will be highly effective in getting him to accept the point you are trying to prove.

For example, suppose that you are arguing against compulsory military training, and are trying to show that such training results in serious injury to men who are drafted by taking them away from their regular occupations for a year. To support that contention, you cite the case of a young doctor, called into military service just after he had succeeded in building up a small practice. You tell about his experiences after his return from the army—how he finds his practice taken over by other doctors, how he discovers that much of his medical knowledge has been forgotten, how he learns that his calloused hands have lost the deftness required of a surgeon. By giving a vivid picture of that one man's experience, you make your listeners realize the extent to which compulsory training would probably injure the individual.

Frequently the illustration is taken from a different field than the one involved by your contention—a field that is *closer to the everyday experience* of the listener. For example, you compare our system of presidential elections, arousing citizens to a more direct interest in their government, to an alarm clock which rings only once in every four years. The idea of an alarm clock which rings so infrequently seems ridiculous to your listeners, and their feeling is carried over to the field of interest in elections. Or, to show the need for government leadership in organizing our production requirements for national defense, you compare the system of private enterprise with a football team without a quarterback—every member of the team doing his best, but accomplishing very little because of the lack of a plan. Your listeners know little about the idea of national planning, but they do know something about a football team; since they know that some one must call signals if a football team is to gain any ground, they will readily believe that the same idea applies to industry.

Note the way in which illustrations have been used in the following examples:

Regardless of anything the affirmative may say, they can't prove to us that there will not be political interference and graft under government management of the railroads. We do not intend to stand here tonight, and tell you that we can prove, beyond the shadow of a doubt, that there *will* be political interference. But if your neighbor has a vicious dog that has been biting strangers again and again for the past five or six years, and if a stranger comes into your neighbor's yard, you can't logically *prove* in advance that the dog will bite that stranger. But, you will agree, you can certainly *expect it*. And in the same way, we cannot positively prove that there will be political interference under government ownership and operation of the railroads. But we can reasonably expect such interference.

———

Before considering directly the affirmative's plan to take from the Supreme Court its check upon constitutionality of legislation, I want to tell you a little story which bears upon our subject tonight. Bill Johnson was an old prospector who lived thirty-five or forty miles back in the hills and came down to Missoula about once a month for supplies. Bill got pretty tired of tramping back and forth on foot, so one day he bought an old, rattle-trap, secondhand Ford car, gave away the burro which he had been using to carry his pack, and drove away happy. There was a pretty good road running up to within less than a mile of Bill's camp, so on the way home everything went lovely.

But a week or two later when Bill started to town again, things didn't go quite so well. Going downgrade he began to have trouble, as green drivers usually do have in the mountains. On the long downgrades, the brakes on his car would heat pretty badly; they would bind and jerk and almost stop the car entirely.

This binding and jerking made old Bill mad. So about halfway down one especially steep grade, he jammed the front end of his Ford against a boulder beside the road, climbed out, and with the aid of a few tools, a crowbar and a great deal of profanity, he jerked those offending brakes right out of that old Ford car. And then, much relieved, he climbed back under the wheel, bit off a generous chaw of tobacco, backed away from the boulder, and started down the grade, free at last of those troublesome brakes.

A few days later, a sheepherder found the car smashed almost beyond recognition at the bottom of a deep ravine near a turn in the highway; and beneath the car was what was left of old Bill Johnson. He'd got rid of his brake trouble, all right; but he'd forgotten to play safe.

Tonight, our friends from Kansas are asking us to do just about the same thing to our government that old Bill did to his secondhand Ford. They tell us that our government has some brakes on ill-advised action in the form of the check on the Supreme Court, and they are suggesting that to get rid of the occasional delays and checks that come from these brakes, we ought to yank them off entirely and go down the grade unchecked. As you consider their argument, I want you to remember the experience of old Bill Johnson.

———

Now, why are too few young men and women going into the medical profession today? Let us look at a young high school graduate called Jim, who is considering the study of medicine. After four years of regular college he must attend medical school an additional four years to receive his degree. But he still cannot practice medicine. He must now spend a minimum of one year as an intern in some hospital for an average wage of about $125 per month. He still cannot practice medicine. If he expects to be a family doctor or "general practitioner" he must spend four more years in "residency" at an average wage of about $200 per month. Of course, if he wishes to be a specialist in surgery, pathology, or some other line of medicine, he must spend seven years instead of four in residency. So, the high school graduate, Jim, faces schooling that will last from 13 to 17 years before he can hope to begin practicing medicine for profit.

But time is not the only factor facing him. His general college degree will cost him no more than would any other A.B. degree, from $1,400 per year on up, depending on the school he attends. His four years of medicine will cost him an additional $2,386 per year on the national average if he remains single, or $3,271 per year if he marries— a total of from $9,500 to $14,000 for his M.D. degree. Jim's chances of helping finance his education by earning while in school are almost nonexistent. Some medical schools forbid it. Scholarships and loans to medical students last year averaged only $500. If Jim asks he will find that last year's medical graduates owed from $2,000 to $5,000 each. And none of them can start paying off this debt for another five years at the earliest. Most will borrow more because the pay for interns and for doctors "in residency" is too small to meet their expenses, even faces schooling that will last from thirteen to seventeen years before he can hope to begin practicing medicine for profit.

Now, Jim sees a minimum of thirteen years of schooling ahead of him if he chooses medicine at an absolute minimum cost of $11,000. If you were Jim's parents, would you advise him to study medicine? You can understand why fewer qualified young people go into medicine than the nation needs. And although nothing can be done to shorten the training period, something can be done about the high cost that will encourage thousands of additional young people to enter the medical profession. Because it's a national problem, the federal government should subsidize the medical student who makes average or better than average grades.

———

Some working men and women want to join a union. Others do not. In either event their choice should be respected. A union is seldom merely a collective-bargaining representative. It is often also partly a political organization, partly a fraternal order, partly a social club and partly an insurance society. When a union donates money to political campaigns or otherwise involves itself in politics, it is just as bad in principle to give it the power to conscript members or to levy assessments as it would be to give the same power to the Republican party, to the Democratic party, or to the Communist party.

Rules for using illustration. The illustration depends for its effectiveness on the *vividness* and *reality* of the picture it gives the listener. It must explain *how the idea works* in a way that the listener will understand and remember. Three methods will aid in making the illustration clear and vivid:

1. To the greatest degree possible, the illustration should make use of the everyday experiences of the listener.

Our clearest mental pictures are those of things we have actually seen, or heard, or touched. Consequently, illustrations become more vivid if they are brought into the *everyday life* and *experience* of the listener. Apply the illustration to some person your listeners know—better still, build it around the listener himself, using the "Suppose you" opening. Have the happening you describe take place in some nearby community, or in the very neighborhood in which the debate is to be held. Base your comparisons on things your listeners themselves do or at least know about firsthand—driving a car, building a piece of furniture, managing a small business, preparing a meal. If the illustration is based on animals or on inanimate things, make them things that your listeners see every day—horses, dogs, tables, alarm clocks, automobiles, houses, newspapers, or similar commonplace things.

2. Give enough details to make the picture complete.

If you use people in your illustrations, give them names. Make them human; have them talk, move about, do things. Make them do the little homely things that people actually do— scratch their chins, blink their eyes, double up their fists, light their pipes—things which have nothing to do with the *idea* you are presenting, but that help make the people *real*. Tell your listeners what they say; use the same words your people would use in real life, and tell what they think and how they feel. Give enough details and descriptive materials so that your listeners can *see* the picture as a whole.

Note the details in the Bill Johnson illustration, on page 65. The old prospector was given a name—Bill Johnson. He bought "an old, rattle-trap, secondhand Ford car"; he jerked off the brakes "with the aid of a few tools, a crowbar and a great deal of profanity"; he "climbed back under the wheel," and "bit off a generous chaw of tobacco." These are just a few examples of the details given. Details stimulate the listener's imagination, and help make the picture you give clear and vivid.

3. Use some element in the illustration that will make the listener remember it.

While the illustration deals with familiar things, there must be something about it that is *different*; something that will make the listener remember it. This element is vital to the effectiveness of the illustration. It may be supplied by using any of a number of devices. You can have something *drastic* and *shocking* happen—one of your characters may be seriously injured or even killed, as in the illustration about Bill Johnson. You can appeal to the *sympathies* or *pity* of your listeners, showing that the situation you picture is extremely bad for the characters you introduce. You can use the element of *familiarity* by introducing local people or local institutions or everyday objects with which your listeners are acquainted. You can introduce an element of *unusualness* by having things take place which would not normally occur—remember the alarm clock which rang only once in four years. You can introduce *novelty* by giving the illustration an unexpected twist; sometimes you can make the illustration striking by the use of *humor*.

Sometimes your comparison will be very brief, simply showing the similarity between the idea you discuss and some commonplace thing. Sometimes it will require several sentences, introducing two or three characters, and using narrative form to show things that might be expected to happen to them if the idea you discuss is put into effect. But in any case, try to include some element that is *striking*. Your illustration will be effective only if the listener *remembers* it.

PART III—STUDYING THE SUBJECT

FINDING MATERIAL

In the preceding pages, we have taken up various items of background information about debate and the methods used to secure belief. In those which follow, that information will be applied to the actual debate situation. The rest of the book will explain in detail, step by step, the processes actually followed in preparing and presenting a debate.

Steps in preparing for debate. Five important steps are involved in preparing for a debate and presenting your arguments to listeners. These steps are the following:

1. Finding the material
2. Planning the case
3. Preparing the constructive speeches
4. Preparing for rebuttal
5. Presenting the debate

Each of these steps will be considered at length in one of the five remaining parts of this textbook. Under each of the steps, definite methods of procedure are suggested. Perhaps the rules laid down may sometimes seem arbitrary. But we shall try to explain in each case why the rules or methods of procedure we suggest are essential to good debating.

Preparation is 90 per cent of successful debating, whether in a formal contest debate situation or in the more important debate situations in the later lives of students. A debate itself takes only an hour or so, but it must be preceded by weeks of careful study, wise planning, and diligent practice. You must study the subject thoroughly, to learn all that is to be known about it. You must analyze the question to determine which arguments are most likely to win the acceptance and belief of your listeners, and the arguments your opponents can be expected to advance. A plan of attack must be laid out; speeches must be at least outlined; in some cases, portions of the debate speeches may be written. Possible arguments supporting the other side of the question must be carefully studied, and the strongest method found to meet each one of them. Then, before the debate itself takes place, hours should be spent in practice debating to develop confidence on the platform and skill in meeting the situations which may arise in actual debate. The more time and effort you give to preparation, the more effective debating you will do.

Information about the subject. The first step in preparation for debate is to get as much information as you possibly can about the subject you are discussing. The more you really *know* your subject, the more effective your efforts. In the televised debates between Senator Kennedy and Vice President Nixon in the political campaign of 1960, both candidates showed an astonishing mastery of a wide variety of subjects—subjects on which differences of opinion might be anticipated. If either had given evidence of insufficient knowledge of any of the score of different subjects which were brought up at different times during the televised series, it would have given a tremendous advantage to his opponent, who was better prepared. In your own situation, the more you read about your subject, and the more you think about various aspects of the subject as you read, the more clearly you will understand the proposal you are to discuss; wide reading likewise brings to light items of evidence which you can probably use effectively in your argument.

In gathering information on any subject, the intelligent debater follows some definite *plan*, to insure that his search for material is systematic and thorough. Aimless reading may turn up a part of the information available, but a hit-or-miss method not only wastes your time but also allows you to fail to discover a great deal of material that might be extremely valuable. To be *certain* of finding the material you need with a minimum of effort and the least amount of wasted time, follow the four steps suggested below:

1. Read for background information about the subject.
2. Prepare a comprehensive bibliography.
3. Collect as much material as you can find.
4. Read and study the materials you have discovered.

If you are working in cooperation with other debaters, you can probably save time by dividing the work involved in steps 2 and 3 with other members of the group, so that needless duplication of effort can be avoided. In going through various bibliographies or indexes which list sources of materials, for instance, one debater may check the references given in one set of indexes, another may take a second group, and so on. Or, when your bibliography has been prepared—presumably the result of group effort—and you have an idea of just what material is available, this list of available materials may be divided into sections, with different sections assigned to each member of the group. To insure that no really important material is overlooked, it is desirable to assign each section to at least two different debaters; to this extent, there may be duplication of effort, but you also have greater assurance that no important piece of evidence has been omitted from your material files.

Preliminary Reading

The first step in your study of the subject is to do enough preliminary reading to get a good general knowledge of the proposition for debate, of its historical background, and of the conditions which make it a matter of current interest. If you are discussing medical care for the aged provided by the federal government, for example, you'll probably find the subject discussed in general terms in fairly recent magazine articles. But as you read three or four such articles, you'll discover that considerably more background information is needed—about the Social Security system, about various plans of voluntary health

insurance, about provisions of bills introduced in Congress dealing with the general field of public health as well as the specific
question of medical care for older people. To get an adequate
background on the entire subject, including these related topics,
it's suggested that you consult in particular the following sources
of information:

1. For general and historical background material:

   Encyclopaedia Britannica

   The Encyclopedia Americana

   Encyclopedia of the Social Sciences

   Collier's Encyclopedia

2. For more recent information:

   Britannica Book of the Year

   The New International Yearbook

   The Americana Annual

   Collier's Yearbook

3. For information concerning conditions during the past
   year:

   Time

   Newsweek

   U.S. News & World Report

   New York *Times*

Encyclopedias and yearbooks are probably the best sources
of background historical information, and at least the *Encyclopaedia Britannica* and *The Americana Annual* are to be found
in practically every library. The *Encyclopedia of the Social Sciences* often contains much valuable information on questions
for debate, since most debate subjects lie in the field of social
science. It can be found in all of the larger public libraries, and
in nearly every college or university library.

The publishers of the major encyclopedias endeavor to keep
them up to date by revising a small portion of the articles in
each new printing. But since most articles are not revised in

each printing, the encyclopedias in your library may not provide information concerning recent developments in the field in which you are interested. To supply more recent information, the publishers of several major encyclopedias issue annual yearbooks, such as *The Americana Annual*, the *Britannica Book of the Year*, and *Collier's Encyclopedia Yearbook*. Another record of events is *The New International Year Book*, originally designed to supplement *The New International Encyclopedia* but now published independently. Files of these yearbooks will give you an account of important happenings relating to the fields in which you are interested.

But even the yearbooks are published only once a year; as a result, they do not cover those events which have taken place during the last few months, and these very recent changes may be of extreme importance. So, a careful reading of the files of such authoritative news magazines as *Time, Newsweek,* and *U.S. News & World Report* is essential. The handiest guide to the information contained in these and other popular magazines is the *Readers' Guide to Periodical Literature*, described on page 81, below. The New York *Times* carries articles discussing nearly all really important current public issues, in addition, of course, to news stories. Like the three news magazines recommended, the New York *Times* is available in nearly every library. Also, the *Times* publishes at regular intervals *The New York Times Index*, which lists all news stories and articles published in any issue of the newspaper, making it easy to locate materials which relate to the subject in which you are interested.

If you have consulted the various sources suggested and have read the materials they provide that relate to your subject, you should have acquired a fairly thorough background knowledge of that topic, as well as of other topics related to the specific subject you expect to debate. Incidentally, if there are several debaters working on the same subject, every member of the group should do *all* of the background reading suggested—this is not a part of the work of preparation that can be divided among the various individuals who make up the group.

All of this preliminary reading should be supplemented by discussion of the subject with others who are interested in the field. Sometimes you can find some older person in your community who has made a special study of the subject or of the general field in which the subject lies; nearly always one or more of the instructors in your school will have a good general knowledge of the field. If such a person can be found, he can give you valuable background information. In any event, your ideas on the subject will round into more definite form if you take occasion to discuss the various phases of the topic with your instructors or with other debaters.

PREPARING A BIBLIOGRAPHY

The second stage in your study of the question will be that of preparing a general *bibliography*. A bibliography is a list of books, pamphlets, magazine articles and other printed materials in which information can be found on a given subject. In most cases, bibliographies are classified, with separate sections for books, pamphlets, magazine articles, government reports, and miscellaneous publications; under each head, materials are listed alphabetically by name of the author or by name of the magazine, for easy reference. In some cases, they are classified according to phases of the general subject or by sub-topics. Excellent bibliographies on many subjects have already been compiled; the Bibliographical Division of the Library of Congress has bibliographies on practically every subject which is likely to be the basis of federal legislation; these bibliographies cannot be purchased, but copies may usually be borrowed for limited periods of time by public or school libraries. Issues of the *Bulletin of the Public Affairs Information Service* cite bibliographies on a variety of subjects, including many not on the Library of Congress bibliographical list. Other ready-made bibliographies are included in books in the Reference Shelf series, published by The H. W. Wilson Company; these books are compilations of articles and addresses on current issues and social trends. Bibliographies are also included in the materials provided by state high school debate leagues, on topics to be used by high schools in various states during the current year.

Preparing your own bibliography. Although published bibliographies are extremely helpful, they cannot completely meet your needs. On many subjects, published bibliographies are not available. Even if they are to be found, they may not deal with the exact aspect of the subject in which you are most interested—and obviously they cannot include references to materials which have appeared since the bibliographies were prepared. So on every subject you study, you'll find it necessary to build your own list of references. Use a published bibliography as a basis, if one is available, but check every available listing of printed materials as well, to find sources which are not included in any of the ready-made lists you are able to secure.

Indexes of published materials. Various government and commercial agencies issue monthly lists or *indexes* to all the materials published in books, pamphlets, magazines, or government documents. In nearly all of these indexes, the articles or printed materials are listed by *subjects*, as well as by titles or under the names of their authors. Consequently, by looking under the subject or subjects to which your question relates— and as a rule, any proposition for debate involves a number of different subjects or general topics—you can secure a complete list of publications or magazine articles dealing with that subject which have appeared during the month or year covered by that index. In nearly all cases, indexes are published once a month; however, materials covered are collected, reorganized and republished in volumes issued once every three months, or once a year, or in some instances, once every five years. This makes it easy to locate materials published during the past several years, or those published even within a period of a very few weeks.

One point should be made clear. None of the indexes attempts to provide references to all of the material published within the period of time it covers. Each index is limited to some one definite type of publication; one lists articles published in a specified list of general-interest magazines; another lists articles appearing in business publications; a third catalogues government publications, and so on. As many of the indexes as are available in your library should be consulted; if your library is not well equipped in this field, it is usually profitable to take the time to visit a larger library in a nearby city.

Some of the major indexes to publications are listed below, classified according to the general fields covered:

1. Books dealing with the subject, listed in
   Cumulative Book Index
   Library of Congress Catalog: Books
   Subject Guide to Books in Print

2. Magazine articles on the subject, listed in
   Readers' Guide to Periodical Literature
   International Index
   Business Periodicals Index
   Education Index
   Agricultural Index

3. Pamphlets on the subject, listed in
   Bulletin of the Public Affairs Information Service
   Vertical File Index

4. Government documents relating to the subject, listed in
   Monthly Catalog of United States Government Publications
   Monthly List of State Publications

As the heading indicates, all or practically all books published in the English language are listed in the *Cumulative Book Index*, and files of this index are to be found in practically every library. The *Library of Congress Catalog* lists all accessions to the Library of Congress—pamphlets as well as books, incidentally—and since the copyright laws of the United States require that two copies of every publication for which a copyright is issued must be deposited in the Library of Congress, the *Catalog* provides an index to all published copyrighted material. The *Subject Guide to Books in Print* is more likely than is the *Library of Congress Catalog* to be found in the average library. Students will find it less unwieldy and will find it likely to contain all important book titles on subjects for debate.

The magazine indexes listed—there are several others, by the way, but the five named cover the magazines most likely to have articles dealing with subjects used for debates—give references to articles published in magazines of various types. The *Readers' Guide* covers magazines of general circulation, and this index at least is to be found in nearly every library. Probably of greater value to the debater is the *International Index,* which includes articles and papers appearing in journals of American and British learned societies in the fields of economics, sociology, and government—the fields from which most debate topics are chosen. The *Business Periodicals Index* lists articles appearing in business publications; the *Education Index* covers periodicals in the field of education; and the *Agricultural Index* lists articles in publications concerned primarily with agriculture. There are also separate indexes covering publications in the fields of law, medicine, fine arts, and technology. If your subject lies in a field relating to government or economics or business or education, check the appropriate index, referring to the general subject in which you are interested and also to related topics, and make your own list of current or past articles relating to those subjects.

Many debaters make the mistake of limiting their bibliographies to books and magazine articles. This is a serious error, since some of the most valuable information on many subjects is published in pamphlet form, or appears in government documents. Most of the available pamphlets are listed in the *Bulletin of the Public Affairs Information Service,* which also includes many book and magazine references and some references to government documents. The *Vertical File Index* lists pamphlets only. The *Monthly Catalog of United States Government Publications* is prepared by the Superintendent of Documents, in Washington, and includes every item of published material issued by any federal department or agency. An annual index appears in the December issue of the *Monthly Catalog.* If your subject is one involving state rather than federal action, the *Monthly Checklist of State Publications* catalogs materials published by agencies of the various state governments.

By consulting the various indexes referred to, you can construct a fairly complete bibliography on the subject in which you are interested. It will not include all of the information available on the subject—encyclopedias, yearbooks, and unpublished materials will not be listed, for example—but it will provide you with references to a large part of the printed material that bears directly or indirectly on your subject.

During the entire time you are preparing for a debate, keep on the lookout for additional references that should be added to your bibliography. You'll run across a considerable amount of additional material in most cases: articles in reference books, pamphlets issued by various organizations which for some reason were not listed in the *Bulletin of the Public Affairs Information Service* or the *Vertical File Index,* and magazine articles or other publications which appear after your first bibliography was prepared. No bibliography is ever *complete;* you should continually add new references as you discover them.

COLLECTING MATERIAL

After you have listed all the references you can find on the subject, your next task is to *get* as much of the material as can be located. From the standpoint of securing it, published debate material falls under two general heads:

1. Material available in libraries

2. Non-library material

If you have access to a good library, most of the materials you need will be found on its shelves. If your local library has limited resources, you should plan to visit a larger library in a nearby city, to find materials to supplement those available locally. But in any case, your first step in collecting material will be to find out exactly what is available in your local library, and later, if necessary, in any larger library to which you have access.

Checking the bibliography. To begin with, check the references in your bibliography against the following lists of material to be found in your local library—and later, if necessary, against similar lists in a larger library:

1. The library card catalog
2. The library's list of periodicals received and on file

The card catalog is a file which includes separate cards for every book, pamphlet, or government document on the library shelves. As a rule, each item will be listed on at least three separate cards: one according to the title of the book or other publication; a second according to the name of the author; and a third according to general subject-matter. The periodical list must be secured from your librarian, or in a large library, from the person in charge of the periodical section; it will list all of the magazines which the library receives, and will indicate the period of years for which files of each magazine are available. If you check your bibliography against these two library lists, you can find out exactly which of the materials listed in your bibliography can be secured from the library whose facilities you are using. Of course, as new items are added to your bibliography, these should be checked at once to see whether your library has them on its shelves.

Reference materials. Your library will also have much helpful material that is not included in your bibliography, that is available in various *reference* books. Mention has already been made of the usefulness of articles on the subject provided in encyclopedias, and in the general yearbooks bringing encyclopedias up to date. Available encyclopedias should by all means be consulted; in addition, those articles on the subject you are to debate provided in such annual publications as the *Britannica Book of the Year* or the *New International Yearbook*. Other yearbooks give information in specialized fields; the *Statistical Abstract of the United States*, published by the Bureau of the Census, gives statistical information relating to characteristics of the population, business conditions, and other subjects investigated by the Census Bureau; the *Yearbook of the United Nations* covers activities of the United Nations, together with information about countries included in that organization. One of the most widely used annual publications is *The World Almanac*, published by the New York *World-Telegram and Sun*. If the subject is one of considerable importance over a period of years, not only current issues of yearbooks should be consulted, but also the articles dealing with the subject in issues of annual publications covering the past several years.

One type of reference book not previously mentioned is that which gives biographical material concerning people who have written books or articles or have made public statements dealing with the subject you are to debate. Some men can qualify as being *authorities* on the subject; others lack the special background of experience in the field, or have not held the public offices or other positions which entitle them to acceptance as authorities. And of course, materials from non-authoritative sources are of little value in debate. Two of the most valuable biographical sources are *Current Biography*, published monthly and later reprinted in annual volumes, and the always-standard *Who's Who;* both give information concerning men and women of outstanding importance on an international basis. *Who's Who in America* provides biographies of outstanding Americans; in addition, many individuals who may have authoritative status in specialized fields are listed in such publications as *Who's Who in the East, Who's Who in the Midwest,* the *Directory of American Scholars, American Men of Science,* and *Who's Who in Commerce and Industry*.

Inter-library loans. Occasionally your bibliography may include a reference to some book or pamphlet not available on the shelves of your local library, but which seems to be of unusual value in relation to your subject for debate. An example might be a doctoral dissertation written on some aspect of the subject, or a legal publication available only in a special law library. With respect to such publications, it may be possible for you to arrange with your local librarian to borrow the publication from a larger or more specialized library. Loans between libraries are not uncommon; in any case, it will pay you to see whether your local librarian can arrange to secure the material on a short-term loan basis. There are dozens of specialized libraries in larger cities—law libraries, medical libraries, libraries of materials relating to railroads, libraries maintained by broadcasting companies, to name a few; in many cases your librarian can secure materials that might be important to you on an inter-library loan basis.

So far, we have considered only materials likely to be available through your local library, or publications already on its shelves. But there are often other materials which your library does not have, which you can secure directly from the publisher, and which are important enough to warrant being purchased, if necessary, or secured simply by request.

Compilations of materials. An important source of debate material is provided by *compilations* on various subjects. Such compilations, published in book form and including reprints of magazine articles and excerpts from authoritative books, are available on nearly every topic which has been widely debated in recent years, or is of current general importance. Probably the most widely known and most useful compilations are those appearing in the Reference Shelf series, published by The H. W. Wilson Company; compilations on five different subjects are issued every year, and a sixth annual volume reprints recent speeches. If the topic you are to debate is one used by your state high school debate league, the state league itself probably makes available a compilation of materials dealing with the subject. In some instances, less formal compilations are available from the extension service of your state university. Debate league and extension service publications are not likely to be listed in the *Cumulative Book Index*, and so may not be included in your bibliography; compilations in the Reference Shelf series, however, will be given such listing. If a compilation of materials dealing with your subject has been prepared, it is almost always valuable enough to justify its purchase.

Government publications. Publications of the federal government will be listed in the *Monthly Catalog of United States Government Publications,* and with few exceptions, any of the government materials listed may be secured at nominal cost from the Superintendent of Documents, Government Printing Office, Washington, D.C. Very often, some government publications will be of extremely great value to you; nearly every conceivable subject will be dealt with in some document, since the government publishes annual reports of every department, commission or regulatory agency, special reports of congressional investigating committees, hearings of committees on pending legislation, and bulletins on an almost unlimited variety of subjects. Since it is not probable that your local library will have *all* of these government publications on its shelves, it is suggested that you write to the Superintendent of Documents, tell him the general subject in which you are interested, and ask him for a copy of the *Price List* of government documents dealing with that field. Price lists have been issued cataloging documents in more than a hundred different fields; each one lists the documents which are available, the date of publication, the number of pages, and the price of each publication listed. The *Price Lists* themselves are sent free, on request.

Sometimes at least some specific documents may be secured without cost, by asking your senator or congressman to supply them. Copies of speeches reprinted from the *Congressional Record,* copies of bills before Congress, and reports of various congressional committees can usually be secured in this manner; sometimes your congressman can send you other materials as well.

If the topic you are debating is one relating to state rather than to federal governmental activities, a list of available published materials is provided in the *Monthly Checklist of State Publications*. Materials from this list must be ordered from the secretary of state of the state issuing the publication.

Publications of propaganda organizations. A third type of material not ordinarily to be found on the shelves of your local library includes pamphlet publications of various organizations and societies, including those organizations actively interested in influencing public opinion with respect to various subjects. There are literally hundreds of organizations in the United States which provide the public with material favorable to causes in which they are interested. *The World Almanac* lists more than a thousand such organizations—in each case, with the name and address of the secretary or executive director of the organization named. Typical are the Association of National Advertisers, the American Trucking Association, the National Temperance League, the Navy League of the United States, the League to Abolish Capital Punishment, or the American Council on Education. Then of course there are numerous organizations which are primarily trade associations, such as the National Association of Broadcasters or the United States Chamber of Commerce, or labor or professional groups, such as the American Federation of Labor and Congress of Industrial Organizations, the American Bar Association, the American Medical Association, or the National Education Association. In some degree at least, each of the organizations listed is a "propaganda" organization, with the sole or more often the partial objective of influencing public opinion with respect to certain causes. Consequently, nearly every organization provides pamphlets—almost always without cost to the recipient—in which are presented the organization's point of view, concerning the subject or subjects in which the organization is most directly interested. A careful check on the list of associations and societies given in *The World Almanac* is almost sure to provide the names of one or two—and in some cases, of half a dozen—organizations which are likely to have published materials available on the subject you are debating; a letter to the organization will nearly always bring available publications, entirely without cost to you.

After you have secured all of the material available, your next concern is to read and study carefully the books and articles you have found. If several debaters are working on the same question, it will not be necessary for each one to try to read *every* item of material you have secured. Time can be saved by dividing the work along the lines suggested earlier in this section—dividing the list of available references into as many parts as there are debaters working on the subject, and assigning one part of the list to each member of the group. In this way, each debater will have ample time to make a very careful study of the material assigned to him, noting the strongest items of evidence and the articles which seem to be valuable enough to warrant their being read by other members of the group.

In studying the material assigned to you, keep four main purposes in mind:

1. Try to learn as much as you can about the subject, and to get the points of view of as many different authorities as possible.

2. Be on the lookout for new ideas and new suggestions for argument, both on your own side of the question and on that of your opponents.

3. Look for specific items of evidence, which might be used as proof.

4. Think while you read. Try to understand not only *what* is said, but *why* the author makes the statement he does.

While you are reading, make careful notes on what you read. Jot down any important facts you find concerning the question, any illustrations or instances or statistical data, any short quotable statements by authorities. The greater part of what you read and write down will not fit in with the particular plan of attack you finally decide to use, no doubt; but much of it will be of value regardless of the type of case you prepare. Detailed suggestions for taking notes are given in the next section. The important thing to remember here is to read carefully, study what you read, and try to understand just what specific things are said.

TAKING NOTES

From the time you begin your study of the question, form the habit of making *written notes* of all of the things you discover which you think may be helpful in making your argument. Jot down references to sources of material, and make notations of every new idea or new argument that is suggested, and of items of evidence that might be useful. In taking notes, follow some definite *system* that will allow you to organize the information you write down and to find it again when it is needed.

One system of note taking, used by many college and high school debaters, has proved especially valuable. It calls for taking down three major kinds of information, as suggested in the instructions below:

1. Make a bibliography card for every book, pamphlet, magazine article or document that you read.

2. Make a list of all reasons advanced supporting the affirmative side of the question, and another list of reasons supporting the negative side.

3. Make an evidence card for each item of evidence you discover which may be used to support arguments on either the affirmative or the negative.

Detailed suggestions concerning each of these types of note taking are given on the following pages.

Making Bibliography Cards

Very often a debater, in preparing his argument on some certain phase of the question, will discover that he needs some specific information to support his contention. And often, too, he has a vague recollection that some book or article read while he was studying the subject contained exactly the information he needs—but unfortunately, he cannot remember just what book or article it is that he wants. Difficulties of that type can be avoided by making a *bibliography card* for each book, magazine article, or other item of published material that he reads during his study of the question. Likewise, when several debaters are working on the same topic, the practice of making bibliography cards is a valuable aid in indicating which articles are valuable enough to be read by other members of the group.

Bibliography cards should be of uniform and convenient size—cards four by six inches are recommended, although three by five inch cards are also widely used—and the following information should be listed on the card made for each separate article or publication:

1. Material identifying the reference, including the author's name, title of the article or book, name of the magazine in which the article is printed, the page on which it begins, and date of publication.
2. Place where the book or other material is to be found, if needed again.
3. A condensed summary of the contents or thought developed in the article, followed by notations of any specific fact items of value which are included.
4. An estimate of the value of the article, to guide other members of the group in selecting articles for further reading. May include information as to whether point of view is affirmative, negative, or unprejudiced.

Figure 1 suggests the arrangement of material on the bibliography card. Identifying material should be placed at the top, with the writer's name at the extreme left. The source from which the publication may be secured may be placed in the lower left corner, and the estimate of the value of the article in the lower right corner. This leaves the center of the card free for a summary of the article and for mention of statistical data, illustrations, instances or other material included.

Ching, Cyrus S. "The Future of Labor Management Relations,"
  Vital Speeches, v15, no19, Jl 15, 1949

  Contents: Discusses the importance of understanding human
    relationships in collective bargaining as a tool for the
    preservation of our economy

  Local Library: Superior analysis of the basic
    Periodical stack   Labor-Management problem

Figure 1. Specimen Bibliography Card

If bibliography cards are prepared systematically for all of the
books or other materials read, it will be an easy matter to find a
source from which any specific information needed can be secured
by glancing through the file of cards on articles read. A separate
card should be made for each book or article read, whether it has
any information of value or not; and the cards should be filed
alphabetically under the names of the writers.

Listing Arguments

A second type of material to be noted in written form consists of the various *arguments* advanced by writers of books or
articles on the subject for discussion, supporting either the affirmative or the negative side of the question. If every new argument
encountered in the course of reading on the question is written
down, a study of the list resulting will give the debater a very
good idea of just what points may be brought up in the debate.

In preparing your file of arguments, it is desirable to place
each argument on a separate card of the same size used for bibliography purposes, or on a separate sheet of loose-leaf notebook

paper. Every article you read will probably suggest one or more *reasons* for believing in one side or the other of the question; even very impartial and objective articles usually list the reasons advanced by those favoring and by those opposing the proposal. List every *reason* suggested for accepting the proposal on a card, headed "Affirmative Argument"; every reason suggested for *not* accepting the proposal on a card with the heading "Negative Argument." As far as your listing of these possible arguments is concerned, it makes no difference whether the writer is a well-known authority or whether he is completely unknown; you're interested in the *idea* he presents, and not in its source.

However, it is highly desirable that for each separate argument listed, you make reference, on the same card, to any published article in which an especially effective development of that argument is included—including of course, name of the writer, title of the article, and exact source. If the plan of attack you finally decide upon calls for use of that particular argument, it will be helpful to you to check back to the article and see just how the writer supported his point.

SELECTING EVIDENCE

A third type of information to be included in your notes consists of the definite examples, statistics, opinions of authorities, and other items which may be used as *evidence* in presenting your argument. These items should be listed on separate *evidence cards,* using a form that will be suggested later. But your first problem will be to select *which items* of evidence are to be included in your notes. Naturally, if you read a hundred different books or pamphlets or articles on the subject, you will probably find several hundred different items which *might* be taken down as evidence. But a great deal of this material will have little real *value* as evidence, and there is no reason to clutter up your evidence file with worthless items. Test out every item you find before taking it down; be sure that it would really have value as *proof* before including it in your notes.

Comparisons and illustrations. So far as illustrations or comparisons are concerned, the problem of selection is not difficult. Any illustration or comparison that is *striking enough to catch your attention* as you read, and which of course relates to a possible argument on the question, is worth taking down. If it catches your attention, it probably would capture the attention of an audience. And if it is striking enough to get the attention of listeners and make the idea illustrated *vivid* to them, it should be available when you are ready to select the particular items of evidence to use in building your argument.

Examples. Almost every *example* or *instance* that you find in your reading should likewise be jotted down, if it relates to any point that might be included in the argument. Usually the number of instances you can find to support any given point will be limited; if that point is to be used in your argument you probably will need all the examples you can find to support it. Of course, if you find that the number of available examples supporting some possible point is extremely great, include in your notes only those which you think would have the greatest value as evidence—those which support your point most *directly,* those which are most *recent,* or those which your listeners are most likely to *know about,* themselves.

Frequently you will find that the same happening will be described in three or four different articles. In such a case, there is of course no need to include all of the different accounts in your notes. Choose the account given on the best authority, or given by the writer your listeners are most likely to believe.

Statistics. The amount of statistical material that should be included in your file of evidence cards naturally will depend on the nature of the question you are debating. For a debate on government ownership of railroads, you would need a great amount of statistical data relating to earnings and operating costs of roads in various countries, including both privately owned and state-owned systems. But if you are discussing the value of interscholastic athletics, very little statistical material will be available. As a rule, you should take down notes on every set of statistics you find that relates to any point that *might* come up in the debate, provided that the figures come from authoritative sources. If statistical data that you think will be valuable is found in an article by some unknown writer, or in one by a prejudiced authority, check up on the figures given in some standard reference work such as the *Statistical Abstract* or *The Statesman's Year-Book*. If the same figures are given in an authoritative reference book of this kind, list them in your notes as coming from that book rather than from the doubtful source from which you first secured them.

If the statistics you find are given in tabular form, make it a practice to take down the entire table, or at least all of it that relates to any point that might be used in your argument. Of course, not all of the figures in the table will be used, but you can't tell when you are taking your notes just *which* of the figures given may be needed when you are on the platform.

Statements of opinion. Most of the evidence you will find will be in the form of statements of opinion by authorities. If you read widely on the subject, you will find hundreds of such statements. Some will apply directly to the subject for debate itself, especially if the writer is definitely in favor of or definitely opposed to the proposal. But the greater number will be statements dealing with some specific phase of the subject—some reason advanced in the article for supporting or opposing the course proposed.

Of course, not all of these statements of opinion should be included in your notes. Take down only those that will be most valuable to you. In deciding which statements to use and which to discard, three tests should be applied. First, take down the statements only of men who are *authorities*—men who are already accepted as authorities by the general public, or men who hold positions which will cause them to be accepted, who have firsthand knowledge about the subject, but who have no personal reasons for prejudice. Don't bother with the opinions of men who cannot be established as authorities. Second, take down only those statements of opinion that are short, definite, and direct. If the writer tells you exactly what he thinks about the subject in twenty or thirty words, his statement will carry conviction. But if the statement is vague and indirect, or if it is qualified, or if three or four sentences would have to be quoted to express the writer's opinion, that will be a good statement to omit from your files. Third, take down only the statements which support points that are important in the argument on the question. You can't afford to fill your evidence files with statements on trivial points that are certain not to come up in the debate.

One other suggestion must be offered with respect to your statements of opinion. Sometimes in an actual debate, your opponent may charge that the opinion you quote does not represent the actual opinion of the authority—that you have taken a single statement, or even only a portion of a sentence, out of context. To be on the safe side, take down *not only* the brief, succinct statement referred to in connection with the second requirement above, but also the sentence preceding it and the sentence following, if they relate to the same material—and *underline* the specific short statement you find valuable as expressing the position of the authority.

What sources are authoritative. Evidence in the form of examples, statistics, or statements of opinion should be taken from sources that listeners will accept—either from books or articles written by men who qualify as authorities, or from other authoritative sources. Which brings up the question: What publications and what individuals should be accepted as competent authorities?

Reference books such as the *Encyclopaedia Britannica,* the *Statistical Abstract,* and others mentioned in the preceding section, are accepted by everyone. Government reports are highly authoritative.[14] Publications of such research agencies as the

---

[14] This does not apply to every statement found in every government publication. Speeches found in the *Congressional Record,* for instance, are not to be considered as official government statements; they are made by individual senators or representatives who usually are strongly prejudiced on the subjects they discuss. Similarly, the testimony given by witnesses in hearings before congressional committees is almost always biased. The value of material from these two sources will depend upon the general attitude of the public toward the individuals quoted.

Brookings Institution, the National Industrial Conference Board, or the Carnegie Endowment for International Peace, will be generally accepted by listeners as worthy of belief, at least as regards any factual materials or statistics given.

Individuals who might be regarded as authorities fall into three general classes. First, there is a very small group of men who are already known and already accepted as authorities by the average listener—men such as the President of the United States, certain members of the Cabinet, leading members of Congress, a few great industrialists, and a number of other men prominent in public life. A second group would include men who are not known to the average listener as individuals, but whom he would accept as authorities because of the *positions they hold.* Professors in leading universities, heads of government departments or members of government commissions, members of the diplomatic or consular service, editors of important newspapers or magazines, representatives of authoritative research agencies, and officers of such national organizations as the American Legion, the American Farm Bureau Federation, or the National Federation of Women's Clubs, would probably be accepted as worthy of belief by most listeners. In every case, of course, it is assumed that the position held by the individual is one which would bring him into contact with the field under discussion.

A third group of individuals who may be accepted as authorities includes men who are as individuals unknown to the general public, but whose views will be accepted by the average listener because of *publications* with which their names are associated. A man who has written a recognized book on a given subject will generally be accepted as an authority on that subject. Similarly, writers for "scholarly" publications such as the *American Journal of Sociology,* the *Quarterly Journal of Economics,* the *American Historical Review,* the *Journal of Applied Psychology,* or the *Annals of the American Academy of Political and Social Science,* may be considered authorities in the fields in which they write.

On the other hand, writers for the popular magazines such as *Life* or the *Saturday Evening Post,* or even for such more serious publications as the *Saturday Review* or the *Atlantic Monthly,* should be checked very carefully. Usually the contributors to such magazines are professional writers rather than experts in the fields about which they write; sometimes, too, their articles are colored to harmonize with the editorial policies of the publication. And, of course, the men who prepare pamphlets or reports for private propaganda organizations are not to be quoted as authorities. No doubt they are well acquainted with the field about which they write, but their articles are always colored by prejudice—they are *advocates,* rather than authorities.

Whenever you find a statement that might be valuable as evidence, check on the man who wrote the article before including the information he gives in your evidence file. Many magazines give you information concerning each contributor in a note at the beginning or at the end of the article, or in a separate section in which all contributors to that issue are identified. If the writer is not identified in the magazine itself—or not sufficiently identified—look up his name in *Current Biography, Who's Who,* or *Who's Who in America.* If these do not list him, try the "Who's Who" in his special field, or look in *Cumulative Book Index* and the magazine indexes to see what you can learn about him from other things he has written. Satisfy yourself that the writer is really an authority before you include in your evidence file any statistics he gives or any opinion he expresses.

Evidence on both sides. Include in your notes the items of evidence you find on *both sides* of the question—not merely that which favors the side you expect to uphold in your debate. If you are one of a number of debaters who are working on the same question, the information you note down will help other members of the squad as well as yourself—and some of the group will be taking the other side of the argument. Even if you are working alone, a file of the items of evidence available to your opponents will help you. If you are acquainted with the materials available to the other side, you can have a pretty good idea of what arguments they are likely to use; and you are likewise in a position to correct your opponents on the platform if their citing of evidence is not entirely accurate.

Evidence Cards

Each item of evidence that you decide to include in your notes should be placed on a separate *evidence card*. Some debaters use notebooks instead of cards; this method is not recommended, since it makes it impossible to organize and classify the different items secured. Cards of uniform size should be used by all of the members of your team, preferably similar to those on which *bibliography* materials are noted. Usually a card three by five inches is used for each item included in your notes.

The information on each card should include the following:

1. A "headline," giving the gist of the evidence noted on the card
2. The name of the authority quoted
3. The position the authority holds, or other reasons for accepting him as an authority
4. The evidence or proof-material itself
5. The exact source from which the item is taken, including name of the publication, page, and date

The form to be used is suggested in Figure 2. Notice that the "headline" is placed in the upper left corner of the card. It should be very concise; three or four words should be enough to suggest the idea given on the card. The name of the authority, and information as to why he is an authority, should be entered in the upper righthand corner of the card. The exact source of the material presented should be placed at the bottom of the card, including title of article or publication, date, and page. And the item of evidence itself is placed in the center of the card—if too long to be included on the front of the card, a portion may be carried over to the back of the card, but leave the "source" entry at the bottom of the front side of the card.

Extent of Programs Produced   Dr. Frank Stanton
    by a TV Network   President, Columbia
                                                Broadcasting System

"The complexity and magnitude of networking are also indicated by the staggering size of the CBS Television Network's annual program output. In 1956, the network—by itself or in association with independent program packagers—will produce and broadcast approximately 2,500 hours of programs. This does not take into account programs broadcast by the network but produced entirely by others. Compare, if you will, these 2,500 hours of programs with the 427 hours which represent the amount of playing time for all U.S. feature films produced for release in 1955. In other words, the program product of the CBS Television Network this year is about six times that of Hollywood's total feature film output."

—Statement before Senate Committee on Interstate and Foreign Commerce, June 12, 1956. (From pamphlet with that title, published by Columbia Broadcasting System, page 15.)

Figure 2. SPECIMEN EVIDENCE CARD

Study the figure until you are familiar with the arrangement of the different items it contains.

If the statement is one giving the *opinion* of an authority, quote the authority directly, using his own words; direct quotations of this kind should be indicated by using quotation marks. If the material consists of *illustrations, comparisons,* or *statistical tabulations,* direct quotation is not necessary. References to *examples* may be quoted directly if they are short and forcefully stated; otherwise the information given by the authority may be given in your own words.

Organizing the evidence. After you have collected a number of evidence cards, they should be classified and filed according to subject matter. Separate filing boxes should be used for affirmative and negative material. In each file, the evidence should be classed under fifteen or twenty subject headings, so that all of the cards relating to each phase of the question are placed in the same section of the file.

To illustrate the method of classification used, the following headings might be found in an affirmative file on the question of compulsory military training:

A. Analysis of the Proposition
   1. Definition of terms
   2. History of the question
   3. Admitted points
   4. Irrelevant points
   5. The issues
B. The *need* for (or points against) the Proposition
   1. Past conditions
   2. Present conditions
   3. Future conditions or possibilities
C. Possible Remedies or Solutions
   1.
   2.
   3.
D. The Remedy Proposed
   1. Practicability of the remedy
      a. How will it operate
      b. Cost
      c.
   2. Desirability of the remedy
   3. *Cure* for the need
E. Counter-Remedies (offered by negative)
   1. Practicability claimed
   2. Desirability claimed
   3. Superiority claimed over affirmative remedy

Make a tentative list of the subject groups into which your evidence cards may logically be divided. This list may be added to or changed as other items of evidence are added to your file:

when you have decided on the plan of attack you will use in
your debate, you may find it desirable to revise your classification system entirely. But some set of subject headings should
be used for organizing your evidence soon after you first begin
taking notes.

Organizing your evidence cards in the way suggested has
several important advantages. First, it makes it easy to eliminate
duplicate cards, and to discover in reading any given article
whether each specific item of evidence found in that article is
already included in your file. Second, it makes it easy to find
any separate bit of evidence when you need it. And finally,
it supplies a convenient means by which you can check your
stock of evidence on each separate subject to see in which fields
additional evidence is needed. If the information listed under
any subject heading is not as complete as you think it should
be, you have a definite idea of what to look for in the way of
added evidence.

PART IV—PLANNING THE CASE

ANALYZING THE PROPOSITION

After you have studied the subject thoroughly, you are ready for the next step in preparation for the debate—that of *planning the case,* or deciding upon the plan of attack to be used in your constructive argument. This step may logically be divided into four phases, as follows:

1. Analyze the proposition you are to discuss.
2. Choose the main points to be presented.
3. Determine the methods of proof to be used for each main point.
4. Prepare a final working outline.

The first of these four stages of the *planning* step in preparation will be discussed in this section; the others in the sections which follow.

Every debate deals with some general subject, such as "compulsory military training," or "a league of American nations," or "public ownership of electric power utilities." But the actual clash of argument centers about some specific proposal upheld by the affirmative team, usually called the *question for debate,* although ordinarily it is stated in the form of a resolution, and it is called a proposition in formal debating. The language in which the question is stated is extremely important; it determines exactly the sort of proposal the affirmative must support. To know exactly what idea you are upholding or condemning, you must study very carefully the meaning of every important word or group of words in the formal statement of the question. You must discover exactly what the resolution means, what ground it covers, what changes it involves from the present system, and what the affirmative is obligated to prove. And you must decide what interpretation may be placed upon the question that will make your side least difficult to support.

Defining the terms. As a rule, the proposition used in any formal debate has been carefully worded; the men who phrased the resolution have tried to define at least the general idea which the affirmative must uphold. But words have various meanings. As a result, the question for debate may be subject to several different *interpretations*. To discover just what the question means, you will have to *define the terms* used in the resolution—the words and phrases which carry the meaning.

This process of *defining terms* is nothing new; you use it constantly in everyday life. Suppose, for example, you ask yourself this question: "Should I give a party for my friends?" Before you can come to any intelligent decision, you have to decide just what you mean by the words you have used. Such words as "should" and "I" and "give" should offer no difficulties; their meaning is clear. But what about the other terms? What do you mean by "party"? Do you mean a picnic, a gathering at your home, a banquet, a formal dance, a line-party at the theater, or something else? And what do you mean by the phrase "for my friends"? Does the term "friends" include everyone with whom you are on friendly terms, or the smaller group of those of your own age or in your own class at school, or the four or five people with whom you are most intimate? You have to define these *terms* and decide exactly what you mean by them, before you can examine intelligently the arguments for and against giving a party.

The same principle applies with respect to the proposition for debate. Every resolution used as a question for debate will include some terms which have to be defined. Suppose that you are debating the proposition, *"Resolved, that the United States should protect by armed force the possessions of its citizens in foreign lands."* Some of the terms used require no definition; their meanings are obvious. But what is meant by the phrase "protect by armed force"? Protect against what? Against acts of the regularly constituted governments in the countries in which the possessions lie? Against destruction by rioters or revolutionists? Or merely against the actions of common criminals? And what is meant by "armed force"? Does that mean simply the provision of special policemen to guard American property, or does it involve sending troops into a foreign country, or does it obligate this nation to go to war, if necessary? "Possessions of its citizens"—what does that term include? Does it include wallets in the pockets of tourists, bank deposits of Americans in shaky foreign banks, American-owned stocks or bonds of foreign business concerns, or concessions and special privileges granted to American concerns by foreign governments—or does it refer only to factories and oil wells that are located abroad? Even the term "in foreign lands" might be given more than one interpretation. Does it mean in *every* foreign country, including nations at war and in danger of invasion—or does it refer only to small Caribbean nations for instance?

You will notice that several of the terms in the resolution have a number of possible meanings. That is true of nearly every proposition for debate. And the meaning of the proposition will vary a great deal, depending on the definitions that are given the terms.

The meaning of the question. Under such conditions, how is it possible to find the *one, exact* meaning of the proposition you are to debate? The answer is that it *isn't* possible. Nearly every question, no matter how carefully it is phrased, can be interpreted in several different ways. And any one of these possible interpretations may be the one that is used in the debate.

In this matter of interpretation, the affirmative has a decided advantage. The affirmative upholds the resolution, so it is the privilege of the affirmative to decide just what interpretation it will support. The affirmative may give the question any interpretation *that the listener will accept as fair and reasonable,* in view of the language in which the proposition is stated, and the negative has no choice but to accept it. Of course, if the affirmative interpretation is *too* extreme, the negative may win some advantage with the audience by attacking it and showing how it is unreasonable—but after this is done, the negative must still debate the proposal on the basis of the affirmative's interpretation. Otherwise, instead of a discussion of the subject, the debate becomes a mere quibble over the meaning of terms.

When your study of the resolution has brought to light all of the possible meanings of each term in the statement, make a list of *all of the possible interpretations* which might be given the question for debate. If you are upholding the affirmative, such a list will help you select the interpretation which will be least difficult to support; if you are on the negative, it will help you discover the interpretation your opponents are most likely to use.

Choosing the affirmative interpretation. Your choice of an interpretation will be determined largely by the side of the question you uphold. If you are supporting the affirmative, three rules should be followed in selecting the interpretation to use in the debate.

1. **The interpretation must be one which the listener will accept as reasonable and fair.**

This is the all-important test. Remember that the basic purpose of debate is to win belief. If the listener feels that your interpretation of the question is not justified by the phrasing of the question, he will refuse to accept it. And once he believes that you are trying to take an unfair advantage of your opponents, you lose all chance of winning his support. Be fair and reasonable in interpreting the question.

2. **Use an interpretation which holds the debate to the subject at issue.**

Occasionally, the proposition for debate may be so phrased that it *could* be interpreted to mean something quite different from the subject the framers of the question had in mind. And sometimes a debate team will use such an interpretation, in an effort to gain an advantage over their opponents. But what about the audience, in such a situation? Audiences come to debates, as a rule, because they are interested in the subject which is to be discussed. And when the debaters make use of a trick interpretation so that the discussion is carried into an entirely different field, the listeners who attend feel that they have wasted their time—they didn't get the information they wanted.

A few years ago two English debaters who were touring the United States were scheduled to debate a Midwestern university on the question, "Resolved, that the American form of government is more dangerous to civilization than is that of Russia." A large audience attended the debate, interested chiefly in hearing what the English speakers could say in behalf of the Russian system of government. But the Englishmen, who had the affirmative, chose to use a trick interpretation of the proposition. Instead of presenting arguments in favor of the Russian system, they took the position that the Russian form of government was highly undesirable—but argued that since other nations were not copying the Russian system, and were copying the system used in the United States, the American system alone was able to harm civilization. Of course, the English speakers demonstrated their cleverness—but their listeners were utterly disgusted. They had come to hear an honest straightforward comparison of two systems of government; instead, they heard only quibbling about the interpretation of the question.

Keep the audience in mind when choosing the interpretation to be given the question for debate. Remember that the purpose of debate is to *win your listeners to a desired belief* concerning the subject under discussion. A tricky interpretation, which carries the debate into entirely different fields, certainly will not help you accomplish that purpose. So use an interpretation that will center the debate on the subject which you have agreed to discuss.

3. Select an interpretation which gives the affirmative as light a burden of proof as possible.

Remember that as an affirmative speaker, you have the burden of proof with respect to the proposal you advocate. And that burden may be relatively heavy or relatively light, according to the interpretation placed upon the question. When the question of placing an embargo on shipments of goods to warring nations was debated a few years ago, some teams advocated that the United States follow a policy of complete isolation from Europe, permitting trade only with nations in the Western Hemisphere. The majority, however, took a more moderate position, and argued only that we should not send American ships into the belligerent zone—a position much easier to support. Similarly, in debating the Agricultural Adjustment Act, some teams argued that the act would *raise* farm prices; a few, however, upheld the bill as a device for *preventing unreasonable declines* in farm prices—an interpretation which followed the actual language of the bill. Naturally, it was much easier to show that the act would prevent decreases in prices than it was to show that it would increase prices.

Do not undertake to prove more than you have to prove is one of the soundest principles of debate. Interpret the question in such a way that you advocate a *moderate* change, not a radical one. Ask for the most moderate change consistent with the real meaning of the question. It is easier to persuade your listeners to take a short step than a long one.

Choosing the negative interpretation. The rules which have been given in the foregoing pages are suggested as a guide in selecting the affirmative interpretation of the question. From the standpoint of the negative, only one rule is important.

1. Make your interpretation as broad and as general as possible.

As a negative speaker, you are bound to accept any reasonable interpretation the affirmative may offer. You cannot know just what that interpretation will be until the debate has actually begun. So in preparing for debate, use an interpretation broad enough to fit almost any analysis the affirmative may present. Plan your case especially to meet the interpretation the affirmative is most likely to use, but make your analysis general enough so that your argument will apply to any other reasonable interpretation.

Once in a long while you will meet an affirmative team which tries to get an advantage in the discussion by using an unexpected interpretation. When that is the case, you will nearly always find that the affirmative has been able to do so by giving unreasonable emphasis to a single term, or by using a very unusual definition for one of the terms of the proposition. Two possible courses are open to you in meeting such interpretations.

First, you may meet the new interpretation directly. Point out the unusualness of the affirmative stand to your listeners; show them that the affirmative, merely to gain an advantage, has supported a proposal quite different from the one suggested by a reasonable analysis of the question. Then agree to meet the affirmative on its own ground. Let your audience know that you are disappointed in the unusual course the debate is taking, but that you are willing to debate this new proposal rather than waste the time of the audience in arguing over what should be debated. In meeting the new interpretation you will probably find that your arguments are not very strong—but you have gained a distinct advantage in winning the support of your audience by your fairness and willingness to adapt yourself to new conditions. Your opponents, on the other hand, have greatly weakened their own position. In most cases the moral advantage you gain will be great enough to offset whatever disadvantage in argument exists.

The second method of meeting a surprise interpretation should be used only when the new interpretation is so extreme as to carry the debate into an entirely different field. It consists of meeting the new interpretation, but also of forcing the affirmative back to a more reasonable analysis. In using this method you first call attention to the unreasonableness of the interpretation, but offer to meet your opponents on the basis of their analysis. However, you add one other item to your comments on the interpretation. Tell your listeners that since they came expecting to hear an intelligent discussion of the subject called for by the proposition for debate, you want to give them that discussion. Explain that by so doing you will make very clear just *why* the affirmative chose such an unreasonable interpretation of the question. Imply that the affirmative was afraid to argue the actual question for debate; the affirmative knew that it could not hope to convince reasonable people in a fair debate. Then do what you have announced you will do; meet your opponents on their new interpretation as best as you can, and spend the major part of your time attacking the plan that a reasonable interpretation would give to an affirmative team. In a majority of cases such a procedure will force the affirmative team to abandon the interpretation it has set up, and to meet you on the original subject for debate. And at the same time it weakens the confidence of the listeners in your opponents. [15]

[15] See Appendix 2, for an example of preliminary planning for the debate case.

CHOOSING THE MAIN POINTS

The purpose of every debater is to make the listener *believe* something concerning the subject for debate. And to get a person to believe a thing, you have to give him adequate *reasons* for accepting it as true. The important *reasons* which the debater gives, become *the main points* or *major contentions* in his argument.

Naturally, every debater should attempt to give the listener those reasons which will be most effective in securing his belief. Or in other words, he should try to select the most effective main points in support of his position on the question. To find the main points which will be most effective, three steps are suggested. First, list as many different reasons as you can, supporting your side of the argument. Second, choose the type of case which is strongest for the particular question to be debated. And third, select the main points which best support that case. These three tasks will be discussed in this section.

Discovering the Possible Reasons

The strongest reasons for accepting an idea are not usually the first reasons which come to mind. To find those which will be most effective in supporting your argument, the best method is to think first of as many different reasons as you can, and then to select from your list those which you find to be the strongest. One very successful method of discovering possible reasons is to ask yourself a series of questions, writing down all of the answers you can think of to each question in the series. The questions to be asked will differ, according to the side you are upholding.

Finding affirmative reasons. If you are supporting the affirmative, list as many answers as possible for each of the following four questions:

1. Why do we need to change our present system?
2. Why will my proposal improve conditions?
3. What other advantages will my proposal bring?
4. Why are my opponents wrong in attacking my proposal?

You will find a number of different answers for each of these questions. Each of the answers you list will be a reason for accepting your proposal.

To illustrate, suppose that you are arguing in favor of the proposal to abolish the present system of grading in your school, and to substitute a system in which each student is marked either "pass" or "fail" in each course. Here are some of the possible answers to the first question suggested above:

Why do we need to change our present system of grading?

1. The present system is inaccurate and unfair to students.
2. The present system defeats the purpose of education by making grades more important than knowledge.
3. The present system causes antagonism between students and instructors.
4. The present system encourages cheating.
5. The present system creates jealousies among students.

Each of the answers to this first question gives you a *reason for believing* that the grading system should be changed. But merely finding reasons for *changing* the present system does not prove that the system of reporting only "pass" or "fail" grades should be the one adopted. Therefore, you must proceed to the second question.

Why will my proposal improve conditions?

1. My proposal is more accurate and fair.
2. It will stress education instead of grades.

3. It will remove one of the causes of antagonism between students and instructors.
4. It will eliminate much of the reason for cheating.
5. It will remove one of the causes of jealousies among students.

The answers to this question give reasons for accepting your proposal. Note that each of these answers corresponds to an answer to the first question suggested. But your proposal may have advantages which go beyond correcting shortcomings in the present system. To make sure that these advantages are not overlooked, see how many answers you can find to the third question on your list.

What other advantages will my proposal bring?

1. It will save much time that would be wasted under any other system.
2. It is in line with present-day educational trends.
3. It follows the system used in actual life.

The fourth question suggests possible "defensive" reasons— reasons for not accepting various arguments which may be made against the proposal by speakers on the negative. Some of these may become "defensive points" in your debate; in any case, as many as possible should be listed, to help you anticipate the arguments your opponents are likely to advance.

Why are my opponents wrong in attacking my proposal?

1. The new plan would not kill the incentive for studying.
2. It would not make it difficult to transfer credits from this to other schools.
3. It would not encourage the "get by" attitude in students.
4. It is not true that some different plan would be more effective.

By studying these questions and listing as many answers as possible for each of them, you have enabled yourself to canvass the subject systematically, and to discover all of the important reasons for believing that the grading system you propose should be adopted. Or at least, you have discovered *most* of the important reasons. To check your thoroughness, compare your list of answers with the list of reasons you discovered in reading on the subject—the list referred to on pages 92-93. You may find additional reasons to be added to your present list. If other answers to any of the questions occur to you later, these should likewise be added to your outline of reasons. The more complete your list of reasons is, the better chance you have of finding the best and strongest reasons to be used as main points in your argument.

Finding negative reasons. Negative speakers should use a different set of questions from those used by the affirmative, to help them discover reasons which support the negative side of the question. Questions which negative speakers may use are the four listed below:

1. Why is there no real need for changing from the present system?
2. Why will the affirmative proposal bring no improvements in conditions?
3. What new evils would be created by adopting the affirmative proposals?
4. What other plans can be offered which are more desirable than the affirmative plan?

If each of these questions is considered in the same manner as suggested for the affirmative, the answers will provide you with a list of the important reasons for accepting the negative point of view in the debate. Check your list of reasons with the list prepared in your study of the materials on the question, and add any additional reasons that you think are important.

Evaluating the reasons listed. The *main points* on which your argument is based will come from the list of reasons you have prepared. The actual main points to be used will not be selected until you have decided what type of case is most advantageous; but your selection of the type of case you will use in your argument likewise depends on what main points are available. So your next duty will be to weigh the various reasons you have listed, and pick out those which are *strongest*— those which can be used most effectively as *main points* in your argument.

Two tests should be applied in making your selection:

1. The main points you select should be those which give the listener the strongest reasons for accepting your position on the question.
2. The main points you select must be those which you can support with effective proof.

Keep the listener in mind in making your selection—remember that your whole purpose in debate is to make the listener believe your side of the question. The strongest main points will be those which, in the opinion of the listener, give the *most compelling reasons* for accepting your position in the discussion. But remember, too, that every point you finally select will have to be *proved*. So include in your list only points which you know you can support with effective proof. Go through your file of evidence cards; see what evidence you have available on each point before including that point in your list of possibilities.

Careful examination of the reasons which make up your list will probably bring to light six or eight which seem to be strongest, from the standpoint of the two tests applied. The points you place in that group of six or eight are the *possible main points* which may be used to support your debate argument.

Choosing the Type of Case

Debating is chiefly a battle of argument and evidence; but argument and evidence are not the only factors involved. As in every other form of contest, *generalship* plays an important part. We think of football as a game in which brawn and skill are important; but the team which selects the best plays to use and the best time to use those plays is the team which generally wins. In debate, generalship is found in your choice of a constructive case or plan of attack; in addition it is found in the use of certain devices which increase the effectiveness of your arguments. These devices for effectiveness will be considered later; for the present, we are concerned with the use of generalship in selecting the case to be used.

Your *case* in debate is simply your general plan of attack—the plan upon which you build your constructive argument. The choice of the *type* of case to be used is a matter of some importance. By selecting the type of case that best fits the arguments available to you, you can center the discussion on points which give you greatest advantage. Or if you are careless in your selection, you may give a similar advantage to your opponents.

The affirmative case. Unfortunately, the affirmative team has little or no choice as to the type of case it will use. There are certain things the affirmative *must* prove in every debate; the affirmative debaters have no choice in the matter.

In *every* debate, the affirmative case must include two main lines of argument. First of all, the affirmative must establish *a need for a change*—that something is wrong with the present system. And second, the affirmative must show that the proposal it advocates would *produce certain benefits*—that it will correct the major evils found in the present system, and possibly bring other advantages as well. These two general lines of argument are *"musts"* in the affirmative case. Sometimes a third line of argument is added. The affirmative may find it desirable to include *defensive* arguments, either showing that the change proposed will not create new evils, or that no better plan exists than the one the affirmative offers. Such defensive arguments are necessary if the listeners already hold definite views along the lines suggested, prior to the actual debate.

The conventional affirmative case, then, consists of two, or possibly of three, elements—arguments showing *need for a change,* arguments showing *benefits* to be secured, and possibly *defensive* arguments. Of course, within this framework, the affirmative has a wide latitude in the selection of *main points* to establish need or show benefits. In some debates, two or even three main points may be introduced to show need for a change; at other times, only one point may be used under this head. Or sometimes, the affirmative may offer two or three main points which show benefits to be gained by adopting the affirmative plan. Rarely, however, will more than one *defensive* main point be included in the argument. Of course, in every debate the affirmative has the privilege of selecting the specific *contentions* which are to be used as main points; the requirements of the case are simply that *at least one* main point be introduced to show need, and that *at least one* main point be used to show benefits. What those points are to be is a matter for the affirmative to decide.

Negative case possibilities. The negative has a much wider range of case possibilities than does the affirmative. Any one of five general types of negative case may be used, as suggested below:

1. The conventional case
2. The case based upon agreement
3. The "eggs-in-one-basket" case
4. The "shot-gun" case
5. The "counter-plan" case

The *conventional* negative case follows the same general pattern as that required of the affirmative—with arguments, of course, supporting the negative point of view. It takes up in turn the need for a change, the benefits claimed for the affirmative plan, and the evils or disadvantages of the affirmative proposal. In general, the negative shows first, that "present conditions do not justify a change from our present system"; second, that "the affirmative proposal would not be of benefit"; and third, that "the adoption of the affirmative plan would make conditions worse." Each of these general arguments is presented through one or more *main points* selected by the negative speakers, but these three general arguments provide the foundation of the conventional negative case.

Note that the negative does not argue that "no evils exist." That would be a ridiculous claim; some weaknesses are to be found in any system. The negative argument, therefore, recognizes that conditions are not perfect, but takes the position that the evils which are to be found are not serious—certainly not serious enough to justify a change. This line of reasoning is followed by arguments showing that the affirmative plan will not better the situation, and pointing out new evils which would probably result from the change proposed.

To illustrate, suppose that you have a cold, and that one of your friends is trying to persuade you to go to a doctor. Refusing to accept his suggestion, you argue first, that your cold is not serious; second, that doctors are not able to cure colds; and finally, that if you went to the doctor, you would have to pay him a fee that is more than you can afford. Stated briefly, your arguments are (1) no need, (2) no benefits, and (3) new evils. These are the general lines of argument in the *conventional* negative case.

When the case based on *agreement* is used, the negative agrees with the affirmative on one or more of the affirmative main points, and centers its attack upon the points which remain. The affirmative must establish *all three* of the points in a conventional case—they must establish need for a change, show benefits to be gained, and show further that no serious new evils will follow the change they suggest. If the negative can overthrow even *one* of these vital contentions, the listeners cannot logically accept the affirmative plan.

To illustrate, take again the question of going to the doctor. You might agree with your friend that your cold is pretty bad, but refuse to go to the doctor on the grounds that doctors cannot cure colds, and that you cannot afford to pay the doctor's fee. You might even agree that your cold is bad and also that the doctor could cure it, and still refuse to take the advice of your friend solely because you cannot afford to have medical care. Or possibly, you might agree that your cold is bad, and agree too that you are willing to spend the money for treatment, and still refuse to go to the doctor on the ground that doctors cannot cure colds. In other words, you can agree with your friend on any two of the arguments he may have given, and still present a good reason for not doing what he asks.

The case based on agreement offers two chief advantages. In the first place, it saves you from being forced to argue against something that your listeners firmly believe. They may be convinced that there are extremely great evils in the present system; they may believe it so strongly that no amount of argument could change their belief. Agreeing with the affirmative on the fact that the evils exist will strengthen, rather than weaken, your case in the minds of such listeners. Second, by agreeing on one point, you have more time available for argument on those which remain—you can center your attack on the points which give you most advantage.

Of course, there are disadvantages to the case based on agreement as well as advantages. The chief one is that your listeners may believe—and your opponents usually will encourage them to believe—that you were *forced* to *admit* the affirmative point. They may feel that your agreeing with the affirmative on the point was a confession of weakness. Never use the words "admit" or "concede" when you *agree* with an opponent. You aren't "admitting"; you actually do "agree." You *believe* as the affirmative believes on the point in question, and refuse to argue about it. But you disagree strongly on other points, which are important enough in themselves so that by overthrowing them, you overthrow the whole affirmative case.

The *eggs-in-one-basket* case is very much like the case based on agreement, in that you center your attack on a single element in the affirmative argument. You may attack need for a change, and nothing else; you may attack only the benefits to be secured; your argument may be limited to pointing out new evils. The *eggs-in-one-basket* case differs from the case based on agreement, in that you never openly *agree* to any of the affirmative contentions. Instead, you simply *ignore* those which you do not attack.

This type of case has all of the advantages of the case based on agreement, and the additional advantage of leaving the affirmative obligated to prove all of the points in the conventional affirmative case, even though you actually attack only one of them. But it has one very important weakness. By concentrating on a single point, you allow the other affirmative contentions to go unchallenged. And your listeners may believe that the two or three points which the affirmative establishes without attack from you are more important than the one point which you overthrow. If you use the *eggs-in-one-basket* case, be sure that the point on which your arguments are centered is one which the *listener* will accept as one outweighing every other element in the debate.

The *shot-gun* case is the exact opposite of the *eggs-in-one basket* case and that based on agreement. Instead of centering attack on one or two points, you scatter your attack over ten or a dozen phases of the debate, making each one a *main point* in your argument. Of course, with so many points advanced, the argument supporting each of them will be rather weak. You simply do not have time to offer enough evidence and reasoning to support so many points effectively. But the fact that you use so many different attacks may have a strong effect on the listener. The mere fact that so many attacks against the affirmative plan are *possible* may be enough to convince many listeners.

The chief advantage of the *shot-gun* case is the position in which it places your opponents. Although they may disprove without much difficulty any five or six of your arguments singled out for attack, they do not have time to attack *all ten or twelve* of them. And the listener is likely to infer that the points they do not attack are valid. On the other hand, the *shot-gun* plan has two major disadvantages. The first is that, at best, the proof you offer to support each of your points must be woefully weak— not enough perhaps to convince your listener that the point is worth considering. Then, too, your points are of little importance individually, because your listeners cannot begin to remember all of them. With an audience of more than average intelligence, or with one which leans toward the affirmative side of the question, the *shot-gun* case would not be effective. Give serious thought to the kind of audience you probably will have before deciding to use this type of case.

All four of the types of negative case so far discussed are based on a "do nothing" philosophy. Each one admits, either by implication or directly, that things may be wrong with the present system, but opposes any steps toward bettering conditions. As a rule, your listeners are quite willing to accept this philosophy; the average man is basically conservative, and resists the idea of change. But sometimes the situation is different. Sometimes your listeners are very much dissatisfied with the existing system, and feel that some change—*any* change—is needed. If that is the situation under which you must debate, your negative argument should make use of a *counter-plan.*

The case based on *counter-plan* follows the method of the case based on *agreement,* but goes one step further. The negative agrees that a change is needed, but refuses to agree that the affirmative has the proper solution. In place of it, the negative offers a plan of its own. Sometimes, the negative will propose an entirely new plan of action; at other times, suggest that the present system be improved in a way that will remove the evils cited. At times, the negative outlines the advantages of the counter-plan offered in detail, and offers evidence to show that it would be effective. More frequently, however, the counter-plan is merely mentioned, since in any event the affirmative speakers must tear it down if its own proposal is to be accepted.[16]

The *counter-plan* case is of greatest value when audiences are highly dissatisfied with the present system, and are directly affected by it. It is strongest where the *shot-gun* case would be weakest. It has least value when used before audiences that are not directly affected by the situation being debated. Its chief disadvantage is that, in using it, the negative accepts a direct *burden of proof* with respect to the plan it advocates. In general it is wise to undertake to prove no more than you are forced to prove in a debate. The counter-plan case increases your bur-

[16] In effect, the presentation of a counter-plan is an attack upon the affirmative use of *proof by eliminating.* The fact that some other alternative can be offered shows that the affirmative's list of possible courses of action is not complete.

den, since you must defend it against affirmative attacks. Be sure of your ground before deciding to use this type of case.

Final choice of case. The final selection of the type of case to be used by the *affirmative* offers no problems; if you uphold the affirmative, your case is already outlined for you. You *must* establish a need for a change; you *must* show that the change you propose will bring definite benefits; you *may* offer one or more defensive points. Except for your decision as to whether defensive points are to be used, and your selection of main points to establish *need* and *benefits,* no choice of argument is open to you. You *must* advance a conventional affirmative case.

But on the negative, several possibilities are present. You may use any one of five different types of case. Which type you use is for you and your teammates to decide. The chief advantages and disadvantages of each type of case have already been mentioned. Cases will vary in strength, depending on the question you discuss and the audience you address. As an aid in making your selection, ask yourself the following questions:

1. How does the audience feel about the system the affirmative wishes to change?

If the audience is fairly well satisfied with the present system, use either the *conventional* or the *shot-gun* case. Do *not* use the case based on *counter-plan.* If your listeners are mildly dissatisfied with the present system, but not affected by it directly, the case based on *agreement* will be effective. If they are very much opposed to the present system, use either the *eggs-in-one-basket* or the *counter-plan* type of case. If the audience is completely indifferent to the question for debate, the *conventional* case is usually strongest, but either the *eggs-in-one-basket* or the *agreement* types may be used.

2. Which of my possible main points will be most effective?

If the attitude of the audience does not clearly determine the type of negative case to use, consider the six or eight possible main points you have selected. Pick out the points which you feel are particularly strong—considering both the strength of the *reasons* they give, and the weight of the evidence with which you can support them. And of course, classify these strongest points according to the elements in the argument to which they apply—separate the points which show *no need* from those showing *no benefits* and those charging *new evils*. If the points supporting the *no need* argument are weak, you probably should use the case based on *agreement* or the *eggs-in-one-basket* case. Or, if these points are weak, and you can discover an effective counter-plan, use the case based on *counter-plan*. If you seem to have two or three very effective points all dealing with the same phase of the discussion, use the *eggs-in-one-basket* case. Or if you find a number of fairly strong points, but not outstandingly strong, the *shot-gun* attack may be the proper one to use.

As a rule, careful consideration of your audience and of the possible main points in your list will help you determine which type of negative to use. But if neither of these factors suggests a case, then use the *conventional* attack. In the long run, you will find it safer and more effective than any other type.

THE MAIN POINTS

After you have selected the type of case to be used, your next task is to choose the main points to be used in your argument, to word them as effectively as possible, and to arrange them in the order in which they are to be presented in your argument.

Selecting main points. The main points upon which you base your constructive argument will be chosen from the six or eight *possible* points previously selected as the strongest *reasons* for believing your side of the question. Just which of these points you will finally use will depend on the type of case that has been chosen, the relative strength of the different reasons from the standpoint of the listener, and the amount and weight of evidence available to support each point.

The main points which you select fall into several distinct groups, each group corresponding to one of the possible *divisions* of your argument. For the affirmative, these possible divisions will include:

1. Arguments relating to need for a change
2. Arguments showing that the affirmative plan will correct existing evils
3. Arguments showing other advantages to be gained by adopting the affirmative plan
4. Defensive arguments, meeting major objections to the affirmative plan which may exist in the minds of your listeners

As you have probably noticed, these four divisions correspond to the four questions used by the affirmative in discovering possible *reasons* supporting the affirmative proposal. In some debates, the affirmative argument may include all four divisions. In every debate, the argument *must* include the first two divisions listed. But the use of divisions three and four is optional; both may be used, one may be used and the other omitted, or both may be discarded.

For every division which *is* included in the affirmative argument, however, *at least one* main point must be included in the case. In some instances, *two* main points may be introduced, both falling in the same division of the argument; occasionally as many as *three* main points may be included in the same division of the affirmative case. But every main point must represent one of these divisions, and every division included in the argument must be represented by at least one main point.

The negative argument may also be divided into four general parts:

1. Arguments upholding the present system, and opposing need for a change
2. Arguments showing that the proposed plan would not remove evils cited in the present situation
3. Arguments showing that the proposed plan would create new evils
4. Arguments upholding a negative counter-plan

As has been indicated in the discussion of negative case possibilities, the negative argument is considerably more flexible than that of the affirmative. Depending on the type of case used, the negative argument may include all four of the divisions named—though the first and fourth are almost never found in the same case—or it may include only three, two, or even one of the divisions listed. Each division that is included, however, will be represented by one or more negative main points. And every negative main point introduced must fall within one of these four divisions of the possible negative argument.

Now the question is, just *what* points should be selected as main points in your argument? In making the final selection of those to be used, five rules should be kept in mind.

1. Do not use too many main points.

Remember that the time allotted your side for constructive argument is limited. Remember, too, that the average listener can hold only a very few ideas in his mind at any one time. Consequently, it is better to present only three or four main ideas—some authorities permit the use of as many as five or six—and to support each one with an abundance of proof, than to attempt to use a greater number in your argument. This applies in every debate situation except that in which the negative uses a *shot-gun* case; then, of course, as many as ten or a dozen main points may be introduced.

2. Taken together, your main points must establish your case.

An affirmative speaker may show that present conditions are unsatisfactory, and that the change he offers would bring no new evils—but these two main points would not establish his case. He must also show that the change he proposes would correct the conditions to which he objects. Particularly when you have the affirmative, be sure that your main ideas establish each division of a conventional affirmative case. Check your points to make sure that you have at least one main point showing need for a change, another showing that your proposal would better conditions, and possibly one showing that no new evils would result from the change advocated.

3. Select main points which give the listener the strongest reasons for accepting your position.

Since you are limiting yourself to presenting only three or four main ideas or reasons for belief in your side of the question, it is obvious that each main point should give the listener the strongest possible reason for accepting your position on the question. Naturally, some reasons will affect the listener more than others. Choose those which influence him most strongly.

But what sort of reason has the greatest power in securing belief? Men are most affected by those things which *directly concern them,* or which concern their way of living, or their families, or their friends. If you are opposing compulsory military training, for example, you may find as possible reasons to support your stand, the following:

1. Compulsory training will rob each drafted young man of a year of his life.
2. Compulsory training will seriously interfere with employment in industries employing young men.

If you are talking to men who are eligible for draft, or to the parents of such men, obviously the first reason will be much stronger than the second—it directly affects them or their families. On the other hand, if you are speaking before an audience of employers, the second reason probably will be stronger—it affects those in the audience through their business interests.

Test each possible main idea on the basis of its compelling power as a *reason,* for the *particular audience* before which you are to speak. And select as your main points those which relate most directly to the lives or the vital interests of the people who will make up the audience.

4. Use main points which you are able to support with ample evidence.

The fourth test to be applied is the amount of evidence which is available to support the possible point. Remember that every main point you present in your case has to be *proved*. No matter how compelling it is as a reason for accepting your side of the question, it is valueless if you cannot support it with evidence enough to make listeners accept it. Check through your evidence file before making your final selection of main points; be sure that enough evidence is available to convince an unprejudiced listener of the validity of every main point you finally include in your case.

5. Every main point must satisfy the rules for either proof by classifying, or proof by eliminating.

Remember that every main point is essentially a *reason* for excepting your position on the question. And as a reason, it must be connected with the proposition you are trying to prove by one of the two types of reasoning discussed in the sections on proof. In other words, it will be a part either of the proof process of classifying, or of that of eliminating. If any of the main points you have tentatively selected do not support your basic proposition either as a classifying statement, or as a statement eliminating an alternative, you must either rephrase the statement so that it does meet this test, or omit it from your list of main points to be used.

Perhaps a general suggestion or two may be inserted at this point. If you are a negative speaker, never include as one of your main points an attack upon the *constitutionality* of the affirmative proposal. It is an unwritten rule in debate that the constitutionality or legality of the plan that is discussed is not a point for discussion. In the first place, the average high school or college debater is hardly well enough versed in constitutional law to give an intelligent discussion of that phase of the question; and in the second place, the listeners aren't interested in the legality or illegality of the measure discussed. If the proposition is sound, if it would benefit the United States, laws can be passed which would make it legal. If necessary, even the Constitution can be amended. So if you are supporting the negative, discard any possible main points which bring up the question of constitutionality.

One other point is important. Remember that good debating implies that the arguments of the two sides will *clash*. Nothing is more disappointing to listeners than a debate in which the two teams fail to meet head on. In selecting your main points, select points with which your opponents *must disagree*, if they are to uphold their contention. If your points are statements which your opponents can admit, you may be sure that they are of little value as main points.

Order of main points. The order in which the main points you select are used in your argument will depend first of all upon the division of the subject under which they logically fall. On the affirmative, main points which show the need for a change obviously should be introduced first. A second group will include any main point or points which show that the affirmative plan will correct the evils cited. If any main point is to be included in the case showing other benefits—benefits in addition to correcting evils in the present system—it will come in the third section of the argument. And finally, purely defensive points, which meet objections which the listener may have to the proposed change, will come last.

On the negative, a similiar organization of points is followed. First come those main points which contend that the evils in the present system are unimportant, and that there is no need for a change. The next group includes any main points which show that the affirmative plan will not curb whatever evils do exist. Main points which charge that new evils will be created come third. And if a counter-plan is introduced by the negative, it logically is introduced last after the weaknesses of the affirmative plan have been shown.

In discussing the order of points, reference has been made to the "one or more" main points which may be used in each division of the argument. If all four divisions are included in either an affirmative or a negative case, the chances are that but one main point will be used in each division.

But frequently, as in the case based on agreement, one or more of the divisions will be omitted completely. When this is the case, the divisions which remain may be represented by two, three, or even four main points.

In the event that more than one main point is to be used in any division—for instance, to show that evils exist in the present system—arrange the points within that division in the order of greatest effectiveness. The place of greatest effectiveness in any group is at the *end*—arrange the main points within any division so that the strongest point comes last. If three or more main points are included in any division, place the second most effective point first. Use this order whenever you have two or more main ideas within any given division of the case.

Phrasing main points. Up to this time, main points have been thought of simply as *reasons* for accepting either the affirmative or the negative position in the debate; no attention has been given to the way in which they are stated. But the language you use in expressing your main points is important. Considerable emphasis will be given to the statement of the main points during the debate; naturally you want to use words which will most strongly impress your listeners. The following rules will help you in finding the most effective phrasing for your main points:

1. Each main point should be a short, definite statement.

Never use a question form in stating your main points; what you are trying to get your listeners to believe is not the question, but *your* answer to the question. Don't use long, involved statements; such statements are hard for your listeners to understand, and even harder for them to remember—and you want them to *remember* your main points and the *reasons* they express. If possible, hold the statement of each main point to ten words or less. Use simple sentences, with only one subject and one verb; a compound sentence conveys two different ideas, and listeners can accept only one idea at a time. And finally, make every statement *specific*. Don't say merely "evils are to be found in our present system"; tell your listener what the evils are, and phrase your point: "The present system encourages graft and political corruption."

2. Phrase each main point in words which carry the greatest meaning for the listener.

In stating your main points, use plain, everyday language. Don't try to "dress up" your ideas by using "three dollar words." Most of the technical terms used in debate have no meaning whatever for the ordinary listener; many other words that sometimes are used are expressions with which he is only vaguely familiar. Make your language forceful, but stick to simple, everyday words which the listener really understands.

3. Each main point must be a statement of belief, not a statement of fact.

No one argues about statements of fact; facts are things which people recognize as true. Phrase your main points so that they are statements of *belief*, rather than statements of fact. If you are arguing for a change in the system of grading in schools, don't use as one of your main points such a statement as, "Some students cheat under our present system." Everyone knows that this statement is true; but in the way it is worded, it is simply a statement of fact, and not a *reason* for believing that the system of grading should be changed. If the same basic idea is expressed in the statement, "The present system *encourages* cheating," you no longer have a statement of a *fact*, but of a *belief*; and the revised statement, if established, supplies a logical reason for changing the system. Watch the form of your main points; see that each one is a statement of belief, which provides a reason for believing something.

PROVING THE MAIN POINTS

The main points used in developing your argument are statements of *belief*. As such, listeners will not accept them as giving valid reasons for believing your side of the proposition, until they are *proved*. Every main point you advance must be supported with reasoning and evidence sufficient to cause an unprejudiced listener to believe it. And after your main points have been selected, your next task in preparing for debate is to plan the exact method you will use in proving each point.

Every main point will be proved by some combination of reasoning and evidence. With very few exceptions, the reasoning will follow the method of *classifying*; that is, the main point will be supported by statements which give *reasons* for accepting it as true. In debate, these supporting statements are called *sub-points*. Every main point presented will be supported by one or more *sub-points*, each sub-point advancing a single reason for accepting the main point as true.

For example, in a debate on abolishing the present system of grading, one possible main point is that "the present grading system is unfair." This, of course, gives a reason for abolishing the present system; but the statement that the present system of grading is unfair must itself be proved. So specific reasons are given for believing that the system is unfair—each one presented as a sub-point supporting the main point. In the outline below, the sub-points are listed below the main point they support:

I. The present system of grading is unfair.
   A. Accurate grades are impossible.
   B. The system penalizes the "slow but thorough" student.
   C. Too much emphasis is placed on very small differences in students' work.

Each of these sub-points has the same relation to the main point it supports that the main points, in turn, have to the general proposition discussed. Each one gives a *reason* for believing that the main point is true. Of course, the sub-points themselves are simply statements of belief; so they in turn must be proved by use of evidence.

Sometimes a main idea which you have selected will seem at first glance to require no sub-points to support it, since you have evidence which apparently applies directly to the point to be proved. For example, if the main point is that "the present grading system encourages cheating," you may not be able to give statements showing *why* the point is true, but have certain examples or statistics or statements by authorities which lead you to believe it. In this case you may decide that the evidence proves the point without the use of reasoning. However, your individual pieces of evidence do not supply the whole proof used in supporting the point. In reality, you make use of sub-points, as follows:

II. The present grading system encourages cheating.
   A. Examples show this to be true.
   B. Statistics support this conclusion.
   C. Authorities agree that it is true.

Note the use of a minimum amount of evidence for the support of a sub-point.

I. There is an evident need for a change from the present electoral college method in the election of a President, because
   A. The electoral college system is contrary to the democratic principles of our theory of government, because
      1. The present system permits the election of a minority candidate.
         a. In 1824, Andrew Jackson, with more popular and more electoral votes than any other candidate, lost to John Quincy Adams when the election was thrown into the House of Representatives because no one had a majority of the electoral votes.

    b. In 1876, Tilden, with a plurality over Hayes, lost the election in the House of Representatives to Hayes.

    c. In 1888, Grover Cleveland, with a plurality of 100,000, lost to Harrison.

    d. In 1960, a shift of 40,000 or 50,000 votes in key states would have given the election to Richard Nixon, though a slight majority of popular vote would still have been received by John F. Kennedy.

2. Minority groups, within large, pivotal states, control and dominate the electoral vote in these states.

    a. Labor organizations in industrial states frequently have the balance of power in these states.

    b. Religious or racial groups in such key states as New York, Illinois or Massachusetts, may determine which candidate gets the electoral vote of those states.

3. The power of political bosses in large cities is often a determining factor as to which candidate gets electoral votes in key states.

    a. Democratic bosses in New York City, Philadelphia and Chicago deliver such tremendous party majorities in those cities that Republican votes in other parts of the states are outweighed, and the electoral votes of New York, Pennsylvania and Illinois go to the Democratic candidate.

In each case the evidence you have collected supports the sub-point; the sub-points in turn establish the main point you are trying to prove.

SELECTING THE SUB-POINTS

Since every main point depends for proof upon the sub-points which support it, your first task after choosing your main points will be that of discovering the sub-points to be used. Consider the idea conveyed in your main point; list as many *reasons* as you can why the main point should be accepted as true. Then, from the reasons you have listed, select those which most effectively support the main point to be proved.

Your choice of sub-points will be governed by practically the same rules which you used in choosing main points for your case.

1. Use only two or three sub-points to support any single main point.
2. Select the sub-points which give the listener the strongest reasons for accepting the main point.
3. Taken together, the sub-points must establish the main point as true.
4. Select sub-points which you can support with an abundance of evidence.
5. Each sub-point must satisfy the rules for either proof by classifying or proof by eliminating.

These rules have been discussed in the preceding section in connection with the selection of main points. One important difference should be noted. In establishing your entire debate case, from three to as many as five or six different main points may be used; but not more than *three* sub-points should be used to support any one main point. The total number of sub-points used in the debate is of no importance.

Check the sub-points you finally select; make sure that each one actually offers a *reason* for believing that the main point is true. A very effective test is to state the main point, then follow it with a statement of the sub-point introduced with the word "because." For example, "The present grading system is unfair" (*main point*) "*because* too much emphasis is placed on small differences in students' work" (*sub-point*). That statement "makes sense"; the contention that too much emphasis is placed on small differences in students' work is a *reason* for believing that the grading system is unfair. And consequently, the contention is an acceptable sub-point. But check this statement: "The present grading system is unfair" (*main point*) "because the 'pass' or 'fail' system saves useless bookwork by the instructor" (*sub-point*). Perhaps you can show that "the 'pass' or 'fail' system will save useless bookwork"—but that statement certainly does not show that the present grading system is unfair—it doesn't offer a *reason* for accepting the main point as true. Consequently, that statement cannot be used as a sub-point to support the contention that the "present grading system is unfair."

Phrasing sub-points. When you have chosen the reasons to be used as sub-points supporting the main point, state each of these reasons in the most effective manner. The following rules are suggested:

1. Each sub-point should be a short, definite statement.
2. Each should be a statement of belief, and not a statement of fact.
3. Each should be a more specific statement than the main point it supports.

The first two rules have been discussed in the preceding section. The third, however, requires some explanation.

Sub-points give reasons for accepting main points as true. Main points are stated in broad, general terms; the sub-points apply to specific, limited fields included under the main point; each sub-point shows *one way* in which the main point is true. Using again the example of the system of grading used in schools, the main point already suggested is that "the present system of grading is unfair." That is a broad statement; the grading system may be unfair in several different ways or to several different groups, all of them included however in the general statement that the system is unfair. Each sub-point offered would suggest *one specific way* in which the grading system is unfair. Sub-points must always be more specific than the main points they support, and must apply to a more limited field— a field that is only a part of the general field covered by the main point.

One application of this rule is suggested in the following statement: No sub-point should *repeat* the statement of the main idea it supports. Perhaps this seems obvious, but debaters often make the mistake suggested. They offer a main point, and to prove it present a sub-point which, in essence, is nothing but the main point stated all over again. For example, they argue that "the present system of grading is unfair" (*main point*) "because grades are unfair" (*sub-point*). Obviously, such argument gets nowhere; the debater is simply arguing in a circle. Make sure that each sub-point applies to a more limited field than the main point it supports, and that the limited field is specifically stated in the sub-point.

The order of sub-points. When you have the sub-points you will use to support each main point, arrange them in the most effective order. The order of effectiveness is that which has been suggested for main points falling in any one division of the argument. If two sub-points are used to support any one main point, use the weaker first, and follow with the stronger. If three sub-points are used, begin with the one ranking second in effectiveness, and use the strongest sub-point last; the weakest of the three should be placed in the middle. The general rule to be followed is that the point giving the listener the strongest reason for accepting the main idea comes at the end, in the position of greatest emphasis.

Choosing the Evidence

Every sub-point is a statement of *belief;* if your listeners are to accept it, it must be supported by *evidence.* So the next step in planning your argument for debate is to select the items of evidence that you will use to support each sub-point introduced.

Finding the evidence. If you followed the method suggested when doing your reading on the question, you will have a file including a considerable number of evidence cards, each bearing one item of evidence which might be used to support your side of the question in debate. Go through the file, and pick out the separate items of evidence which support each sub-point to be proved. If you arrange the evidence in separate groups, one for each sub-point included in your case, you will find that you probably have a great number of cards supporting some sub-points, but hardly any to support others that are vital to your case. If the evidence available on any point is not sufficient, two methods may be suggested of finding additional items.

1. Examine your bibliography cards for sources of additional evidence.
2. Consider the use of comparisons and illustrations to support your points.

Very often an examination of your bibliography cards will give you sources from which additional evidence can be secured. If they were properly prepared, they include references to any especially valuable materials in the books or articles covered. By checking through your file of cards and noting references to those materials which relate to the specific field in which you are interested, you can usually discover several publications which have the information for which you are looking.

In addition, consider each sub-point that has to be proved, and see whether you can figure out some illustration or comparison which would help prove that point. Don't depend on your card file alone for comparisons and illustrations; very often you can simply "think up" comparisons just as effective as any you can find in an article you read. And the same thing often is true of illustrations. After all, your illustrations and comparisons must fit your own particular audience, and you are in a better position to know more about that audience than any writer of articles on the question for debate.

Selecting evidence. When all of the possible evidence to support each sub-point has been collected, select that which is strongest. The following general rules will help you:

1. The types of evidence used should be varied enough to hold interest.
2. Use two or more types of evidence to support each main point.
3. Use as much evidence as time will allow to support each sub-point.

No one type of evidence should be used throughout the debate speech to the exclusion of the other types available. Variety makes for interest; use several types of evidence in your speech. To support a single sub-point, you probably will use two or three pieces of evidence, all of the same type; but use other types to support other sub-points relating to the same main point in the case. As to the third rule suggested, remember that *enough* evidence must be given to make the listener believe in the point. Since it usually is difficult to know just how much evidence is needed to make the listener believe, the safest rule is to give all you possibly can in the time you allot to that particular point in the argument.

Illustrations and comparisons are valuable as evidence because they make the reasoning vivid to the listener. Because these are not often found in an evidence file, too many debaters fail to include them in the types of evidence used in proof. Take advantage of their value as proof; try to use either a comparison or an illustration to support some sub-point under every main point in your argument. If a good illustration or comparison is used, no further evidence will generally be needed to support that particular sub-point.

Examples and statistics, on the other hand, have value because they show that your reasoning is based on *facts*. Isolated facts have little significance; but several facts, all of which point to a single conclusion, have tremendous weight with your listeners. Use one of these types of evidence to support at least one of the sub-points in every group. And of course, be sure that in using examples, you use several different examples to support the point you are trying to prove.

Statements of opinion by authorities are valuable principally to show the listener that some important man agrees with the conclusion you have established by some other method of proof. Such statements should usually be used with other types of evidence; use examples or statistics or a comparison to *establish* the point, and then follow with the opinion of a competent authority who supports the conclusion already established. If a sub-point is proved by statements of opinion alone, quote three or four or five different authorities whose ideas on the subject agree. Your listener is more likely to accept the opinions of several men than the opinion of a single authority.

Section 4

THE WORKING OUTLINE

Up to this point, you have analyzed the subject and selected the interpretation to be given it; you have chosen the main points you will use and arranged them in the most effective order; you have selected the sub-points needed to support each main point; and finally, you have chosen the specific items of evidence to be used as proof of each sub-point. Probably, as you have taken these various steps in preparation, you have written the main points down, and noted under each the sub-points you will use to support them. Without being conscious of it, then, you have practically built the *outline* of your case.

Assemble the sheets on which your points have been noted, and arrange them in the order in which they are to come in the debate. The result will be a working outline very similar in form to the one in the example below:

AFFIRMATIVE CASE OUTLINE

QUESTION: *Resolved, that the federal government should own and operate the railroads of the United States.*

I. Private ownership of railroads cannot save them from bankruptcy.

   A. History proves it.

   B. The entire industry faces bankruptcy today.

II. Private ownership will not adequately protect the public welfare or provide the facilities required for national defense.

   A. It cannot keep the railroads on a high plane of efficiency.

   B. It has failed to improve service in keeping with the progress made in other industries.

   C. Financial difficulties have prevented the railroads from fulfilling their obligations to labor.

III. Government ownership would provide finances needed to meet these problems.
   A. Bankruptcy would no longer threaten.
   B. Railroads could be kept at a high level of efficiency.
   C. Railroads would fulfill their obligations to labor.

IV. Government acquisition of the railroads would not be a dangerous move.
   A. The government could stand the expense.
   B. Service would not suffer under government ownership.

V. No other plan will save the railroads.
   A. Direct subsidy without ownership would lead to inefficiency.
   B. Stricter regulation will not solve the problem.

The five arguments preceded by Roman numerals are, of course, the main points in your argument; those preceded by capital letters are sub-points. You have only to list under each of the sub-points the items of evidence you will use to support it, and your general *case outline* will be complete.

Listing evidence. In listing the various items of evidence, simply make brief notes of the items to be used—enough to help you identify them, or the *evidence cards* on which the complete items are found. For instance, your list of evidence supporting the first main point in the case outline presented above might take the following form:

I. Private ownership of railroads cannot save them from bankruptcy.
   A. History proves it.
      —Testimony: Brown, that railroad failures caused three major depressions.
      —Statistics: bankruptcies, 1900-1941.
      —Statistics: railroads in receivership today.
      —Testimony: Interstate Commerce Commission.
   B. The entire industry faces bankruptcy today.
      —Statistics: loans from federal government.
      —Statistics: decline in passenger miles traveled, 1945 to 1960.
      —Statistics: combined profit and loss figures, 1959.
      —Testimony: Owen Clarke, chairman, Interstate Commerce Commission.
      —Testimony: Senator Magnuson.

In listing your evidence under each sub-point, arrange the items in the most effective order. Sometimes chronological order will be used, as with the statistical materials given under sub-point "A" above. Often it is wise to use a strong statement by an authority as the final item, as has been done under both of the sub-points above. In other cases, you may use the device of "strongest last, next strongest first, weakest in the middle." Decide on the best order in which to present the items you use, and list your evidence in that order.

Dividing the case. So far, your entire debate case has been treated as a unit, as though the whole argument was to be given in a single speech. But usually, a debate team is made up of two speakers. So each of the two will be expected to handle a *part* of the case. Your next step in preparation is to agree with your colleague on how much of the total argument each one of you is to present.

First of all, consider how much *time* will be available for constructive argument in each of the speeches for your side. As a rule, two or three minutes will be needed by the opening affirmative speaker for introducing the debate. If the affirmative proposal is one which the audience will probably oppose, even more time may be required for the first speaker to win the good will of his listeners and to create a receptive attitude. If he has been allotted a ten-minute speech, not more than six or seven minutes will be available for actual argument. In the same way, the time available to the first negative speaker, after allowing for the requirements of introduction, will usually be seven or eight minutes; that of second speakers for either side probably eight to eight and a half minutes. Of course, these estimates will vary according to various factors in the situation; you will have to decide for yourself just how much time will be available in your own situation, for your own and your colleague's constructive arguments.

Consider, second, the time that will be required to develop each main point in your case outline. You will have to take three factors into consideration:

1. The relative importance of the point
2. The listeners' attitude toward it
3. Your opponents' attitude toward it

Generally speaking, the more important the main point is, compared with other points in your argument, the more time must be devoted to it. It would be ridiculous to give only a minute or so to your strongest argument, while taking five or six minutes to establish a point that is relatively weak. Again, the time required will be determined in part at least by the attitude your listeners will take toward the point. If they are inclined to accept it without much argument, don't waste time in supporting it with more evidence than is needed. On the other hand, if the point is one that they will be reluctant to accept, more time is required. Be sure to allot enough time to each point to get your listeners to believe that point.

The attitude of your opponents is another factor which must be considered. If you think your opponents are likely to agree with you as to need for a change, don't waste several minutes in establishing that need. Support the point briefly; if your opponents attack it, you can offer more evidence in rebuttal. On the other hand, some points are almost certain to be strongly attacked by your opponents. Allow plenty of time for your development of points which are sure to be attacked.

On the basis of the suggestions given, estimate the approximate time that will be required to present each main point in your case. Then, making due allowance for the time required for speech introductions, divide the case into two parts. In dividing the arguments between the two speakers, keep the following suggestions in mind:

1. Give the first speaker as much of the case as his time will permit him to handle.
2. A single main point may not be divided.

Assign as much of the case to the first speaker as he can crowd into his speech, considering the time which must be reserved for a speech introduction. In most debates, the first speaker will cover all of the points relating to the need for a change, and possibly one point dealing with benefits to be secured. Possibly you may find that by crowding points into the opening speech, the second speaker will have time to spare. Do not let that worry you; free time of that sort can always be used for rebuttal.

A more serious difficulty may result from the fact that the argument upholding any one main point may not be divided between the two speakers. All of the sub-points and evidence supporting any main point must be included in the same speech. Otherwise there will be a ten-minute break in the argument on that point—and in ten minutes your listeners will have forgotten almost everything the first speaker said about it.

This fact may cause you to make some serious readjustments in the plan of your case. For instance, you may find that the first speaker can finish the second main point in your outline, with two minutes still available, while the third point you plan to use will require three or four minutes. In such a situation, one of two things must be done. If possible, cut down the time devoted to those first two or three points, so that all three can be presented in the opening speech. Otherwise, you must expand your proof for the two which come first, and present only those two in the opening argument, leaving the third for the closing speech of your side. Occasionally, an inspection of the main points to be used may show that you can change the order in which they are presented, to give you a better division of points between speakers.

The speech outline. When you have finally decided just what main points are to be handled in each of your two speeches, divide the case outline into two parts—one covering the points to be given in the opening speech, the other including the remaining points which are to be presented in the second constructive speech for your side. Do what revising is needed in regard to order of points, or the amount of evidence to be used. Note down in the right-hand margin, opposite each point, the number of minutes allotted to the discussion of that point. Provide in the outline for your speech introduction and conclusion, and note the time to be reserved for each. The result is the *working outline* from which you will develop your speech. [17]

[17] A specimen working outline is given in the Appendix, on pages 327-329.

PART V—WRITING THE SPEECH

THE SPEECH INTRODUCTION

After you have laid out the detailed *plan* to be followed in your constructive argument, the next step in preparing for debate is that of *writing your constructive speech.* As will be suggested in a later section, your speech will probably be delivered *extemporaneously,* with ideas expressed in the language that comes to you at the moment of delivery. But even though the extempore method of delivery is to be used, the speech should be written out in full as a step in preparation. Writing the speech gives you a more accurate idea of the time required to develop each argument, and helps you check the strength of your proof for the points introduced. And writing also gives you a chance to work out the language to be used in places where exactness of phrasing is essential. Write the speech; revise it once or twice, if you wish, for better balance or for greater clarity in expression; then go back to your case outline and talk extemporaneously.

One section of the speech that demands particularly careful preparation is in the *speech introduction.* Your introduction is one of the most important elements in your speech. It gives the listener his first impression of you and of the ideas you present, and either helps you or hinders you in getting him to *believe* your ideas.

Prestige. Whether you accept a statement and believe that it is true, or whether you reject it entirely, depends in very great degree on the person who makes that statement. If you *like* him and *respect* him, you usually believe what he says. But if your attitude is one of *distrust* and *suspicion,* you tend to resist his ideas; your mind unconsciously tries *not* to accept his statements. Your listeners in a debate react in just the same way. The more they *like* a speaker as a *person*, the more likely they are to believe him. The liking and respect and confidence that a debater is able to command from his listeners, are referred to in a single term as the debater's *prestige* with the audience.

Naturally, the degree of *prestige* that a debater enjoys is of vital importance in debate. In large degree, it determines whether or not his arguments will be accepted by the listeners. And the first important function of the *introduction* of a speech is to *build up the speaker's prestige* with his listeners.

Prestige is influenced by many things—the speaker's appearance, his voice, his platform mannerisms, his attitude toward his opponents are all important. But prestige is strongly affected by *what the debater says,* and his attitude toward his audience. If he *compliments* his listeners, or the community in which they live, they appreciate his friendly attitude—and he takes on increased prestige. If he establishes a *common ground* with his listeners, showing them things which he has in common with them, again he increases his prestige. The use of *humor* generally builds prestige, particularly if the speaker makes himself the target of his own shafts; listeners appreciate his good nature and his sportsmanship. An attitude of *fairness* likewise increases a speaker's prestige; if he assures his listeners that he wishes to take no advantages, but to debate the subject entirely on its merits, their confidence in him is increased. And listeners respect the debater who is *quick-witted* and *alert,* who is able to pick out weaknesses in the arguments of his opponents, and attack them effectively; his ability to think under pressure increases his prestige.

The introduction of the debater's speech gives the listeners their first impression of him as a *person*—and first impressions may determine their attitude toward him during the entire debate. So include in your speech introduction material that will build up your prestige with your listeners.

Of course, the introduction has other functions. It introduces the subject for discussion, or supplies a link with what has gone before. Elements that may be used in introductions to various speeches are discussed in the paragraphs which follow.

FIRST AFFIRMATIVE INTRODUCTION

Inexperienced debaters sometimes begin the opening speech in a debate by stating the question, defining the terms, stating the points on which both sides will agree, and so on. *That is probably the worst way in which a speech could be introduced.* It ignores the need for creating a favorable attitude toward the speaker; and while it does introduce the subject, it presents it in such a way as to destroy any interest the listener might have in the question.

Remember that the very first purpose of your introduction is to *create a favorable attitude* on the part of your listeners—to *build prestige.* And remember that you must also introduce the subject, *in a way that will make it interesting to your listeners.* A first speech introduction that will accomplish these two purposes will probably include the following five steps:

1. An approach
2. An introduction to the problem
3. An expansion of the problem
4. An introduction to the affirmative proposal
5. An explanation of the proposal

On first thought, an introduction including these elements may seem much too long. But remember that the introduction determines, in very great degree, the attitude your listeners will take toward yourself and toward your subject during the entire debate. Usually, the introduction takes only a minute or two; but if it takes half of the entire time allowed you for your speech, the time you give it is probably time well spent. The willingness of your listeners to *believe* depends on the attitudes you create in your introduction.

The approach. The first part of the introduction is the *approach,* in which the speaker's sole purpose is to secure the good will and personal liking of the listeners—in other words, to build prestige. In the first affirmative speech, the approach usually follows one of three methods. First, the speaker may use a *personal introduction,* talking about himself and his feelings in a way that will put him on good terms with his listeners. Sometimes he may make use of humor at his own expense; sometimes he speaks of his pleasure in having an opportunity to appear before the audience—an indirect form of complimenting the listeners. Frequently he uses some material to put him on common ground with his listeners—telling them of experiences he has had which parallel those of his listeners, mentioning his former residence in the community, or referring to other respects in which he and his listeners are alike. Examine the examples listed below for suggestions as to the use of the personal type of approach. And remember that the more hostile the audience may be to the speaker's proposal, or the more unknown the speaker is to his listeners, the more important will be his part of the introduction.

In each of the examples given, the italicized statement suggests the situation in which the example was used.

(Visiting debater, before an audience hostile to his proposal)

My first very pleasant task, Mr. Chairman, is to say on behalf of my colleague and myself that we are very pleased and proud to be here this evening, and to tell you how grateful we are to Iowa State University and the organizers of our visit here, and to Sigma Kappa, Delta Delta Delta and all the other sororities, fraternities and their attendants who have made our stay here a very pleasant one. I believe, myself, that these international debates are the kind of thing that help forward friendship and understanding between our two countries. Mind you, an auditor of these debates, hearing what was said about "poor old miserable England" might gather the opposite. Indeed, very little is more ferocious than some of the American attacks on England that we have heard during these debates—except perhaps the attacks on America which we have given in return. Sometimes, indeed, I feel that my colleague and I have only to prolong our stay in America a little longer for an outbreak of hostilities between the two nations to become inevitable. But I do think that these debates help us get a better understanding of America. We now understand, we think, the American language. We know what a "jitterbug" is, and it is not, in fact, an insect, but merely a human being behaving like one.

(Speaker well known to his audience; listeners interested in the subject, but opposed to the speaker's proposal)

I'm in a pretty tough spot, tonight. We are discussing a question on which I have some definite ideas and conclusions. I realize, too, that a lot of you are thinking about this subject, and that you have some very definite ideas about it. And I know that a great many of you are not going to agree with me. But I'm going to express my views honestly and frankly, and I know that I am expressing the opinion of a great many students both here at Kansas State and throughout the country when I advocate a program of de-commercializing college athletics.

(Visiting speaker; audience but little interested in subject)

On behalf of my colleague and myself, I want to express our appreciation of the opportunity to be here this evening, representing the University of Pittsburgh, and to present the case for the non-company industrial union. For some months, we have been looking forward to this opportunity to come to Columbia, and we have planned on it and thought a lot about it. So you can imagine my surprise when we pulled into the station at St. Louis yesterday, and my colleague turned to me, and throwing out his arms, said, "Well, here we are in Kansas."

A second method of building prestige in the approach is that of *complimenting the debater's opponents*. Speaking well of them creates confidence and respect; people like debaters who are friendly toward their opponents. Notice the use of this type of approach in the following example.

(Speaker before home audience, referring to visitors)

This evening's debate, as you probably know, marks the fifth and final in a series of five with the gentlemen from England. We have enjoyed our association with our guests from across the waters. We have found them to be delightful companions and genial opponents on the platform. We have enjoyed their comments on American customs and our American speech, and even their criticisms of our American ways of living. The most peculiar thing about Americans, Mr. Sharp suggested the other day, is the way we drive our automobiles on the wrong side of the street all the time, without having more collisions. But now at the end of our series, we're happy to welcome our guests to our own home campus, and we hope that their visit will be a delightful one.

A third method of creating prestige in the approach is that of complimenting the audience. A flattering reference to the audience itself, to the community in which the listeners live, or to some organization to which they belong, will usually arouse a feeling of friendliness.

(College debater, speaking to a high school audience)

In opening this debate before this very fine audience this morning, I am somewhat at a loss for the proper form of introduction. It reminds me of the predicament of the famous lecturer who was called upon to address the prisoners at Sing Sing. He started off, "Ladies and Gentlemen," but looking at his audience, he discovered that he was speaking before an all-male audience. Then he selected, "Fellow Americans," but he saw immediately that that form of address could not be used, since a large part of his listeners were obviously foreigners. Finally, in desperation, he shouted, "Well, anyway, I'm glad to see so many of you here."

Well, Mr. Brown and I feel that way about seeing you this afternoon. It is a pleasure to speak before such a fine audience. And I want to congratulate you on this wonderful school. Just before the debate, I had the privilege of looking through your building and seeing the facilities you have here—and I was simply amazed at what I saw. No wonder this school has won the reputation with the faculty of the State University of being the finest high school in the state.

(Debater speaking to audience in a small town)

This is my first visit to Marysville; my first visit, in fact, to this section of your state. I've been in your city only three or four hours. But from what I have seen of you, and from what my good friend, Judge Bennett, has told me about you, this visit to your town will not be my last. I'm delighted with the beauty of your community—with its lovely homes and its beautiful trees and its fine public buildings. And I've been warmed and thrilled by the spirit I've found here. This is the kind of town I'd like to call my home. I'm coming to visit you again next spring, and right now, I'm thinking very seriously of hanging out my shingle here in Marysville after I graduate from law school next June.

The approach sometimes uses only one of the methods suggested; more frequently, two or even all three are combined.

Occasionally, some other method is used to create prestige. But *some* effort must be made in every opening speech to win the friendship of your listeners. The more opposed they are to your proposal, or the less interest they have in the subject, the more important is this part of the introduction to your speech.

Introducing the problem. The second portion of the speech introduction is used to introduce the problem discussed in the debate. The problem should be presented in such a way that it not only *arouses the listener's interest,* but also *gives him a desired point of view* concerning the problem. Usually, one of three methods is used. The first is to begin with a *striking statement,* showing in a single sentence the serious nature of the problem. The second method is to offer an *illustration* which makes the situation vivid to the listener. And the third possible method is to *refer to a local example.* Any of these methods is effective in arousing interest; if properly handled, any one of them can give the listener a desired attitude concerning the subject. Note the examples below, which illustrate the methods suggested. In each case, remember that the material given has been preceded by some form of *approach.*

During the past twelve months, automobiles in the United States have killed more than 35,000 persons. Half, almost, of those who were killed were pedestrians, or children who were riding bicycles or crossing the street. The cars involved were not to blame—only 8 deaths in each hundred were caused by poor brakes or mechanical faults. The roads and streets were not to blame—only 20 per cent of the fatal accidents occurred on streets that were wet, and the death car skidded in only 5 per cent of the cases. The cause of death in nearly 90 out of each hundred cases was carelessness on the driver's part—reckless driving, driving at too high speeds, and drunken driving menace the safety of every child in this nation today.

———

The gerontologists promise us that most of you in this audience can expect to live past 90, your children can expect to live to 100, and your grandchildren may well live to be 150. Medical science is advancing the life span tremendously. But just as booming birthrates cause food problems in some countries, America's continued increases in number of older citizens pose the problem we are debating tonight—the problem of too few doctors.

———

This is my first visit to the East Coast. As we drove into your city today I noticed a road sign announcing "Boston, population 697,000." And the road map told me that the highest point of ground in Boston is eleven feet above sea level. I could not help thinking how vulnerable you are to atomic warfare—how one bomb set by time-fuse 50 miles off your shores and 2 miles deep would put your highest point of land under 89 feet of sea water. How your 697,000 people would have *no* chance of survival. To you people on the coastal plains the problem we are debating tonight is more vital than a mere problem of shelters, or will the city be a target, or can we escape fall-out. To the coastal plains of America atomic war is unthinkable. And whatever must be done to abolish such warfare is absolutely essential.

Elaborating on the problem. The third part of the opening speech introduction elaborates on the problem, to make the listener realize its importance and seriousness. Sometimes a history of the development of the problem is used; at other times, amplifying details are given. Especially when the striking statement method of introducing the problem is used, the expanding step is sometimes included with the problem introduction. And, if the audience is already interested in the problem and aware of its importance, the step is often omitted entirely. In most debates, however, the extent and the seriousness of the problem entitle it to all the emphasis you can give it.

To understand just why this question is significant, let us go back to the early years of our nation's history. As you all know, a hundred years ago, the consumer was largely self-sufficient; he churned his own butter, he made his own clothes. One farmer noted in his diary that all he had to pay out in cash was ten dollars a year; that was for salt and for nails. But today, that pattern has changed. We find people living, 70 per cent of them in cities, buying every single thing that they use, from shoes to milk. We even find farmers buying their butter and their feed. The change that has taken place in the pattern of our social and economic structure is one that makes the consumer dependent on the market for his very existence. And that dependence on the market has placed him, to a very large extent, at the mercy of the producer and the businessman.

———

Now, these periodic business recessions deserve careful study. It is bad enough that they occur periodically. But a study of those hitting the American economy since World War II is even more frightening.

We have had four business recessions since that war—in 1949, 1954, 1958, and again in 1961. But recovery in each case from the lowest point of recession has been less than it was in the preceding recession. For example, *U.S. News & World Report* tells us that the percentage of recovery in gross national product was 27 per cent after 1949, 13.5 per cent after 1954, 11.5 per cent after 1958 and only 10.5 per cent after the 1961 recession. Unemployment declines in the same order were 46.5 per cent, 29.5 per cent, 24 per cent, and only 23 per cent after 1961. You may analyze recovery from these recessions from any standpoint you choose—production, personal income after taxes, wages and salaries, corporate profits, retail sales, total business sales or what have you— and the story is always the same. Recovery has been less in each recession, percentage-wise, than it was after the preceding recession. This is the real danger that threatens us from periodic recessions.

Introducing the affirmative proposal. After the *problem* has been outlined, and its seriousness impressed upon the listeners, the next step in your introduction is to suggest a remedy for that problem—the affirmative proposal in the debate. Sometimes the affirmative proposal is stated formally in the language of the proposition for debate; sometimes only the general idea is mentioned. The transition from problem to remedy is made by the use of such phrasing as, "In view of the seriousness of the situation, it is appropriate that we should discuss tonight the proposition, Resolved, that . . . ," etc. Or sometimes the phrasing used is "To meet this problem, Mr. Smith and I believe that . . . ," etc.

Explaining the proposal. After you have introduced the proposal the affirmative is supporting, offer any explanation that may be needed. If the terms of the question are not clear they may be defined; but in nine debates out of ten, definition of terms should be omitted. If a specific plan is being upheld, it may be outlined at this point in your speech; however, most teams prefer to present it later in the discussion, usually late in the second affirmative speech. Sometimes a definite statement of the position the affirmative is taking is included with the explanation of the proposal.

The complete affirmative introduction. The following example illustrates the use of the five parts of the introduction of a first affirmative speech. For your convenience, each of the five steps is numbered.

1. I feel just a little embarrassed, and so, I am sure, does Mr. Rose, in speaking here this afternoon. It seems a little presumptuous for two mere males to try to impose their ideas on more than two hundred women, especially when we must argue with the two charming young ladies who represent the negative. But nonetheless, we appreciate the honor you have given us in asking us to speak here. The Century Club has long been known for its active interest in civic affairs; and for the powerful influence it has exercised for better government. We're glad to have the privilege of being here today.

2. Last week, I spent an evening at the home of a married sister. Her son, little eight-year-old Billy, entertained me most of the evening. His line was impersonations. Sometimes he was a gangster, shooting me with a toy pistol and leaving me to die. Sometimes he was Buck Rogers, and I died from the discharge of an atomic ray. Sometimes he was an aviator swooping down on me from above, and filling me full of bullets from an imaginary machine gun. But always, the pattern remained the same. I died; he was the killer. I asked his mother about it; and she seemed very much concerned. "All the children he plays with are constantly killing each other," she said. "They see it every day on programs on TV."

3. Now, friends, little Billy's case is anything but unusual. You mothers of eight- or ten-year-old children know the situation yourselves, first hand. All over the United States, children watch television. They're influenced by what they watch and hear, they imitate the men and women on their favorite programs. Research shows that they spend more hours in a year before television sets than they spend in the schoolroom. And *some*—in fact many—of the programs they watch do not establish high ideals of living, to say the least. Some programs are definitely harmful. And those harmful programs are molding the attitudes of impressionable boys and girls, by the millions.

4. That sort of situation demands some attention. The welfare of our nation, the sanity of future generations, demand some sort of action. And it is because such organizations as your own Century Club have a powerful influence in our nation, that I ask you this afternoon to go on record in favor of rigid supervision of materials broadcast.

5. May I make myself entirely clear. I do not advocate a system of government censorship. The content of programs must be regulated by broadcasters themselves. But broadcasters are guided by public opinion; and women's clubs can exert a tremendous influence. So my

suggestion is that these clubs, throughout the nation, set up their own machinery for evaluating children's programs, and exert the power at their command to see that harmful programs are not allowed to go on the air.

FIRST NEGATIVE INTRODUCTION

If you are giving the opening argument for the negative, a somewhat different type of introduction will be used. There is no need to introduce the problem or the proposition for debate; the first affirmative speaker has done that for you. But in addition to linking your argument to that which has gone before, the introduction to your speech helps you in three important ways. First, it gives you an opportunity to *build prestige,* and place yourself on good terms with the listener. Second, it allows you to *lessen the effectiveness of your opponent's arguments* already given—to weaken your opponent's prestige and also to divert the attention of your listeners from his arguments. And third, it allows you to *create a listener attitude favorable to the negative.*

As a rule, your introduction will include four distinct steps:

1. An approach
2. Minor point rebuttal
3. Attitude-building material
4. Statement of negative position

Each of these steps will be considered separately in the following paragraphs.

The approach. The first affirmative speaker opens his introduction with an *approach,* intended to create prestige and to put him on good terms with his listeners. Your speech introducing the negative argument should open with the same sort of material. You can *compliment your listeners;* you can *speak well of your opponents;* you can use a *personal reference* to yourself or to your feelings; you can use material that will establish a *common ground* between you and your audience; you can make use of *humor;* or you can use a combination of several of these

methods. But you *must* make use of *some sort* of approach at
the very beginning of your speech.

This part of your introduction has two major purposes. To
begin with, of course, it builds up your own *prestige* with your
listeners; that is just as necessary for you as it was for the first
affirmative speaker. But in addition, it *diverts the attention* of
your listeners from the arguments your opponent has presented.
It gives them a chance to forget the things he has said. For
this reason, it is even more important than the approach for the
first affirmative speech.

Don't make this part of your introduction too short. Give
your listener an opportunity to forget the affirmative points before asking him to accept those you will advance. And be careful not to mention any *specific* affirmative contentions in your
approach. You can talk of your opponents in a general way,
but not of their actual arguments.

The examples below will illustrate two types of approach
which the opening negative speaker might use. In the first, the
speaker has combined *common ground* material with material
complimenting his opponents; in the second, *personal reference*
has been used, in connection with *humor.*

I am sure that we have all been interested in Mr. Waterman's
argument. He has given a very able defense of the government's plan
for farm relief—a reasonable, intelligent argument. And I know that
Mr. Waterman is sincere in what he says. He believes in the proposal. But, Ladies and Gentlemen, I'm just as sincere as Mr. Waterman is, in opposing the government's plan. I'm a farm boy; my home
is on a farm in central Illinois. I know the farmer's problems first
hand, just as you Iowa farmers in this audience know them. And of
course, we're interested in these plans that are being proposed for farm
relief, because the things that finally are done affect us directly. That's
one advantage that we have tonight over Mr. Waterman. I know that
he's sincere in what he tells us—but he doesn't really know the situation
as you and I know it, first hand.

————

I'm very happy to be here this morning. And I want to thank
you for that fine applause—even if I do know that you're enjoying
this debate principally because it gets you out of your classes in algebra
or history. It gives me a better feeling about appearing before you

this morning. Because, for the last hour or so, I've been pretty doubtful about what you'd think about the chances of a 130-pound college freshman debating against a couple of husky football players like the gentlemen from Nebraska. I've had some *reason* to be doubtful about that, too. You see, after we arrived this morning, your principal introduced me to several of the members of your high school debate team. And one of them—a very attractive young lady—said, "Oh, are you Mr. Hughes?" I said I was. "Not the Mr. Hughes we heard in those debates over the radio?" she said. "Yes," I said, "I'm that Mr. Hughes." "Oh," she said, and I could sense the surprise and astonishment in her voice, "Oh, why I thought from your voice on the radio, you were a *man!*"

Minor point rebuttal. The second step in your introduction will be the introduction of *minor point rebuttal*, for the purpose primarily of *weakening your opponent's prestige* with the listeners. Of course, this part of the introduction cannot be prepared in advance; it will have to be planned while your opponent is speaking. It will consist of an attack on one or two minor points in the arguments he presents—possibly you will expose his lack of proof for some contention, or his inaccuracy in quoting an authority, or possibly you may call attention to some inconsistency in his argument. The point attacked will not be important; your only purpose is to *shake the confidence* of your listeners in your opponent, and so neutralize the effect of the first affirmative speech. The methods which may be used are discussed in the sections on rebuttal, but an idea of the use of minor point attack is given in the example below.

Before opening my argument this evening, I want to call your attention to a statement made by Mr. Tate while attacking right-to-work laws. As nearly as I can quote him he said, "America's wealth and the high wages in America have progressed in direct ratio to the strength of American labor unions. We cannot have one without the other." Now, I'd like to call Mr. Tate's attention to the fact that most economists agree that America's economy and high wages are due to our free institutions, to large capital investments, to scientific research, to inventions, to labor-saving machinery, to better management techniques, and to American know-how—not to the strength of labor unions. Merely because labor unions have grown at the *same time* that our economy and wages have risen does not mean that the unions are the *cause* of our economy. Cigarette consumption in America increased in direct ratio to the increase in teachers' salaries, too. But no one would argue that the smoking habit is the *cause* of higher teachers' salaries. If labor unions were the dominating factor in creating high wages and prosperous America, why is it that England, France, and other European countries where labor unions experienced earlier and more powerful development do not surpass the U.S.A. in wages and material wealth? So it is evident that Mr. Tate is very much mistaken in arguing that strong unions mean a strong America and high wages for its citizens.

Attitude-building material. The third part of the introduction will consist of material directly intended to create a listener attitude favoring your side of the question. A *vital interest* of the audience may be emphasized; a *striking statement* by an authority may be introduced; an *illustration* or *comparison* may be effectively used. Whatever the method used, it should present a vital objection to the affirmative proposal, in a way that will *fix it strongly* in the listener's mind. The more strongly the objection is impressed on the listener, the greater the probability that he will be *biased* in favor of the arguments you present in the body of your speech. Note the use of various methods of *building attitudes* in the examples which follow:

As I looked over your college campus this afternoon, I was very much impressed with your old, ivy-covered Main Hall. It isn't the last word in college buildings, to be sure. It's old; its corridors are dark; it isn't air-conditioned; it probably has many shortcomings from an architectural standpoint. But it's solid and substantial; it has plenty of space for offices and classrooms; it serves its purpose in a completely satisfactory manner. Now, suppose Mr. Johnson were to come here tonight, and say, "Let's tear down that old building; let's build something more modern." Well, you probably would feel that a new building isn't needed; you know that the old one is entirely adequate for your needs. You'd have no assurance that Mr. Johnson's new building would be much improvement, and you'd know that his new structure would cost the school a million dollars or more which the college cannot well afford. Now, Mr. Johnson hasn't suggested this evening that we tear down your old Main Hall. But he has told us that our governmental structure is old and drafty, and he wants us to tear it down, and put up something modern, as he puts it, in its place. We oppose the change he offers, because we know we don't need it, because we believe it will bring little improvement, and because the American people can't afford the tremendous costs that would result.

———

And at this point I want to call to your attention one vital fact. This is not an academic question before us tonight. It's a matter that is real; one that affects every man, woman and child in this city. If we put the federal government into medicine, *you* are the ones who will suffer. If politics and red tape and perhaps graft get into medicine, *your* life and health, and the health of your children, will be endangered. If we socialize medicine, *you* will see *your* taxes mount to pay for it. If doctors become assigned, rather than chosen by the patient, *you* are the ones who will have to accept assigned doctors. And I want you to keep these things in mind as you consider the arguments this evening.

———

Ladies and Gentlemen, the problem before us tonight is not a simple problem of the cheapest method of handling those new-born unfortunates who have no chance at normal life. It is not a matter of ridding the parents or society of a difficult problem. The Supreme Being has told us, "Thou shalt not kill!" And no doctors, group of doctors, or society of doctors were exempted by this admonition. Keep this in mind as you listen to the arguments on mercy killing tonight.

Statement of position. The fourth part of your introduction includes the material you introduce to make clear the negative position in the debate. Possibly you wish to agree with the affirmative as to need for a change—making clear, however, that you are opposed to the *specific change* the affirmative advocate. Possibly you want to tell the listeners just what attitude you take toward the affirmative proposal. Or possibly, you may wish to outline the reasons you will develop for opposing the affirmative stand. Any material you introduce that makes your position clear goes into this final step in your introduction. Several types of such material are suggested in the examples below.

The members of the affirmative team have wasted a great deal of your time this evening. They have taken nearly twenty-five minutes to tell you that there is a railroad problem. You all know that we have a railroad problem in the United States; there is no getting around that fact. The railroads are in bad shape; in bad shape financially. We know that. We are not going to try to dodge that fact. We are going to meet the issue squarely. But we are going to see which is the best way to meet that financial problem.

———

In opposing the 30-hour week in America, Mr. James and I want to make perfectly clear at the outset our reasons for opposing. First, we are opposed because at this time in our history America dare not cut production by one fourth. Second, we are opposed to the tremendous hardship it would work on taxpayers forced to hire one-fourth more teachers and other public servants. Third, we oppose the 30-hour week because it would widen the unfair gap in the work week of those hired and those self-employed in businesses and professions. As first speaker on the negative, I want to discuss the first of these points.

———

As first speaker on the negative, I want to make perfectly clear that we are not upholding the status quo—we do not favor our present foreign policy. I ask the affirmative to remember this point. Nor do we argue that stockpiling nuclear weapons is the best method of preserving peace. Our position tonight is simply that World Federal Government is not a good solution. We oppose joining a World Federal Government for three very vital reasons. First, in joining such a government we would be giving up the very freedom we are trying to preserve. Second, such a federation would reduce America's standard of living to that of the rest of the world. And finally, a world federation would ultimately fail, bringing the very nuclear war we are trying to avoid. Let me take up these points in order.

The complete first negative introduction. The following example will illustrate the four steps in an introduction to the opening negative argument, as used in debate. The four steps have been numbered for your convenience.

1. We have come a long way to take part in this discussion tonight. But I want to say that I'm extremely glad that we have come. I'm glad to visit the campus of the university which can claim more beautiful girls among its students than any other university in the country—and I'm glad to say that my observation entirely justifies that claim. In fact, I had decided that I was progressing very nicely in developing a beautiful friendship with a couple of your co-eds, when Mr. Sanders very rudely interrupted me and reminded me that it was time for us to come here for the debate.

2. Perhaps the first affirmative speaker, Mr. Hall, was confused by the attractive ladies in *this* audience, because he could not have meant all of the things he said tonight. For example, he told you that medical care is not available to most of our older people, but later in his speech told us that fine medical care is keeping these same people alive longer. He told us that our senior citizens have little money and cannot afford medical care. In almost the next breath he told how these same citizens waste 500 million dollars a year on worthless drugs and quack cures. At one time he told you that medical costs are high because of the shortage of doctors, and then went on to argue that we should increase the shortage by giving more medical care to the aged through Social Security. We ask Mr. Hall to be consistent in his arguments during the rest of this debate so that you may know which argument he really believes.

3. Before outlining the negative case, I want to make one point very clear. The question we are debating concerns more than sympathy for the aged. It concerns your pocketbook because *you* will have to pay the bill. Increased Social Security taxes will not come from our older citizens, because those citizens no longer pay Social Security taxes. And making medical care free to one class of citizens, the older people, makes doctor shortage that much greater for you and all other citizens. Don't forget these things as you listen to the arguments tonight.

4. And let me make one other point very clear. Mr. Sanders and I do not oppose *adequate* or *needed* medical care for the aged. We simply argue that guaranteeing free medical care through Social Security is not the solution. We maintain, first, that such a plan is bad because it is the first step towards complete socialization of medicine. Second, we will show that the plan would bankrupt our present Social Security Fund, or else we must increase the Social Security tax to prohibitive levels. And finally, we will show that there are better ways of insuring adequate care to our senior citizens. Let me take up the first two points of the negative case.

INTRODUCTION TO OTHER SPEECHES

Since the later speeches in the debate are in effect continuations of the opening speeches, elaborate introductions are not necessary. Some sort of introductory materials should be used to nullify the effect made by the preceding speaker and to link up the speech with arguments already presented. Introductions of the later speeches in the debate should include two steps:

1. Minor point rebuttal
2. "Tie-up" with preceding speeches

The introduction of these later speeches in the debate will usually be opened with rebuttal of minor points in the preceding speaker's argument. Such rebuttal serves two purposes: first, it links the speech being introduced with what has gone before, and second, it weakens the prestige of the opposing speaker and makes his argument less effective. The methods that may be used are discussed in a later section. Of course, since your attacks must be aimed at specific points in your opponent's argument, this part of your introduction cannot be prepared until your opponent is presenting his speech. All you can do in preparing your speech is to hold a minute or two of your time free for this part of the introduction.

The second part of your introduction will consist of material linking up your constructive arguments with the main points presented by your colleague who has already spoken. Usually, the "tie-up" step is simply a short summary of the points he has advanced. The method is illustrated in the example given below.

Complete second speech introductions. The two steps which make up the introduction to the later speeches in the debate are indicated in the following example. The parts are numbered, for your convenience.

1. The gentleman who has just left the floor has somewhat heatedly accused Mr. Wilson of favoring direct government censorship of radio-TV programs. He has made that charge over and over again, using the words "government censorship." I am sorry that the gentleman did not listen more carefully when Mr. Wilson explained the plan we advocate. I believe Mr. Wilson made our proposal entirely clear; I'm sure that Mr. Smith is about the only person here who did not understand it. But we want Mr. Smith to know what he is attacking, so I'm going to take the time to explain the plan briefly again. Mr. Smith, we do not advocate government censorship. We advocate regulation of the content of programs by the broadcasters themselves. All that we ask that the government do is to clarify the standards already imposed on broadcasters, so that the broadcasters will have something more definite to go on than the vague requirement of satisfying the "public interest, necessity, and convenience." But with a clear statement of the requirements imposed by the government laid down for their guidance, we want the broadcasters themselves to apply those regulations to their own program structure, exactly as they are doing today.

2. Now that we've straightened out that matter for Mr. Smith, let's return to our argument. Mr. Wilson has told you of the unsatisfactory conditions under which TV is operated today—especially the failure of the Commission to provide clear and definite rules to govern broadcasting. I want to continue the argument, and to suggest the exact manner in which such rules might be applied.

THE BODY OF THE SPEECH

The *body* of the speech, or the speech proper, includes all of the reasoning and evidence you present to prove your side of the proposition for debate. It is based directly upon the outline of arguments that you prepared as the final step in planning your constructive case. Since the outline indicates the points to be advanced, and the evidence used to support each point, your task of writing out the body of the speech is largely a matter of organization of material, and effective phrasing. Of course, your arguments must be well organized, so that your listeners have no difficulty in following your ideas. And it is equally important that your ideas be expressed in interesting and effective form.

Of course, with the speech delivered extemporaneously, the language you use in presenting the speech will not be that which you use in writing it. But a written draft helps fix ideas in your mind; and if the language you use to present a point in the written speech is particularly striking, you will probably find yourself using almost the identical words when the speech is finally delivered in the debate.

Suggestions on the organization and phrasing of your arguments are given in the pages that follow.

ORGANIZING THE ARGUMENT

Listeners, as a rule, are mentally lazy. They do not attend debates in order to work. They prefer not to exert themselves in listening to any speech. If your ideas are presented in a way that is easy to follow, your listeners will understand. But, if your arguments are presented in such a way that it is difficult to follow, your listeners will simply sit there and fail to understand. They refuse to put forth the effort that is required to understand relationships that are not clearly stated, or to follow your meaning from point to point. So clarity of organization—obvious clarity—is a first requirement of effective argument.

Your outline lists the main points and sub-points that are to be included in your argument. Your problem of organization is to make those points, and the relation between them, stand out clearly in the written speech. Fortunately, that problem is easy to deal with if you think of the speech as a series of arguments, each one corresponding to one of the sub-points in your outline. Each sub-point and its supporting evidence makes up a *unit of proof* in your speech—a unit complete in itself.

To aid you in keeping these units separate in your mind, follow the practice, when you write your speech, of writing each unit on a separate sheet of paper. And be sure that each unit includes three separate parts:

1. An introduction, linking the sub-point to the main point
2. The body of the argument, presenting the evidence
3. A conclusion, repeating the sub-point proved

As you will note, the structure of each unit of proof corresponds exactly to that of an entire speech, with an introduction, a "body," and a conclusion. Of course, each part will be shorter than the corresponding part in your speech—after all, the speech will probably contain six or eight proof units.

The introduction. The introduction to each unit of proof will include two elements: *transitional material*, which links the argument with the main point it supports (or with the preceding sub-point that has just been proved), and a *statement of the sub-point* you are about to develop in this new unit.

Each of the following unit-introductions contains both of these elements. The transitional material in each case is reproduced in italics, while the statement of the point to be proved is in roman type:

In proving that we should adopt the Medicare Plan for the aged, I want first to show that the problem of medical care for the aged is a very serious problem today.

I have just shown you how serious the problem is at present; now let's look at the future and we will see that the problem will be multiplied several times over during the next twenty years—be many times as great as it is today.

———

But not only is there a tremendous shortage of classrooms, there is also a tremendous shortage of teachers. *Let me give you dramatic proof.*

———

In supporting our proposal for world-wide disarmament, I have shown you the disaster that will come from nuclear war. Now let me show you why continuation of the present armament race is certain to end in nuclear war.

———

Body of the proof unit. The body of each unit of proof will contain, of course, the evidence you use to support the sub-point. Just what evidence is to be used is indicated in your speech outline. It may be examples, or statistics, or statements by authorities, or it may be a long illustration; frequently two or more types of evidence will be used in a single proof unit.

The *order* in which different items of evidence are used depends as a rule on their relative strength. If four or five examples are to be mentioned, give the strongest one last; the same principle applies if several statements of opinion are introduced. If one or more statements by authorities are to be used in connection with some other form of evidence, give the other evidence first. Opinions of authorities are most effective if offered after the listener has already been given reason to believe the idea the opinions support.

The *language* in which your items of evidence are expressed is a matter of considerable importance. Your statements should be direct and vivid, to have most effectiveness with the listener. Ideas should be expressed clearly, and in the smallest number of words possible. And of course, necessary connectives must be inserted, so that the whole discussion reads smoothly. Requirements of effective phrasing will be discussed in detail in a later part of this section.

The *length* of the argument presented will depend on the time you can give for the development of the sub-point in question. If the point is important, as much as two or three minutes might be devoted to a single proof unit, including the two or three sentences required to introduce and conclude the argument. Less important sub-points may be developed in as little as a hundred words. In the first draft of your speech, the length of the unit is of secondary importance; you can rephrase the argument for greater compactness or if necessary omit some of the evidence when you revise the speech.

Concluding the proof unit. The conclusion of each of your units of proof includes only one essential element—a final definite *statement of the sub-point* developed in that particular argument. Occasionally, reference is also made to the main point which the sub-point supports; but the single *necessary* element is a final effective statement of the sub-point. Note the following examples.

So, the problem of medical care for the aged is a very serious problem today.

———

And it is obvious from these facts that the problem of caring for the aged will be many times as serious in the future, unless we take steps to prepare for such care in advance.

———

Therefore, you see there is a tremendous problem in teacher shortage, as well as in classroom shortage.

———

The examples I have just given you make it obvious that armament races have inevitably ended in war throughout history, and we can expect war again—nuclear war this time—if the arms race between Soviet Russia and the United States is permitted to continue.

The complete proof unit. The following example shows the form of a complete and well-constructed unit of proof; the numbers 1, 2, and 3 indicate the introduction, body, and conclusion of the unit, respectively.

1. In supporting our case for exemption of teachers' salaries from federal income taxes, I want first to point out that low teachers' salaries constitute one of the gravest problems facing this nation today.

2. Let us look at teachers' salaries. In 1957 the President's Committee on Education Beyond the High School made its now famous *Second Report to the President*. The Committee was composed of 35 of the finest minds in education and in business in the nation. It made the most comprehensive study of higher education ever made in the United States. And while the report dealt with college education only, you must understand that college teachers have higher average salaries than do public school and high school teachers. Here is what that Committee reported about our highest paid teachers—those in our colleges:

> The most critical bottleneck to the expansion and improvement of education in the United States is the mounting shortage of excellent teachers. Unless enough of the nation's ablest manpower is reinvested in the educational enterprise . . . specialized manpower shortages in every field will compound. . . . To restore teaching to a competitive position in the professional labor market comparable to that which it occupied before World War II would require an average increase in faculty salaries of something like 75 to 80 per cent. And to maintain this position, once restored, would probably require by 1970 an average rise of 100 to 125 per cent above present faculty salary levels.

And I point out that such increases would take teachers' salaries only to levels comparable to those of 1940, a year in which it was recognized that teachers' salaries were far too low.

To make the inadequacy of teachers' salaries more vivid, the Committee reported:

> The plain fact is that the college teachers of the United States, through their inadequate salaries, are subsidizing the education of students . . . by an amount which is more than double the grand total of alumni gifts, corporate gifts, and endowment income of all the colleges and universities combined. . . . Unless this condition is corrected forthwith the quality of American higher education will decline. No student and no institution can hope to escape the consequences.

I ask you, Ladies and Gentlemen, what stronger indictment of teachers' salaries is necessary? And when we remember that the need for unskilled labor in America is falling each year, while the need for engineers, mathematicians, scientists, and the like increases by leaps and bounds—it follows that anything which threatens our training program, our schools, is a problem of national survival. It is common knowledge that teachers are underpaid in America, and that because they are underpaid too few of our best young minds go into the teaching profession.

3. So my first point tonight is that low teachers' salaries constitute one of the gravest problems facing America today.

Organizing main point units. So far, we have considered only the units of proof in which sub-points are developed. But the body of the speech is composed of larger arguments, supporting main points. And some attention must be given to the structure of these larger units.

Each main point unit of proof, like those in which sub-points are developed, consists of three parts: an introduction, a body, and a conclusion. The body of the main point unit consists simply of the two or three proof units in which sub-points are presented. These units of proof have already been discussed; no further explanation should be needed.

Introducing a main point. Each main point included in your argument is given a separate introduction. This introduction includes two elements, corresponding to the two which make up the introduction of the sub-point. First, *transitional material* must be used to link up the main point with the position you take on the question for debate. And second a definite *statement of the main point* presented must be included. The following examples will illustrate some of the forms which may be used:

Mr. Jones and I take this position because we believe, in the first place, that the present system of private medical care is not adequate to meet the medical needs of the nation.

———

Now let us take up, one by one, the reasons which we have outlined for adopting a system of state-supported medicine. To begin with, the present system of private medical care is not adequate to meet the medical needs of the nation.

———

For the past fifteen years, medical authorities and various private foundations have made exhaustive investigations of the problem of medical care in the United States. On the basis of these findings, they recommend that the United States should supplement its present system of private medical care with an extensive system of state-supported medicine. In their reports, they have given us several major reasons why such a system should be adopted; and Mr. Jones and I will present those reasons to you tonight. In the first place, their reports show that the present system of private medical care is not adequate to meet the medical needs of the nation.

In the illustrations given, transitional materials are printed in italics, while the statement of the main point advanced is printed in roman type. Note that in each example, the main point is stated in complete form. And note too that an ordinal numeral showing the order in which the particular main point comes in the series to be used is included in the transitional material—in the second example, the expression "to begin with" is used in place of the ordinal number "first." The proposition for debate may be stated or omitted, as you wish. The introduction to the point is usually somewhat longer than the sentence used to introduce a sub-point; material usually is added to give the point greater emphasis.

Concluding the main point unit. After the proof for the main point has been presented—in the form of proof units developing the various sub-points which support the main point—some form of conclusion is necessary. Sometimes this is little more than a final direct statement of the main point itself; occasionally the conclusion may be expanded for greater effectiveness. In every case, however, *the conclusion must include a statement of the main point which has been proved.* Note the following examples.

So, Ladies and Gentlemen, it is evident that the present system of private medical care is not adequate to meet the medical needs of the nation.

Now, Ladies and Gentlemen, we have shown you that health conditions in the United States are highly unsatisfactory, and that these conditions are a direct result of the system of medical care we have today, in which medical attention is available only on a hit-or-miss basis, and at a cost beyond the reach of the average man. The conclusion is inescapable: the present system of private medical care is not adequate to meet the medical needs of the nation.

Remember, in writing or in presenting your speech, that every main point you present *must be concluded.* Introductions and conclusions make it easy for the listener to follow your thought; and effectively worded conclusions give a final force to your arguments which makes the listener remember them. If a point is worth proving, it is entitled to the added effectiveness which comes from a striking conclusion.

The complete main point. The following example was taken from an actual debate speech delivered back in 1947. Although some of the evidence used is now old, it is an excellent example of a complete and well-constructed main point. We have inserted the numbers 1, 2, and 3 to help you identify the introduction, the body, and the conclusion of the main point, respectively.

1. We uphold and defend the United Nations for three reasons: First, because it is the only plan that is acceptable today, and because it is flexible enough to be used tomorrow; second, because it is established and recognized by all the countries of the world; and, third, because it has the strength to take care of the problems of today.

2. The negative upholds the status quo and believes that the United Nations is the answer of today. We believe that the world in its confused state can take no other type of organization, because of nationalism, nationalism that is well illustrated by such slogans as "Vive la France," "Fight for the Four Freedoms," "There Will Always Be an England," and Premier Stalin's statement that only books, movies, and songs about the state should be shown. But we also believe that as political and social programs gather momentum, and as peoples and governments learn to work together toward their fullest capacity, the United Nations Charter will gradually be changed. This is provided for in Chapter XVIII, Article 108, which reads this way:

Amendments to the present charter shall come into force for all members of the United Nations when they have been adopted by a vote of two thirds of the members of the General Assembly and ratified in accordance with their respective constitutional processes by two thirds of the members of the United Nations, including all the permanent members of the Security Council.

The negative feels that this power that the Charter has to change itself as the world changes is very much in its favor. Perhaps the Charter cannot take care of the problems of tomorrow, but we believe it can take care of the problems of the here and the now. As Anthony Eden at the San Francisco Conference pointed out, "We cannot here produce a complete scheme, perfect in all elaborate details, for the future order of the world under all possible circumstances. I am persuaded to the contrary, that we shall be wise to settle ourselves within the compass of our immediate possibilities." That's what we believe the United Nations is; it is an organization within the compass of our immediate possibilities.

Our second contention is that the United Nations is established and recognized by countries of the world. No one can question the fact that the United Nations is a reality, for fifty-five nations have agreed to meet in a common assembly to thrash out their problems peacefully rather than pout until they explode in their own backyards. At the San Francisco Conference fifty-one delegates representing fifty-one nations, got up, one after another, and voiced their country's approval of this organization. The negative doubts very much whether fifty-five nations would ever be for a Federal World Government.

We believe that one of the nations which would be most heartily against it would be the United States, because we would have to get our Senate to ratify such a bill, and it is up to the Senate, not to Carl Van Doren or anyone else that the affirmative mentioned, as to whether a Federal World Government could go into effect.

As proof that the United Nations is recognized today as a body that handles controversial questions, five questions have been submitted to the Security Council. They are the Iranian question, the Greek question, the Indonesian question, the Syrian question, and the Spanish question.

3. In summing up the negative's proposition on the question, *Resolved,* that the United Nations should be changed into a Federal World Organization, I should like to restate our positions.

First, we uphold the United Nations because it is flexible by its own legislation, and because it suits the needs of the status quo, for the world is in a groping state of nationalism and will accept no other plan;

Second, we defend the United Nations because it is recognized by fifty-five nations, and because it has received problems of the world like the Iranian case, and handled them successfully; and

Third, we uphold the United Nations because it has the strength and power to deal with the problems of today.

THE LANGUAGE OF THE ARGUMENT

Not only must your arguments be clearly organized so that they are easy for the listener to follow; they must also be expressed in the most effective language possible. Your speech must be interesting, so that it captures and holds attention; ideas must be made vivid, so that listeners remember them. And interestingness and vividness are largely a result of the way you express your ideas—the language you use. In the following paragraphs, a number of devices will be suggested which will aid in making your ideas vivid and interesting.

Directness. Remember that in debate, you are talking directly to your listeners. So when you write your speech, use the same informal style that you would use in carrying on a conversation. Don't use formal, stilted language; use the words you use in talking. Keep away from big words, unless they're words you use every day and that your listeners understand. Use the personal pronouns "you" and "we." Think of the audience not as a group of people, but as some individual person you know; talk directly to him.

Four devices will aid you in getting directness: the *"you attitude,"* the *use of questions*, the *use of commands*, and the device of *"reminding" your listeners*. The first of these devices—that of the *"you attiude"*—consists simply of the frequent use of the pronoun "you" throughout your speech. A former director of talks of the Columbia Broadcasting System tells us that a radio talk is never good unless the word "you" appears at least four times on every page—that's about one time in each two or three sentences. It makes the listener feel that the radio speaker is talking directly to him. And that same frequent use of the pronoun "you" is just as essential in your debate speech as it is in radio talks. Don't put things in the third person; apply your ideas to your listeners; use the pronoun "you."

The second device—using *questions*—also aids you in securing directness. Don't be afraid to ask your listeners questions, even if the answers are obvious. Whenever you ask a question of your listener, you make that listener *think*. And if you can get him to think—especially along the lines you have suggested in your question—he will be more likely to see things the way you do.

A third device for directness is that of the *command*. Tell your audience to "think," or "picture," or "imagine," or "remember" something; nine listeners out of ten will try to obey your command. If someone says to you, "Think of that last picture show you saw; do you remember the way . . ." and so on, you start thinking about the picture show. You hardly ever resist a command. And your listener responds the same way that you do. When you give him a command, you make him think; and he's much more likely to agree with your arguments.

A final device that helps make your speech direct is that of *reminding* the audience of things they already know, rather than telling them the same things as if they were new. People rarely object to being reminded of things; but sometimes they do object to being lectured. Give your listeners credit for knowing all about the things you discuss. Even though they may not, they will believe that your statements are true, and that they should have known about them.

Notice, in the example below, the use of the various devices which have been suggested to secure directness. Even though the selection is short, the word "you" occurs four times; one idea is expressed in question form, and the "you remember" device is used in three sentences. These devices make the argument more direct and more vivid.

You all remember an incident which received little attention from the average American citizen—the Pan American Aviation Congress in Peru. You will recall that the United States initiated that congress; that we sent seventy-eight army planes roaring down there in formation over the trackless jungles and the towering Andes mountains. You read of them sweeping down over the cheering crowds at the congress, of how they put on a glorious show for the people who came, and displayed the might of the United States and the wonder of our aircraft. But did you read that little item in your paper some three weeks later, which tells us better than anything else of the final results of that congress? The item told of the sale to Peru of six bombing planes—by Italy. The United States made no sale. We put on the demonstration; Italy walked off with the contracts.

Interestingness. If you are to hold the attention of your listeners, your speech must be *interesting*. And interest, like directness, is secured by applying certain principles or using certain techniques. In general, a thing is interesting if it has one or more of four characteristics: if it has *picture-quality*, if it *affects us directly*, if it is *striking* or *shocking*, or if it offers *variety*.

Probably the most important of these interest factors is the one we call *picture-quality*—the quality which builds up clear, distinct *pictures* in the listener's mind. We're interested in pictures; we *think* in terms of mental pictures; but we simply can't be interested in things we can't imagine. Take the expression, "patriotism," for instance. We believe in patriotism, of course— but we get pretty tired when a speaker talks on and on about the beauties of patriotism, and the need for patriotism, and the importance of patriotism to democracy. We simply can't "see" patriotism; the word doesn't build any picture in our minds. But suppose the speaker *applies* the idea in some definite situation. Suppose he tells us about the half-starved, freezing soldiers at Valley Forge, or about the heroic Texans who died in the defense of the Alamo. Those things are real; they build up pictures in our minds—and we're interested. The greater the power of any idea to create a distinct, vivid picture in the listener's mind, the more interesting that idea is to him. If you give your idea *picture-quality,* that idea captures interest.

Now, how can your presentation of an idea be given picture-quality? Three suggestions will help. First, apply the idea to a concrete situation. Second, give enough details to make the mental picture of that situation complete. And third, use specific words, not general terms, to convey your thought.

Let's take a concrete example. Suppose that you are trying to tell your listeners that "the public is opposed to electric utilities companies." That's not very interesting; your listener can't possibly build up a mental picture of "the public" or of "utilities companies." He can't even get a picture from the word "opposed." So apply your idea to some definite case—real or imaginary. Tell about some man who refused to let an electric company build its lines across his farm. That's more interesting; it's an idea your listeners can visualize. Add enough details to round out the picture; use specific words, rather than general terms. And you give the listeners a clear-cut picture, of a "grim-faced, weather-beaten farmer, gun in hand, telling the foreman of the Central Power Company's construction gang to 'get that truck off my land, or you'll be spendin' the next few hours gettin' bird-shot picked out of your hide!'" That's something definite; your listeners can "see" it; it has a high degree of *picture-quality.*

Contrast the way in which ideas are expressed in the sentences given below, and decide for yourself which sentence in each pair is more interesting.

General	*Specific*
New inventions make it possible for machines to take the place of numbers of men.	Every time that Ford's engineers perfect a new machine to stamp out metal, a hurrying, red-faced foreman says, "Sorry, Bill, but we'll have to let you go." And Bill and five hundred other fathers and husbands are given blue envelopes to take home to their hungry families.
Many of the 5 million unemployed in the U.S. in 1962 are unable to keep their families together.	Picture Henry Smith, after the last weekly unemployment check has been spent, and the last long day of job hunting is over, returning wearily to his little home and telling his wife, "Mary, we've spent our last dime. We can't pay the rent. I can't even buy a loaf of bread. We'll have to leave little Mary with that welfare worker, and you and I will hit the road till something turns up."
The race to land the first man on the moon is tremendously expensive. The U.S. will spend $5.6 billion in this race during 1963.	And what is this race to get the first man on the moon costing America? The Space Administration has earmarked $5.6 billion for 1963 alone. This amount would increase every public and high school teacher's salary in America by more than $4,000, an increase of about 80 per cent. Or it would run all the colleges and universities in the land, with enough left over to pay for tuition and books for every college student in the U.S. And for what? So that we Americans can pound our chests, grin, and say, "But *we* put the first man on the moon."

A second method of securing interest is to show that the thing you are talking about *directly affects the listener.* Every man is interested in the things that affect his health or his home or his pocketbook. If someone comes to you and tells you about a way to make some money, you're interested. If you even overhear someone mention your name, you try to hear what is said—if someone is talking about you, you're interested. Anything that concerns you personally, is interesting. So, to make your ideas interesting in debate, show how they affect the listener. If you are talking to an audience of laboring men about British trade methods in Latin America, show how those methods are cutting down demand for American goods, and throwing American workmen out of jobs. Whatever can be shown to affect your listeners, will interest them.

A third device for securing interest is the use of statements that are *striking.* If an idea surprises us or shocks us, we're interested in that idea. The more striking it is, the greater the amount of our interest. It may be merely something strange or unusual; it may be something we hadn't thought of before; it may be merely a new way of stating a well-known fact. For instance, if you tell a boy that smoking is an expensive habit, you probably won't surprise him—and it's doubtful whether you will interest him very much. But if you show him that he is spending ten dollars a month for tobacco, the idea is more surprising, and more interesting. And the same idea is expressed in an even more striking way if you tell him that with the money he spends on tobacco, he could buy $25,000 worth of insurance during his lifetime, and build up a $25,000 estate. That's even more surprising, and much more interesting. Whenever you are presenting an idea in debate, try to express it in a striking manner.

The final requirement of interest is *variety.* We notice things that change; they capture our attention. That is why advertisers on television change camera shots every 3 to 10 seconds, and that is why advertisers use electric signs that flash on and off. We're interested in things that are different, that "break the monotony."

Keep that fact in mind as you develop your arguments. Thoughts developed in the same way throughout a speech are monotonous and uninteresting to your listeners. So work in as much *variety* as possible in your arguments. Change your ways of saying things frequently. Use a different type of introductory material for each new point you present. Vary the types of evidence used to support points that follow one another. Use variety even in the methods you use to secure interest—the use of the same device over and over again makes your arguments monotonous. Use at least one interest method in every argument in your speech; but change the methods you use. In one paragraph, use a striking statement; in the next, show how your idea affects the listener; in a third, depend chiefly on the picture-quality of your explanation.

Emphasis. The third group of suggestions on methods followed in writing your speech includes those which relate to emphasis. Certain things that you say are more important than others; you want them to stand out, and to be remembered by your listeners. To give such ideas greater emphasis, use one of the three devices suggested below.

The first technique for securing emphasis is the use of *repetition.* The more frequently you repeat an idea, the more firmly you impress it on your listeners. You can repeat it in exactly the same words, or you may use different words in restating the same thought. But by pounding the same idea home over and over again, you fix it in the listener's mind. Notice how repetition has been used in the following example:

Every Secretary of Agriculture since Henry A. Wallace in 1933 has had his pet plan of legislating prosperity for the farmers of America. Wallace, Wickard, Anderson, Brannan, Benson, and now Freeman— each has had his plan, and each has failed to legislate prosperity for the farmer. You will remember that we tried plowing under the cotton and burning the pigs; the plan failed. We tried buying the surpluses and taking them from the market; the plan failed. We tried paying farmers to let land lie idle; the plan failed. We tried setting allotments and fining farmers who planted more than allotted; the plan failed. We tried price supports; the plan failed. The very fact that we are debating the plight of the farmer tonight is proof that the best brains in agriculture have failed to find legislation that produces prosperity. Ladies and Gentlemen, you cannot legislate prosperity.

A second device for securing emphasis is the use of *exaggeration*. Facts are exaggerated deliberately—to such an extent that the listener immediately knows you are overstating them. He knows, too, that you do not expect him to accept what you say as literally true; you exaggerate merely to make your point more striking and more vivid. The following example shows the way overstatement is used:

The college student doesn't study, and he doesn't learn. He seldom reads and he never thinks. He spends much money, and he earns not one cent of it. In short, he is the best example we have—together with prisoners, the insane, and people on relief—of the "pure" consumer.

Naturally, your listener knows that you do not expect him to believe such a statement as literally true. He knows that you are exaggerating, to make your point vivid. But he knows also that there is an element of truth behind your exaggeration; and the fact that you have overstated the real conditions, impresses that element of truth on his mind.

Sometimes, your use of exaggeration goes in exactly the opposite direction: instead of overstating the facts, you understate them. But the understatement is so obvious that your meaning is quite clear. Note the following example:

It is contended that Russia desires peace and she is willing to cooperate with other nations in every possible way for the maintenance of a peaceful, communistic world! Russia reminds one of the young lady who maintained that she was willing to cooperate—provided she had her way!

A third device for securing emphasis for your ideas is that of using *comparisons*. Much has already been said about the use of comparisons as evidence. But comparisons have equally great value as a means of making an idea impressive. You simply compare the idea you are presenting to things or experiences in your listener's everyday life. To show school children how a legislature works, you compare it with a student committee; to impress housewives with the effects of prohibition, you compare the situation with little Johnny's reactions when he is forbidden to do something. Note the use of comparison in the following example:

Whatever the United Nations is today, it is not, and the men working with it admit that it is not, a sovereign international authority. The United Nations and its components may be allegorically described as a forum of world opinion, the eyes and ears of the world, or the stepping stone to peace, but they must not be described as world government.

We're not pacifists. We of the affirmative want peace badly; however, we're not idealists. We recognize today there is a conflict brewing. It's bound to brew when you have two diametrically opposed substances in one world. In chemistry we know what happens—an explosion. You're bound to have an explosion when you have two diametrically opposed ideologies in the same world. . . .

One is reminded, when listening to those speaking about the higher standards of living, of a cartoon that appeared some years ago, in which was portrayed the lowland nations of Europe in a rowboat. The back end of the rowboat had a leak in it and the three leaders of the world at that time, England, France, and the United States, were represented by three figures standing at the prow of the boat. As they turned around, they were saying, according to the caption underneath the cartoon, "Thank God it's not *our* end of the boat that's sinking." But yet, Ladies and Gentlemen, we have seen in the past few years how it *is* "our end of the boat" that is sinking. . . .

Loaded words. The final suggestion on the language used in presenting your arguments relates to your choice of words. Words are important. They convey ideas, and they also build up *feelings* on the part of your listeners. Some words may create bias in favor of your idea; others may build up a feeling of distrust and opposition. For example, what are your own feelings toward the two words "plan" and "scheme?" In general, they have the same meaning; but they arouse entirely different *feelings*. Words which have power to arouse such feelings are called "loaded" words.

Be careful, in describing your own proposals, to use words which create pleasant feelings on the part of your listeners. Your plan is "sensible," or "intelligent," or "logical." It has been "tested and proved by experience." It is "democratic," and "economical" and "American." There are scores of other words which may be applied to it—simply in describing it—which arouse similar feelings in your listeners' minds. Use those "pleasant" loaded words, in describing your own ideas, or presenting your own solutions.

On the other hand, try to use words that create unpleasant feelings in describing your opponents' proposals. Refer to their plan as a "scheme" or as a "cure-all." Refer to their points as "contentions," which they have "tried to make their listeners believe." Use adjectives that arouse listener-opposition, when you mention their ideas—adjectives such as "visionary," or "radical," or "untried," or "foreign." The use of such expressions should not be carried to an extreme; but tossing in a loaded word occasionally in presenting your argument sometimes has a surprisingly great effect in determining your listeners' attitude toward your proposal.

Note the use of loaded words and expressions in the following examples. To help you identify them, the expressions which probably will creat feelings have been printed in italics. Determine for yourself which ones create a pleasant, and which an unpleasant feeling toward the idea presented.

Everywhere the *Communists press* forward stronger. Khrushchev, *vowing to take over* the world for communism, and acting with all *the confidence of a winner, threatens* to *put an end to civilized survival* for the world if we do not *let him have his way.* . . . The question for which I urge your attention is *spawned from the ugly union* of communism's *unswerving ambition* and its *unscrupulous methods.* The implications of this question have put a *chill into the hearts* of millions *who yearn for peace,* yet it is spoken by few of us.—Senator Margaret Chase Smith, *Representative American Speeches: 1961-1962* (Reference Shelf. v 34, no 4. 1962) p 28-29.

Men no longer debate whether armaments are a *symptom* or a *cause* of tension. The mere existence of modern weapons—*ten million times more powerful* than anything the world has ever seen, and *only minutes away* from any target on earth—is a *source of horror,* and *discord* and *distrust.* . . .

In short, general and complete disarmament must no longer *be a slogan,* used to resist the first steps. It is no longer to *be a goal without means of achieving* it, *without means of verifying* its progress, *without means of keeping the peace.* It is now *a realistic plan,* and *a test*—a test of *those only willing to talk* and a test of *those willing to act.*—President John F. Kennedy, *Representative American Speeches: 1961-1962* (Reference Shelf, v 34, no 4. 1962) p 44-45.

————

We *need imagination* in programing, *not sterility; creativity, not imitation; experimentation, not conformity; excellence, not mediocrity.* Television is filled with creative, imaginative people. You must strive to *set them free.* . . .

The *power* of instantaneous sight and sound is without precedent in mankind's history. This is an *awesome power.* It has *limitless capabilities for good*—and *for evil.* And it carries with it *awesome responsibilities, responsibilities* which you and I *cannot escape.*—FCC Chairman Newton N. Minow, *Representative American Speeches: 1961-1962* (Reference Shelf. v 34, no 4. 1962) p 77.

Strategic Devices

Our discussion of the debate speech, would not be complete without some mention of the use of *strategy.* The term *strategy* includes those devices sometimes used to increase the effectiveness of certain arguments, or to place opponents at a disadvantage. Some of them are intended merely to cause an opponent to waste time which might more profitably be used for argument; others are used to center attention on some argument on which the debater has a strong advantage.

Time-wasting strategy. The first general type of strategy is used for the purpose of causing opponents to waste time in a discussion of trivialities of no particular importance in the debate. This strategy takes two principal forms. In its first form, a detailed *burden of proof* is presented, including not only the issues which are vital, but also points relating to minor details.

In attempting to show that the government should take over the railroads, our friends of the affirmative have undertaken a tremendous burden of proof. To establish their proposition, they must prove beyond question that there are serious evils in private ownership; that these evils are inherent in the system; that they cannot be corrected without discarding private ownership entirely; that government ownership would completely correct them. They must show that the benefits of government ownership would be great enough to balance the enormous cost to the taxpayer; that a method could be found of taking over the railways without injustice to their present owners; that the credit of the government would stand the tremendous strain imposed upon it. But even this is not all. They must prove that operation by the government would increase efficiency; that it would provide better service; that the roads could be operated at a profit. And finally, they must show that the great force of railroad employees would not be used as a powerful political machine to keep corrupt officials permanently in power.

This is a tremendous burden, Ladies and Gentlemen. Yet our friends must prove every point to your entire satisfaction if they hope to establish their case. I challenge them to accept the task, and to prove the points I have presented.

When the second form of time-wasting strategy is used, a number of *questions* are asked relating to minor details of the opponents' plan; then the opponents are invited to explain each point in detail.

Before we can agree to spend billions of dollars to build these so-called fall-out shelters throughout the country, there are a number of questions we need to have answered. First, how are the affirmative planning to get people into these shelters in the twenty-minute period available after warning of an attack? Do they plan on building completely equipped shelters within twenty minutes' running distance of every citizen in every city and town? Who will stay outside to direct traffic headed for shelters? Can you provide a doctor for every shelter? And second, how will you check those wanting in for contamination? Or will you let all in to contaminate the others? What will you do for heat, light, power and water if no one is left outside to run these facilities? What about normal sickness and births and deaths during the two-week period that all America will be underground? Will you have hospital facilities in every shelter? What about policing within the shelters during this two-week period, when presumably 180 million Americans will be crowded into them? I could go on and on with questions that need to be answered before we decide that building fall-out shelters is a workable plan. You can think of many more questions, I'm sure. But I challenge the affirmative to answer even these few I have raised, before they ask us to decide to spend billions to build shelters that would shelter us not.

The question form of time-wasting strategy is usually more effective than that in which a burden of proof is imposed. If questions are asked in apparent good faith, they can hardly be ignored; undoubtedly the same questions have been raised in the minds of your listeners. But if time is taken to answer them, your opponents have less time to consider the really important points at issue in the debate.

Strategy of emphasis. The second group of strategic devices includes those used to *emphasize* some point in your argument— a point on which you have a definite advantage. The two principal forms are the *challenge* and the *dilemma question*.

When the *challenge* is used, the main point to be emphasized is developed completely, and supported with an abundance of evidence. Then, in concluding the point, you issue a direct challenge to your opponents to meet you on that issue.

Ladies and Gentlemen, this question of financing the system is the one really vital point in this debate. It makes no difference how desirable the affirmative plan might be, it makes no difference whether it would work or whether it wouldn't, if money can't be found to put it into effect. Upon this one point, the entire discussion must hinge. So we challenge our affirmative friends to meet us squarely upon this issue. We challenge them to show us exactly how they'll raise the money to pay for the system they suggest.

If your challenge is ignored, it is renewed in every speech that you and your colleague give until your opponents are forced to take it up. Continued repetition of the challenge centers attention upon that one point as the vital point at issue in the debate. If the point is one that gives you a definite advantage in argument, the use of this method may greatly increase the effectiveness of your case.

A second method of centering attention upon some particular issue is that of asking a *dilemma question*. The word *dilemma* means literally two horns; a dilemma question is one that involves your opponents in difficulties no matter how they may answer it.

The affirmative, in advocating control of atomic energy by the United Nations, is faced with a troublesome dilemma. As we see the problem, the United Nations either has the power to control the war potentials of atomic energy, or it does not. If we assume that it has the power, or that the power can be given to this body by the several nations, the United States and her allies, if any, would be at the mercy of the communistic and self-seeking nations who could—and would—use this power to advance their own economic, ideological and nationalistic interests.

If, on the other hand, the United Nations does not have the power to control and must depend only upon its alleged "great moral force," it would be extremely dangerous for the United States to surrrender its atomic secrets and potentiality to this body. Power politics, as of old, will determine the use of atomic energy, and the less scrupulous nations will control this deadly energy for their nationalistic and ideological interests.

As we see the problem, the affirmative is faced with these two alternatives and there are no other possible solutions to their plan. It will be interesting to hear which of the two possibilities the gentlemen will follow, and, more intriguing, how they propose to justify their untenable position.

If the dilemma is strong, force your opponents to reply to it by demanding a reply in every speech until it is met. Constant repetition increases the difficulty in which your opponents are placed.

The place of strategy. Strategy may be used at almost any point in the constructive speech. Such devices as the use of *questions* or of a *burden of proof* are usually placed either near the beginning or near the end of the first negative speech, although the *question* device can also be used by the affirmative in relation to the negative stand. A *challenge* or a *dilemma question* should be introduced immediately following the argument it is intended to emphasize. If additional arguments are introduced by the same speaker, the *challenge* or *dilemma question* should be brought up again in the conclusion of the speech.

Strategic devices are often very effective in debate. But their value depends entirely upon the situation. Unless the question is one which allows you to use some device effectively, don't use strategy at all. And it is almost never desirable to use two types of strategy in a single debate argument. Use strategy if you are sure it will help you; but use it sparingly.

THE SPEECH CONCLUSION

The conclusion of the speech should give you little difficulty. Its sole function is to sum up briefly the points which have been established, and to give a final statement of the proposition you support in the debate. The conclusion of the second speech for your side will be somewhat longer than that of the opening argument; the entire case must be summed up, rather than the arguments in a single speech.

Two general types of speech conclusion are commonly used. In the first, a concise summary of your main points is presented, followed by a final statement of your main proposition. In the second, the same organization is used, but in addition, a striking statement by an authority or a reference to an illustration already presented is used to provide a final "punch" in the conclusion. The two types are illustrated in the examples below:

(1) So, in summary, we would reiterate that:

If the ultimate aims of Russia and the United States are diametrically opposed and cannot be reconciled,

If compromise between these countries is not possible unless the United States is willing to risk its future,

If, as has been abundantly illustrated, the United Nations is entirely too weak to justify complete faith in its power by the United States,

If the nations refuse to disarm, and we see an armament race today between Russia and the United States,

If Russia insists on securing control of every government in the world in order to feel herself secure, and finally,

If Russia, instead of desiring peace, has the desire for war,

If, as we've maintained, all of these reasons are true, we submit to you that war with Russia *is* inevitable within a generation.

---

(2) To summarize and generalize the affirmative arguments for the proposed amendment: We are convinced that the safety and welfare of this nation demand the abolition of the electoral-college system of electing

Presidents. This system now denies a majority of our people any effective voice in the election of Presidents. The proposed amendment would remove the overpowering incentive in the present system to coddle and corrupt organized minority groups in the pivotal states, since under the proposed amendment, there would be no pivotal states. The proposed change would remove the incentive to buy those who may be for sale to the highest bidder, because their votes would not mean a balance of power and the election of a President. Under the proposed change, there would be little or no compulsion or incentive for fraud and chicanery in national campaigns. Such campaigns would no longer be sectional. The general welfare would then become a party's paramount concern. Principles would then inevitably rise above politics, and statesmanship would then count for more than mere political expediency.

Let us act before it is too late.—Ed Gossett. *Congressional Record.* July 21, 1947.

Making the summary. Some sort of summary is included in nearly every conclusion. In summarizing your case, observe the following suggestions: First, *do not make the summary too long.* Don't repeat evidence; don't even mention the sub-points you use. Simply review the ideas you have presented as main points in your argument. A long, detailed summary merely bores the listener.

Second, *avoid unnecessary formality* in summing up your points. "Thus far in the debate, Mr. Hart and I have proved four main points: first, that protection from Germany is necessary . . ." and so on, is not a desirable form. Avoid all reference to the idea of debate—you're trying to make your listeners *believe.* Don't use any form of the word "prove" in your conclusion. If you *have* proved your points, your listeners believe them; if you have failed in your purpose, it doesn't help you to *say* that your points have been proved. The very suggestion that a point has been "proved" diverts the listener's attention from the *belief* you have tried to establish. Even the use of numbers such as "first," "second," and "third," is better avoided. State your main points as *facts* from which your conclusion is drawn; and make the whole summary as informal and easy as you can.

Note the following formalized conclusion and how much weaker it is than the recast version of the same material in (1) above.

So we see, in brief summary, that the affirmative case is merely this: First, the ultimate aims of Russia and the United States are diametrically opposed and cannot be reconciled to prevent war. Secondly, compromise is not possible unless we are willing to risk the future of the United States. Third, the United Nations today is entirely too weak for the United States to place its faith in. Fourth, disarmament? Rather than disarming, Russia and the United States are arming. . . . We'll accept that. And the last thing before a war is what? An armament race, and that's what is going on today according to the negative. Fifth, the political moves of Russia today are not defensive in nature! We cannot see how it is feasible for any nation to have to control every government in the world in order to feel herself secure. And sixth, rather than the desire for peace, Russia certainly has the desire for war. For those reasons we maintain that war with Russia is inevitable within a generation.

Third, *never mention a point which is still to be proved.* Don't tell your listeners what your colleague is going to do. Some situation may arise which prevents him from so much as considering the points you have outlined. And in any event, a point not yet established gives the listener no reason for accepting your final conclusion. Sum up the main points you have given, or if you are concluding the argument, those presented in both speeches for your side.

Concluding statements. Follow up the summary with a concluding statement of the proposition you have upheld in your argument. Sometimes, it may follow the language of the debate resolution. But that language need not always be used. Often you can use a quotation from an authority who expresses exactly the idea you have been trying to prove. Sometimes you can use a simple comparison, which makes the idea vivid. But always, tie the loose ends together by definitely stating the proposition you want your listeners to believe.

The possibilities for the first time are such that we can actually envy our grandchildren rather than pity them. We have shown that the probabilities of atomic war are against its occurrence. We have

shown, furthermore, that the possibilities of peacetime use of atomic
energy are the greatest of any possibilities up to date. We see that this
is just the light under the door for the new atomic age—benefits never
before imagined; and we feel that the development of atomic power is
an exceptional impetus to the enrichment of life. We feel that our position, furthermore, is well echoed in the first chapter of Genesis: "For
God looked at all He made and behold it was very good."

After-conclusions. The summary and the concluding statement make up your conclusion proper. But occasionally, you
may want to add some additional material, following that
conclusion, and tacked on, for emphasis, at the very end of the
speech. For example, you may wish to repeat a *challenge* made
earlier in your argument; possibly you may wish to state a
dilemma question, and demand that your opponents reply to it.
And very frequently, you may wish to present a final effective
illustration, which sets forth your position in a striking way.
Material of this kind, which follows the regular conclusion, is
called an *after-conclusion*. The following examples show the
use of such after-conclusions in actual speeches and debate:

In the present struggle of ideas, the cold war, I am not afraid
that you will know too much; I am only afraid that you may know
too little. Communism may thrive on ignorance, but democracy thrives
on knowledge. So I would say to you as you commence your adult lives,
beware of half-truths, slogans and shibboleths. Beware of those who
sow race hatred in the name of universal brotherhood. Beware of those
who sow religious and class dissension in the name of equality or freedom. As students, you have learned the importance of an inquiring
mind. I hope that you will continue to be analytical and critical in
politics as you have had to be in your studies here, for you are now
entering the main stream of human society. Your responsibility for
intelligent thought and considered action is all the greater because you
are among the potential leaders of your generation.

Your mission as intelligent, active citizens of America is no less significant than the courageous mission of our armed forces who crossed
the English Channel on D-Day. I would, therefore, repeat to you the
"Order of the Day" issued by General Eisenhower on June 6, 1944:

"You are about to embark upon the great crusade toward which
we have striven these many months. The eyes of the world are upon

you. The hopes and prayers of liberty-loving peoples everywhere march with you."—Andrew G. Clauson, Jr., president, Board of Education, New York, N.Y. *Vital Speeches of the Day.* 15:442. May 1, 1949.

[THE GLOBAL DANGER] Do we actually think that a Russian imperium in Asia would be less dangerous to America than a Japanese?

It would be more dangerous. The Russian geopolitical situation is more advantageous than the Japanese. The manpower and resources of Russia excel those of Germany and Japan combined, if we exempt the Japanese holdings in China, from which she drew a third of her war materials. Russia sits in the heart of Eurasia, with adequate internal resources to arm and equip her million-numbered armies, already distributed at all the peripheries and beyond. In Europe she is at the Danube and the Elbe; in Asia she is at the Yangtze. Everywhere her agents are spying and undermining morale. In some places their impudence is boundless. In France, Maurice Thorez, Communist member of the French Assembly, dares publicly to invite the Russian armies to enter France as liberators, in case of conflict with the Soviet, and to lay down the thesis that "by definition, the Soviets are never the aggressors." He is backed up by Togliatti in Italy. The French hesitate to try Thorez, twice a traitor, lest they make him a martyr. The Russians, however, are not afraid to make martyrs.

[CONCLUSION] It would seem from the facts of our vast strength and wealth, in the service of a nation dedicated as no nation ever was to human liberty, that America's destiny was to lead the world. So the whole world has thought. But wealth and strength are not power. Power is will and direction.

And a nation not perpetually jealous of its own security cannot lead the world. In the end, it cannot even lead itself. Backing and filling, its leaders afraid, even, to tell their own people the truth, it will gradually find itself pushed off every political and military beachhead, until, at last isolated, and without allies, it will be forced to take a stand as hazardous as any stand that might today be made by the Chinese Nationalists, risking its very life against the alternative of passing, for generations, and perhaps forever, out of history.

Every state that falls in Europe or Asia brings that terrible dilemma closer. And every state that falls brings closer, also, the danger that, having sacrificed the liberties of others for our own peace, we shall finally have to give up all our own liberties for the sake of our fundamental security.—Dorothy Thompson. *Vital Speeches of the Day.* 15:438. May 1, 1949.

Because of the nature of international politics as we have now examined them, I would propose a new syllogism concerning international control of atomic energy. It is: atomic energy can be controlled only by a sovereign government; the United Nations is not a sovereign government; therefore, the United Nations cannot control atomic energy. And the correlated conclusion naturally follows: if the United Nations cannot control this civilization-destroying force, it should not be given control of it.

———

When he was entertaining our boys in the South Pacific, Joe E. Brown sat all night at the side of a dying American soldier. Just before he died, that kid asked the actor one question. "Joe," he said, "What's this all about?" What's this all about? Well, all right, what was it all about? How would you answer that boy tonight, if you could? Was it so we could spread new hate, new malice? Was it so we could fight Russia in twenty years? Is that why that boy fought and died? Is that what it was about? No, surely we could face him squarely and say, "It was for peace." It's up to you and me this time, Friends—that peace. This is our last chance. If we are to keep faith with those dead, if we are to preserve hope for those living, we must not fall weakly to our knees and moan that a third world war is here. With industry, with understanding, with vision, we can prevent such a monstrous thing. We must and we shall prevent it. There need be no war with Russia in this generation or in any generation.

PART VI—REBUTTAL

REFUTING ARGUMENTS

The earlier sections of this book have dealt with the *constructive* part of your argument in debate—the part in which you give your listeners reasons for believing your side of the proposition. But debating is a *two-sided* affair. While you were giving the listener reasons for favoring *your* side, your opponents were busy giving him reasons to favor the *other* side of the proposition. So, you have two more things to do before you can expect the listener to agree with you (instead of your opponent): (1) You must show that the reasons given by your opponent are not valid; and (2) you must defend your own arguments against attacks made by your opponents. In other words, *rebuttal* must be used.

The importance of rebuttal in debate cannot be emphasized too strongly. In nearly every debate the question is so evenly balanced that neither side can gain much advantage in the constructive argument. The reasons which may be given favoring one side are just as strong as those favoring the other side, but no stronger. Consequently, the final beliefs of the listener will depend very largely on the strength of the *attacks* made on the various constructive arguments, and on the way in which attacks are met. The team which is strongest in rebuttal is usually the one whose position is accepted by the audience. Rebuttal is a vital factor in debate.

Perhaps at this point we should examine the meaning of the words *rebuttal* and *refutation*. As used in this book, both words mean exactly the same thing—*the process of attacking an argument.*

According to the rules of contest debating, a *rebuttal speech* must be devoted entirely to rebuttal or refutation; the entire time of the speech must be taken up with attacks on your opponents' arguments or in defending your own constructive arguments from your opponents' attack. No *new arguments* (arguments not made earlier in the debate) may be brought up in the so-called "rebuttal speech." The rules of debate are very rigid on this point.

However, the rules of debate *do permit* rebuttal arguments to be used in the constructive speeches. That is, a debater in delivering his constructive speech may include attacks on points already made by his opponents. *Refutation* may take place in the constructive speech as well as in the rebuttal speeches.

A *rebuttal argument,* then, may be defined as one in which an opposing argument is attacked or refuted, whether it be given in the constructive part of the debate or in the rebuttal speeches.

Types of rebuttal. The rebuttal arguments used in debate fall into three general classes:

1. **Direct rebuttal**
2. **Counter rebuttal**
3. **Minor point rebuttal**

Direct rebuttal is a term used to refer to the attacks you make on the important points or contentions in your opponents' constructive case. *Counter rebuttal* is the defense you offer against the attacks made on your own important arguments. *Minor point rebuttal* refers to your attacks on minor points, not vital to your opponents' case; minor rebuttal arguments of this kind are used chiefly as a convenient way of introducing speeches.

To illustrate, suppose you are supporting the negative side in a debate on government ownership of railroads. Your opponents have offered three main contentions or *reasons* for government ownership: that there is need for a change, that government operation would increase efficiency, and that government ownership would further our system of national defense.

If these contentions are allowed to stand, your listeners probably will accept the affirmative proposal. So each of the three contentions must be attacked, and either overthrown entirely or greatly weakened. Your attacks upon these important opposing contentions would be the *direct* part of your rebuttal.

In the same discussion, your own case may be based on four important arguments: that the cost of buying the railroads would be prohibitive, that government operation would increase political corruption, that government operation would result in huge operating deficits, and that the proposal is a step toward socialism. Each of these points will probably be attacked in your opponents' *direct rebuttal*. To keep your own arguments as effective as possible, you will have to meet the attacks against them, and possibly reinforce each point with additional evidence. Your replies to your opponents' attacks will be *counter rebuttal*, or rebuttal directed against rebuttal.

Direct and *counter rebuttal* are the two forms of greatest importance; they include your refutation on all of the *important* points of disagreement. But *minor point rebuttal* is important, too; it helps you win the respect of your listeners, and sometimes to weaken the listeners' good opinion of your opponents. Even though the contentions or arguments attacked are of little importance in themselves, effective minor point rebuttal sometimes has much to do with your success in winning listeners to your point of view.

Methods in refutation. Two distinct methods are possible in attacking an opposing point. The first is to *attack your opponent's proof* for the point he has advanced—to *tear down* his argument by showing weaknesses in his reasoning or by attacking the validity of the evidence used. In our discussion of rebuttal, this will be referred to as the *tearing-down process*. The second method, called the *building-up process*, follows an exactly opposite procedure. To attack an opposing point by this method, you advance a contention of your own that is a direct denial of your opponent's contention—usually the opponent's point, stated in the negative—and proceed to support it with entirely new reasoning and evidence of your own.

To illustrate, suppose that the debate is on the question of disarmament, and that in opposing the proposal, you wish to refute the affirmative contention that an arms race inevitably brings on war. Using the *tearing-down* method, you would analyze the reasoning your opponent has used to support his point, and the various items of evidence on which the reasoning is based. Then you would attack either the evidence he has used, or the reasoning from that evidence, and show that his own proof has failed to establish his contention. If you use the *building-up* method, on the other hand, you would directly contradict his conclusion, telling your audience that nuclear weapons will deter war; then advance reasoning and evidence of your own to support your statement.

Many debaters make the mistake of using only the *building-up* method in attacking opposing arguments. Although this method is sometimes satisfactory, it should be considered a secondary method, rather than one to be used in every rebuttal argument. Now and then your opponents' proof is so strong that you cannot attack it successfully, and the *building-up* method is necessary. However, whenever it is possible, attack the opposing point by *destroying your opponents' proof*, using the *tearing-down* method. You will find this possible with most of your opponents' arguments. And if the point is an important one, it is usually best to use *both* methods in attacking it—first tearing down your opponents' proof, and then building up proof of your own to support a contrary conclusion.

METHODS OF ATTACK

This is probably the most important section in this book. We have already said that rebuttal usually decides the winner of a debate because constructive arguments of the two teams are so nearly equal in strength. Therefore, complete understanding of the *methods* of rebuttal, and an ability to use these methods effectively, are the most important requirements of successful debating.

This section takes up the various methods of refutation. Most of the ideas discussed will be new to you. Most of us are not practiced in finding weaknesses in the arguments of others. Therefore, you may not be able to grasp and fully understand some of the methods described at the first reading. But if you are really interested in doing effective debating, it will be worth your while to *study* every one of the methods until you understand exactly how it may be used. It will pay you to use each of these methods over and over again in practice debating, until you have thoroughly mastered it.

Rebuttal is most effective when it employs the *tearing-down* process, in which you attack the *proof* your opponents have advanced. In attacking an important opposing argument by this method, you may center your efforts either on the *reasoning* used —the *reasons* given for accepting the contention—or on the *evidence* from which the reasoning proceeds. If either the "facts" (evidence) or the reasoning can be shown to be faulty, your opponent's contention is no longer *proved,* for it takes both to complete the proof process. Most of this section will be devoted to explaining the methods of attacking either evidence or reasoning.

ATTACKING THE EVIDENCE

Evidence is the basis of all proof; it is composed of the "facts" from which the speaker reasons to his final conclusion. If you can *tear down* the evidence, you destroy the entire argument; naturally the conclusion cannot be accepted if it is based on evidence that is faulty. So the first important method of attacking an opposing contention is that of *tearing down the evidence* on which the contention is based. Usually, this method is more effective than any other which may be used; to the listener, evidence is tangible—it is easy for him to follow you when you show that the evidence is not true.

Evidence may be attacked in five important ways, as suggested below:

1. Show that the evidence is not sufficient.
2. Show that the evidence does not support the conclusion.
3. Show that the evidence is distorted or inaccurate.
4. Show that the evidence comes from an unreliable source.
5. Show that, in the case of illustration or comparison, a different conclusion may be reached if the idea is carried further.

Of course, it must not be supposed that the evidence supporting *any* contention can be destroyed by using just any of these methods. For every argument that you attack, you'll have to analyze the evidence your opponent has used, and find out whether or not some one of the methods suggested can be used.

Attacking insufficiency of evidence. Sometimes your opponent may fail to offer any evidence whatever to support his contention. More frequently, some evidence will be given, but not enough to be conclusive. Perhaps only one or two instances have been given, or the use of testimony has been limited to the opinion of a single authority. Or possibly, statistics used as evidence may cover too limited a phase of the subject. If the *quantity* of evidence is noticeably small, the point you are attacking may be overthrown by calling attention to the *lack of sufficient evidence to justify the conclusion.*

The method is illustrated in the following selection from a rebuttal argument:

Next, Mr. Baird tells us that our present system of amateur athletics in schools and colleges teaches the players to lie and cheat. This is a sweeping charge; but to prove it, Mr. Baird mentioned just two instances in which college athletes lied about their amateur standing. Do you believe that two instances out of all the splendid athletes who attend our colleges and universities, prove that the system trains these men to lie and cheat? You might find two judges who are dishonest, but you would not conclude that our system of courts trains judges to be crooked. I might find two Italians with red hair, but that would not prove that all Italians have red hair. We cannot base such sweeping conclusions on such a small number of cases. Until Mr. Baird offers us stronger proof for his point, we cannot accept his statement that our present system trains athletes to lie and cheat.

Attacking misapplication of evidence. Sometimes it happens that the evidence your opponent uses is entirely true, but does not logically support the conclusion which he draws from this evidence. To illustrate, your opponent may read a statement by an authority who says that the atom bomb is the most destructive weapon ever invented. He may then draw the conclusion that we need a single world government. Here, obviously, the evidence does not support the conclusion drawn; throughout history *some* weapon has been "the most destructive yet invented," but that did not prove we had to have a single world government. Whenever your opponent makes such an error, his argument may be overthrown by showing that the evidence is misapplied and does not lead logically to the conclusion. The following will illustrate:

Mr. James' third important contention was that socialization of industry increases production. That is a very interesting argument, so let us see how Mr. James tried to prove his statement. He gave us just one bit of evidence—the fact that from 1942 to 1946, during the war, production of armaments and foodstuffs in the United States was larger than ever before in history. Of course, Mr. James forgot to tell us what happened to the production of civilian luxury goods, but we won't quibble over that point. We will agree that during the last war, production of armaments and foodstuffs in the United States was greater than ever before in history. But this does not prove that socialization of industry increases production; there is one weakness in his argument. During the war our industries were not socialized, they were still in private hands as far as ownership and operation went. The profit motive plus that of patriotism were still in operation, government contracts were let to privately owned business, and competition for that business was keen. You all remember these facts. By no stretch of the imagination can our wartime production be credited to socialized industry. So Mr. James has failed to give any valid proof for claiming that socialization of industry increases production.

Attacking distortion of evidence. Sometimes your opponents may be careless in quoting items of evidence. The language used by authorities in statements of opinion may be slightly changed, or part of a statement omitted. Errors may be made in presenting statistics. The facts concerning examples cited may be distorted or exaggerated. Extreme cases may be given as typical, or "hand-picked" statistics may be used. If the error is simply a slip of the tongue, or if the distortion is of minor importance, it is generally best to ignore it—listeners do not enjoy hearing you quibble over trivialities. But if your opponents *deliberately* distort the evidence they give, or if an unintentional error in statement *greatly strengthens their case,* you may attack the argument by calling attention to the lack of accuracy in your opponents' evidence.

Next, Mr. Clark told you that insurance companies are *not* conspiring to hold up premium rates on group insurance. To prove this contention, he told you that only eleven of the more than five hundred insurance companies in the United States have so far joined the "Conference," the members of which have identical rates and policy provisions. I am afraid that Mr. Clark is not very familiar with his insurance companies, or he would not have been misled by these figures. What he apparently does not realize is the fact that the eleven companies which have joined the "Conference" are the *big* companies— together, those eleven companies have sold over 96 per cent of all the group insurance in force today. Most of the other insurance companies either do not sell group insurance at all, or sell only very little of it. The nearly five hundred companies which are not members of the "Conference" have, combined, sold less than 4 per cent of the total. Under the circumstances, we cannot accept Mr. Clark's conclusion that insurance companies have not conspired to hold up the premium rates on group insurance.

Attacking the source of evidence. Statements of opinion, statistics, and accounts of actual instances must all come from highly reliable sources to be worthy of the listener's belief. If the *source* is weak, the value of the evidence is small. Consequently, when your opponent quotes some authority who is unknown, or who can be shown to be unreliable, or who is prejudiced, the evidence taken from that source is open to attack. Usually the attack upon the evidence will be followed by a *building-up* process, in which contrary evidence is given from a more reliable authority.

In arguing that the federal government be empowered to establish minimum national scholastic standards for all public and private schools, Mr. Dary claimed that only through *federal* standards can American education compete with education in the rest of the world. To support this argument, he has given you two bits of evidence: first, he quoted Vice-Admiral Rickover on the low quality of American education; second, he quoted the U.S. Commissioner of Education as favoring federal minimum standards. No doubt, Mr. Dary gave you the strongest evidence he could find to support his argument, so let us look at his evidence. Vice-Admiral Rickover is certainly a national hero and an outstanding submarine commander, but he is hardly an authority on American schools. His life has been spent in the Navy and in developing nuclear propulsion of ships. He has had no direct contact with schools since he was graduated from the U.S. Naval Academy in 1922. We submit that we cannot assume that our great American school system is sub-standard merely because a Vice-Admiral in the Navy says so. And the only other evidence Mr. Dary offered was a statement by the Commissioner of Education. Now, with all due respect to federal employees, it is obvious that they are biased in favor of federal regulation. We do not charge that the good Commissioner consciously plans to increase his own power by asking for federal power to set minimum educational standards—presumably to be set by his own office. But we do submit that federal employees can hardly be accepted as unbiased authority on need for more federal power. One might as well quote the president of U.S. Steel on the need for price increases in that commodity, or quote labor leader George Meany on the need for wage increases, as to quote governmental officials on the desirability of more federal power. We are sure that all of these men are honest and well meaning, but they cannot be accepted as unbiasd.

So neither of Mr. Dary's authorities, Vice-Admiral Rickover or the Commissioner of Education, can be accepted as an authority on this question tonight. One has too little knowledge, and the other has reason to be biased. If these are the best authorities Mr. Dary can find to support his argument, we have no reason to believe that American education is sub-standard, and that the federal government should be empowered to set educational standards.

Carrying the idea further. When your opponent's evidence consists of a comparison or an illustration, it is often possible to destroy its effectiveness as proof by carrying the idea further, until an entirely different conclusion is reached from the one presented by your opponent. Sometimes the tables can be turned completely, and the illustration or comparison turned into a weapon which may be used against the opposing case.

The following selection will illustrate the method of turning the point of a comparison by carrying the idea further:

The young ladies from Bryn Mawr have set forth through an analogy the idea that World Federal Government would prevent war because our American federal government has been able to preserve the peace between the states since 1860. Very well, let us accept this analogy and see what the ladies want the United States Government to give up in order to keep the peace we have had since 1860. As you know, the states in the Union are no longer sovereign units, they are just *divisions* within the United States. They have very, very little power. Would you be willing to see the United States reduced in power to the position of the state of New Jersey or Nevada or Florida? Would you be willing to have the capacity of our right for independent action reduced to this level? Would you like to have a world senate made up of two representatives of the United States, Mexico, Japan, Bolivia, Iran and the other nations deciding what minimum wages are to be in all the areas of the world? Deciding the length of the work week, the size of American income taxes, the size of old-age pensions from Social Security, and all of the other things our own federal government has the power to decide for people of this country? Would you? I think not! And that is what the ladies from Bryn Mawr admit must be true of any World Federation when they compare it to the American federal government. We are glad they used this comparison, for it proves the major argument that we have been making all evening—the United States dare not join a federal union. To do so, we must give up our very basis of freedom—self-rule.

One word of caution. Too often beginning debaters attempt to attack *all* of the *evidence* offered by an opponent. They try to convince the audience that nothing the opponent says is true.

Obviously, a debate question has two sides—two equally good sides—or it would not be a question for debate. There is much good evidence in support of both sides. Usually, the *evidence* given by an opponent in debate is true, well selected, and sufficient for its purposes. In most cases it is the *reasoning from* this evidence that is subject to attack. The beginner should analyze the evidence offered by an opponent carefully, and select for attack only those items of evidence that can be attacked honestly and successfully. More often he will find that the *reasoning*—not the *evidence*—should provide the basis for rebuttal.

Attacking Proof by Classifying

While the method of *attacking evidence* is an effective form of rebuttal, you more often find situations in which the *reasoning*, rather than the evidence, should be the object of attack. Perhaps your opponent has supported his contention with *so much* evidence that time will not permit you to attack all of it; perhaps the evidence will show *no major weaknesses* which would make a successful attack possible; or perhaps your analysis of the argument shows that while the evidence is open to attack, an even *more effective* attack might be launched against the reasoning. In any of these situations, your rebuttal should be directed against your opponent's reasoning, rather than against his evidence.

First, note the type of reasoning that has been used. If the method of *proof by classifying* has been used, it may be attacked by one of the following methods of refutation:

1. By carrying the reasoning further

2. By rephrasing the classifying statement

3. By showing that the sub-point supports a different conclusion

Check the argument to see whether one of these methods can be used. The three possible methods are described briefly in the following paragraphs.

Carrying the reasoning further. When this method of attacking reasoning is used, the same principle suggested in the argument is applied to some *extreme* case, one in which the conclusion is obviously impossible or ridiculous. This method of refutation can be used against a large proportion of the arguments based on classification, and when properly used is extremely effective. To illustrate, suppose your opponent has argued against socialization of major industries because of graft and red tape claimed to be typical of government operation. Applied to socialization of industry, the argument sounds reasonable enough. But, if graft and red tape are enough to stop socialization of industry, they are also enough to stop other governmental progress. You find graft and red tape in city government, therefore we should have no city government. You find it in state government, therefore we should have no state government. You find it in *all* government, therefore we should have no government, no police force, no courts. For us to accept such reasoning is ridiculous on the face of it.

Whenever your opponent presents an important argument based on classification, see whether the conclusion cannot be made ridiculous by carrying the same line of reasoning further, and applying it to more extreme cases.

Mr. Ellis has also attacked the whole theory of farm price control by declaring that it is class legislation, intended to benefit a single economic class. I cheerfully agree that it is intended to benefit the farmer directly. But, Ladies and Gentlemen, is that a valid reason for objecting to farm price control?

Suppose that we accept the idea Mr. Ellis has presented, and condemn every type of legislation that benefits only one economic group. We'll have to condemn the tariff; it favors the producer as against the consumer. We'll have to condemn all labor legislation. We'll have to condemn our widespread consular service, because it benefits the merchant who sells goods abroad. We'll have to condemn highway construction, because highways are of value only to the owner of an automobile or truck. We'll have to condemn railroad regulation, because rate fixing benefits the railroads rather than the general public. We'll have to condemn GI education bills, because the GI is the only one benefited. We must condemn unemployment relief or old-age pensions because these are "class legislation." In fact, we'll be forced to condemn nearly every bit of legislation and nearly every policy our government has put into effect in the last century and more, because nearly all of them benefit one economic group more than others.

So unless Mr. Ellis is willing to bring in a blanket indictment, condemning all of these things, he cannot logically condemn farm price control on the ground that it aids one particular class.

Rephrasing the classifying statement. Often an argument may be very effectively attacked simply by using *different words* to describe the general class in which the proposal is placed by your opponent. The language in which an idea is stated can make a great deal of difference in people's attitude toward that idea. If you say that some public official has been "economical," and that he has "saved the public millions of dollars," you may be describing exactly the same actions as if you said that he was "tight-fisted and niggardly" in supporting public institutions, that he had "crippled the schools of the state," and had "refused to give aid to thousands of men and women on relief." But the difference in your choice of words in describing the action will make a very great difference in the attitude of your listeners toward the actions of that official.

When your opponent uses the method of classifying, and places the proposal in what seems to be a "good" class, see whether it is not possible to make the same class "bad," simply by using different language to describe it than that used by your opponent.

Mr. Houser's second argument seems to be that Russia is justified in entering Iran and taking control of oil fields because—and I quote him—"Russia is forced to use such means to *preserve her economic stability*." Those are high sounding words, Ladies and Gentlemen—but just what do they mean? They mean just this: Russia *needs* what Iran *has*. Well, I am badly in need, just now, of something the First National Bank has; but I imagine that if I *take it*, you would say I was *stealing*, no matter what high-sounding words I used to justify this theft. All that Mr. Houser has really argued, then, is that Russia needs it, so she should be permitted to take it. Ladies and Gentlemen, regardless of Mr. Houser's polished diplomatic phrases, Russia's seizure of Iranian oil is still stealing, exactly the same as if I robbed the First National Bank. Mr. Houser may be right in saying that Russia needs this oil— but he is wrong in saying Russia has the right to steal it.

Drawing a different conclusion. A third method which may be used in attacking *proof by classifying* is to show that the classifying statement really supports a different conclusion from the one presented by your opponent—a conclusion, of course, favorable to your own side of the argument.

Debaters should remember that much of the time a given piece of *evidence* will support *both* sides of the question for debate, depending on the *reasoning* used. For example, in a debate over more rigid speed laws on the nation's highways, does the *evidence* of more arrests for speeding in states with low maximums prove the *failure of low speed laws,* or do these increased arrests prove the *success* of such laws through enforcement? Or, do higher earnings by those having college degrees prove that *education is worth while,* or does it merely prove that *our smarter young people get college degrees?* Does evidence on low teachers' salaries prove that *our teachers are of poor quality,* or do such figures prove that *our teachers are dedicated persons* who put teaching above high pay? Does a quotation from Red China criticizing the Soviet Union mean that *the Communist world is split,* or does it mean that the *the Communists are lulling us into false security* by appearing to be split? In each of these cases the *evidence* is a fact, but its *meaning*—how we reason from it—is a matter of opinion. Factual evidence can be used to prove opposite things. Therefore, it will pay you to examine carefully the reasoning of your opponents to see how their own evidence can be used to prove exactly the opposite of the conclusion they have drawn.

Suppose, for instance, that in debating the question of World Control of Atomic Energy, an affirmative speaker argued that such control is necessary because "Russian bombs now threaten the peace of the world." In attacking the proposition, you might accept the classifying statement given—that Russian bombs now threaten the peace of the world—but use this statement as a reason for *not* favoring World Control of Atomic Energy, on the grounds that with such a threat existing, we dare not rob ourselves of protection by turning over our atomic energy plants to the United Nations. In this type of attack, the classifying statement is accepted, but is used as a reason for drawing a different conclusion from the one your opponent has drawn.

Next, Miss Clark tells us that a large school offers greater advantages to its students than a small one, because the faculties of large colleges have more outstanding men—men who have written important books or carried on important research. I am glad to agree that the faculties of large colleges *do* write more books and carry on more research than the faculties of small colleges. But, Ladies and Gentlemen, this very fact proves my argument that the small school offers more advantages to its students. Men who spend their time in writing or in research certainly can give little time to teaching; and it is a widely accepted fact that good research men are almost never good teachers. Therefore, the proportion of *good* teachers is greater on small campuses. The small school, not the large, offers better training to its students.

Examine the reasoning used by your opponents. If they make use of the method of *classifying*, as is done in most arguments, check their reasoning to see whether it can be successfully attacked either by carrying the reasoning further, by rephrasing the classifying statement, or by drawing a different conclusion from the reason given. Arguments based on *classifying* can often be successfully torn down by using one of these three methods of attack.

ATTACKING PROOF BY ELIMINATING

If the reasoning is based on the proof method of *eliminating*, it can nearly always be attacked by one of two methods:

1. By showing that not all the possible alternatives have been considered
2. By upholding a discarded alternative

The method of *eliminating* consists, essentially, of enumerating all of the possible courses of action, and then eliminating all except the course advanced as the correct one to follow.

In most cases, the number of possible courses will be very large;
consequently it is usually possible to use one method or the
other of attacking the reasoning.

Alternatives not considered. The most common use of the
method of *eliminating* is by affirmative speakers, in supporting
some plan advanced for "correcting existing evils." But as a
rule, there are a number of possible methods by which the evils
cited might be corrected; very rarely does a speaker list every
method that would be *possible,* and show it unworkable. But
from the standpoint of proof, if another single possible course of
action is workable, then the entire reasoning method breaks
down, and the speaker's conclusion does not logically follow. If
your opponent uses the method of eliminating, note carefully
the alternatives which he considers, and see if you cannot find
at least one alternative or course of action *which the audience
will consider sound enough to accept,* which has not been mentioned. If you can show that six or seven courses are possible,
but that your opponent has considered only three or four—even
if you can mention only *one* course that has not been considered
—you will have overthrown his argument, even though you
make no effort to show that any of the new alternatives you mention is better than the one he suggests.

First of all, Mr. Daly tells us that the plan he advocates is necessary. I was astonished at the method Mr. Daly used to prove it
necessary to have socialized medicine. He simply told you that private medicine has broken down because people don't get all of the
medical care they need. And he argued that we can take our choice
of only two things: private medicine or socialized medicine. Since
private medicine is failing, he argued, we must have socialized
medicine.

Now, it may or may not be true that people don't get all the
medical care they need at the present time—I'll touch on that later.
But even if this *were* true, is socialized medicine the only thing
left for us to adopt? Mr. Daly has failed even to consider half a
dozen other possible courses of action we might take. We might
lower taxes so the poor can buy more medical care. We might train
more doctors so that more medical care is available. We might
increase the number of organizations such as the Blue Cross. We
might spend millions on medical research, so that part of present

disease is eliminated and medical care is unnecessary. We might sponsor gigantic radio-TV campaigns, teaching hygiene—striking at the *cause* of disease, rather than guaranteeing people free medical care after they become ill. We might let the states handle their own medical problems instead of adopting some federal plan. Or we might lower medical costs, by regulating prices people must pay for it. In other words, even if it *were* true that people don't now get all the medical care they need, it is no proof of the desirability of so-cialized medicine. There are many other ways we might handle the problem. So Mr. Daly's argument that things aren't perfect today in *no way* proves that we must adopt *his* solution—federal socialized medicine.

Upholding a discarded alternative. If your opponent *does* enumerate all of the possible courses that your listeners would consider reasonable, a second method of attacking his reasoning may be used—that of upholding one of the alternatives which he has discarded as unworkable. In most cases, his attacks on the discarded alternatives will be comparatively light—he probably will not have time to present much evidence or reasoning to support attacks on each of three or four alternatives—and you will have little difficulty in overthrowing his argument, so far as one of the alternatives is concerned. And, of course, if you succeed in meeting his attacks on any of the discarded alternatives, your opponent's argument based on *eliminating* is overthrown.

Mr. Reichley has mentioned three possible courses of action open to the United States with regard to a balanced budget. And he argues that America must follow one of these. First, we can continue to have an unbalanced budget which leads to bankruptcy; second, we can discontinue governmental services and cut costs to equal income; third, we can increase taxes to the point where the budget is balanced. Mr. Reichley argues rightly that the first is unthinkable. But he goes on to argue that the second is impossible, so we must of necessity raise taxes.

Now, if what Mr. Reichley told us about lowering governmental costs were true—if that *were* impossible—I'd agree to the increase in taxes. But it is not true. We *can* cut federal expenditures in order to balance the budget.

This year's budget calls for spending some $93 billion, or $7.5 billion more than we expect to take in. And this amount does not include money transferred to the Social Security trust fund, the railroad retirement trust fund, refunds to taxpayers, and the like. A budget of $93 billion or $7.5 billion more than we take in. What *could* we eliminate if we wanted to? Well, $4 billion of this budget is earmarked to go to other countries. It's fun to be Santa Claus, but not if it drives us to bankruptcy. Surely *some* of the needed $7.5 billion to balance our budget could be made here. Another $48 billion are to be spent on national defense—more for defense in peacetime than we spent any year during World War II. We could balance our budget from this one item alone, and still leave $40.5 billion for national defense. And for 1963 we have earmarked $7.6 billion to put a man on the moon. Now it's nice to be able to say "we got there first," but again it's of little profit if it bankrupts us. Certainly, we could save some of the needed $7.5 billion here. And of course there are other places in our budget where savings could be made. Our farm price support program will cost us $3.5 billion this year. And we are spending more than $10 billion to run what we call "independent federal offices" when we used to spend only $1.5 billion as our total budget for the best government on earth. In short, there are many ways in which we could cut federal expenditures to meet our income—if we only will.

Now, Ladies and Gentlemen, remember that Mr. Reichley's argument in favor of increased taxes was based on the assumption that there is no other way to balance the budget. Since I have shown a number of ways to cut expenditures to meet income, we cannot agree with his conclusion that an unbalanced budget forces us to raise taxes.

While the method of upholding a discarded alternative is usually effective, it should be used with a great deal of caution. For, when you support an alternative your opponent has discarded, you accept a *burden of proof* with respect to that alternative. So far as your listeners are concerned, you accept the responsibility of upholding that particular alternative as *better,* from every point of view, *than the plan your opponent has proposed.* And as a result, the debate resolves itself into a comparison of the merits of *two possible systems,* rather than a discussion of the good points and bad points of the system your opponent has proposed. Unless you are prepared to support the plan you have upheld throughout the debate, and show it to be better than the one your opponent has offered, the method of upholding a discarded alternative is not a safe one to follow.

Using the Building-up Process

So far, our discussion of the methods of refutation has been limited to various attacks on the reasoning or the evidence used by your opponents, all applying the *tearing-down* idea of rebuttal. Nearly always, careful examination of an opposing argument will bring to light some weakness which can be attacked. But what is to be done if the evidence supporting an opposing point is too strong to be overthrown, and if you can find no effective way to attack the reasoning? If your opponent's proof is too strong to be torn down, one of two things must be done: either you must accept the contention as true, or you must depend entirely upon the *building-up* process of rebuttal to attack the contention. *Destructive* rebuttal should be used only when the proof really is open to attack.

The building-up process, as has already been suggested, is essentially the building of a complete *constructive argument*, supporting a statement which is a direct denial or contradiction of the contention you are trying to refute. If your opponents contend that the present system is unsatisfactory, you offer proof to show that the present system is satisfactory; if they charge that being first to send a man to the moon is necessary, you offer evidence and reasoning to show that being first is not necessary. Your argument is constructed—except for the introduction, tie-in rebuttal, and conclusion—in exactly the same manner as if it were an argument in your constructive case.

While the *building-up* method of refutation is very effective in meeting some contentions, it has one very serious weakness. When used alone, it is rarely *conclusive*. If your opponent offers the listener good, logical reasons and unquestionable evidence for accepting a certain contention, the listener will probably believe him. And when you offer a contradictory statement, no matter how strongly you support it with evidence, his tendency is to reject your argument and to be loyal to his first belief. The most you usually can hope is that you may *weaken* his acceptance of the opposing contention, simply by confusing him, and making him wonder which one of you is telling the truth.

For this reason, the *building-up* method should generally be used after some form of the *tearing-down* process has been applied to the opposing proof. If you destroy or even weaken the reasoning or the evidence which supports your opponent's contention, you shake the listener's belief in the validity and correctness of the conclusion your opponent has drawn; then, if you follow with proof to support a contradictory conclusion, the listener is more likely to accept your position on the point at issue. Particularly if the opposing point is an important one in the debate, try to combine both methods in your refutation—use the *tearing-down* process first, and then follow with a *building-up* process to establish the conclusion favoring your side.

The following will illustrate both the *tearing-down* and the *building-up* types of refutation. Numbers have been given to the two types of rebuttal to aid in distinguishing them.

1. Mr. Bellamy has argued that it is essential for the United States to be first on the moon, regardless of the cost, because of the valuable things we will learn there. To support this argument he quoted Dr. John A. O'Keefe, assistant chief of the space administration, as telling *U.S. News & World Report* that sending a man to the moon will cast some light on the structure and on the fundamental laws of the universe. But the point we are debating tonight is not whether we can learn from the moon; our question is whether the United States should race Russia in order to be first. Mr. Bellamy forgot to tell you that *U.S. News & World Report* also asked Dr. O'Keefe why *he* thought that the United States should be first. Listen to the unscientific reason he gave:

> It made a tremendous difference who got the first satellite up. The Russians rubbed that in for years afterward, and they're still rubbing it in. And I'm sure that they'd rub it in the same way if we were second on the moon.

And this was the only reason this great scientist could give for spending more than $20 billion to be first—Russia might "rub it in" if we are second.

2. Now what do other scientists say about the necessity of getting a man on the moon? *U.S. News & World Report* also questioned Dr. R. L. F. Boyd, Britain's leading space scientist. Dr. Boyd's

prestige was not at stake, and he could look at the whole project objectively. Listen to what Dr. Boyd says about putting man into space at this time:

> From a purely scientific point of view, there is really no need at present for sending man into space. There is so very much that one can do with instruments. As far as the preliminary exploration of the moon is concerned, I would think that men are not necessary. . . . I question whether there is much advantage in having man in space at all. In fact, he's really rather a nuisance, because his movements upset the angular position of the spacecraft. This would make much of the astronomy we want to do from space vehicles impossible. . . . I have no doubt at all that if the money that is at present being put into the Apollo project, the Mercury project, and the others, were put into pure scientific research, the rewards would be vastly greater. . . .

Now, here is the unbiased opinion of a great scientist who is not personally involved in the race into space. He believes that sending a man to the moon is not only needless, but an actual nuisance, and that vastly more could be learned by spending the money on pure scientific research.

Ladies and Gentlemen, please note that my opponent quoted a scientist to the effect that much can be learned from the moon. But this very authority could think of only one reason for wanting to be first—fear of Russia "rubbing it in" if we were second. Certainly, Mr. Bellamy has not proved by this authority that the United States should spend more than $20 billion in order to beat Russia to the moon. On the other hand, we have quoted Britain's top space scientist, who tells us that man in space is a nuisance, and that we could learn vastly more by spending our money on scientific instruments and research. Under the circumstances I am sure that you will agree that the United States stop its foolish waste of money in trying to beat Russia to the moon.

Organizing a Rebuttal Point

Every attack that you make on an important opposing argument is a separate *rebuttal argument*. And like every other element in a debate, a rebuttal argument must be clearly organized.

It must be introduced and concluded. Usually, the organization will follow the plan suggested below:

1. Introduction to the rebuttal argument
2. A "tearing-down" process
3. A "building-up" process
4. Conclusion to the rebuttal argument

The introduction always includes a statement of the opposing point which is to be attacked. Usually it also includes certain transitional material, which shows the relation of that point to the whole of the opponents' argument. Methods of introducing rebuttal arguments are suggested in the following examples.

> The second main contention advanced by the affirmative was that free trade between non-Communist nations would benefit the United States by creating wealth in friendly nations that would permit them to maintain better armies and navies with which to deter communism. . . .

> Our second main contention this evening was that free trade with non-Communist countries would lower the American standard of living to that of the rest of the free world. The gentlemen from Michigan have attacked this point in two ways. First, they have told you American technical knowledge and industrial know-how would hold our standard of living to present levels. . . .

The *body* of rebuttal argument usually includes both a *tearing-down* process and a *building-up* process, as already suggested. If the time available for attacking the point will not allow you to use both methods, one of the two may be omitted. But if the point you are attacking really is important, both processes should be included in your rebuttal; the importance of the point demands that you give it enough time to make your attack as strong as possible. When both processes are included in a single rebuttal argument, use the *tearing-down* method first, and follow with use of the *building-up* process.

The *conclusion* of the rebuttal argument gives a final definite statement of the point you want the audience to believe—a direct denial of the point which has been attacked. The following will suggest the form generally used in conclusions.

So it is evident that the United States is in no immediate danger of Russian attack by atomic bombs.

———

So you can see, Ladies and Gentlemen, that our friends from Dartmouth have not proved that free trade would provide money for bigger armies and navies to deter communism. In fact, all the evidence indicates is that the United States would so suffer that the only armed forces in the world today deterring communism could no longer be maintained.

Never weaken the force of your conclusion by using such phrases as "I think," or "I believe," or "We feel." State the point as an *established fact,* without qualification.

Given below is an example of a complete rebuttal argument, including the four steps suggested. The four parts are numbered to correspond with the steps in the outline.

1. Mr. Carroll's second main contention against the right-to-work laws was that these laws are strangling the labor unions.

2. To support this charge, Mr. Carroll gave us three bits of the many items of evidence he claimed to have. I assume he intentionally chose what he believed to be the best evidence on his list. Very well—examine his evidence with me. The first evidence he used was a quotation from labor leader Meany to the effect that unions could not exist if right-to-work laws abolished compulsory membership. Now, you all know that Mr. Meany is very biased on this subject, as are all other labor leaders. We cannot conclude that right-to-work laws strangle the unions, merely because labor leaders say so.

The second bit of evidence offered by Mr. Carroll was the findings of a 1963 poll of Boeing Aircraft workers by the Mediation Board, which showed that the 85 per cent union membership in that company objected that their dues help non-union Boeing workers. Now this reaction is no more surprising than it is to find businessmen believing that all other businessmen should join the Chamber of Commerce. But that union members do not like open shops does not prove that right-to-work laws are strangling the unions, the

point Mr. Carroll was trying to make. In fact, when 85 per cent of
the Boeing workers join the union through choice, it would seem
that force is unnecessary. Mr. Carroll's evidence seems to prove the
very opposite of the point he was making.

The only other evidence offered by Mr. Carroll on this point
was that during the past ten years union membership dropped off in
the garment workers' unions, the various railroad unions, and in the
United States Steel Workers' Union. It is true that membership in
these unions dropped between 1951 and 1961. However, these drops
were not due to right-to-work laws because the majority of members
in these unions reside in states that do not have right-to-work laws.
Actually, technological changes in these industries cut the number
employed, and we could expect fewer union members with fewer
employed workers. So, all three of Mr. Carroll's bits of evidence
failed to prove that right-to-work laws strangle labor unions.

3. But let me give you some acceptable evidence on this point,
and show conclusively that right-to-work laws do *not* strangle labor
unions. Between 1951 and 1961, when most of our right-to-work
laws went into effect, 43 of our unions having more than 25,000
members *increased* their membership by 2,204,000, according to reports by the AFL-CIO to *The World Almanac*. In those same years
only 39 unions lost membership, totaling a loss of only 1,720,000.
And total union membership in America in those years *increased*
10.6 per cent, although the number of people employed in the U.S.
increased only 9.6 per cent. So you see that in spite of the passage
of right-to-work laws in 17 states, membership in unions increased
more rapidly during the ten-year period than did general employment.
And what about union finances? Are the unions going bankrupt?
According to union reports filed with the United States Labor Department in 1962, the unions value their assets at more than 1.5 *billion*
And this does not include 55 *billions* more deposited in
employees' pension funds, welfare funds for employees, and the like.
Further, Labor Department figures show that all types of unions are
wealthy: national unions reported assets at 785 millions, local unions
at 670 millions, and other unions at 102 millions of dollars. If
time permitted, I could detail figures on union wealth, union membership growth, and on high salaries paid union leaders. But it is
obvious from what I have pointed out that the labor unions in the
United States are *not* being strangled, either in membership or
wealth, by right-to-work laws, or by any other law.

4. So, Ladies and Gentlemen, we cannot accept Mr. Carroll's
second main charge against right-to-work laws. Mr. Carroll is wrong in
concluding that right-to-work laws are strangling the labor unions.

MINOR POINT REBUTTAL

Most of your rebuttal time should be devoted to attacks on the *major* arguments of your opponents—the main points in their constructive case, or the important attacks they have launched against your own major contentions. These are the arguments of greatest importance in the debate, so of course most of your attention should be centered on them.

But some of your time must given to the rebuttal of *minor points*—points which, in themselves, are not important. An effective attack on a very minor statement or relatively unimportant item of evidence may shake the listener's *confidence* in an opposing speaker, or in other words, may seriously weaken *prestige* of that speaker. And in the long run, the *prestige* enjoyed by a speaker has a great deal to do in determining whether listeners will accept or reject the *important arguments* presented by that speaker. If you can seriously weaken an opponent's prestige, you lessen the possibility that your listener will accept the opponent's major points. Consequently, some time in every debate should be used for attacks on minor points with the purpose of destroying or weakening prestige.

These minor attacks in your rebuttal may take various forms. They may consist of refutation of *individual statements* made by your opponent, or attacks on *single items of evidence* he has advanced as proof. They may consist of exposing your opponent's use of *unsupported assertions,* or his *misrepresentation of facts.* They may consist of calling the attention of your listeners to serious *contradictions* in your opponent's arguments; or they may take the form of exposing his *attempts to evade* some important issue.

All of these attacks, however, must meet two requirements. First, they must be *short;* and second, they must be *striking.* You can't afford to take much time in minor point attacks;

most of the time available for rebuttal must be used in attacking the important arguments in your opponent's case. And the attacks you do make on these minor points must be striking; they must make a vivid impression on the listener if they are to weaken your opponent's prestige. So for minor point rebuttal, pick out for attack those points which show serious weaknesses. If your opponent has really laid himself open to attack, you won't need much time to expose the weakness in his argument to your listeners; three or four sentences at most should be needed for a smashing attack.

While the primary use of minor point rebuttal is in attacking the prestige of your opponents, the methods you use to meet certain types of strategy are also considered under this head. Both types of minor point rebuttal will be discussed at length in this section.

Position of minor point rebuttal. Whether it is used to weaken the prestige of an opponent or as defense against some type of strategy, minor point rebuttal is most effective when placed at the very beginning of a speech. In fact, it is probably the most effective way of opening either a constructive speech, or a speech in rebuttal. It provides an excellent tie-up with the speech which has gone before; and it serves to take the attention of your listeners away from whatever important argument your opponent has just concluded. And of course, if its purpose is to weaken prestige, it serves to take away much of the strength of your opponent's arguments, and to offset any prejudice against your own side of the proposition which your opponent has been able to create.

Use an attack against one or two minor points to open every speech—except, of course, the first constructive speech for the affirmative. It will increase the effect of the arguments you present later.

Attacking Prestige

The type of attack to be used against minor points to weaken the prestige of your opponents depends, of course, upon the nature of the weakness attacked. The principal methods are outlined below.

Attacking statement. When this method is used, some single statement is selected from your opponent's argument, and shown not to be true. No attention is given to the relation of that statement to the rest of the argument from which it comes; it is considered simply as an independent contention. Since the statement attacked is of minor importance, time need not be taken for *thorough* refutation; your rebuttal will consist of a single attack, using the method of building up a contrary conclusion. The method is illustrated in the following arguments:

Mr. Charlston tells us that "a house divided against itself cannot stand" and that the world cannot exist half Communist and half free. Ladies and Gentlemen, peace is no longer a political plum; it's a necessity for survival. Disarmament is a *must;* life in a world that also contains communism is a *must.* And whether we like it or not, in spite of all the fine nineteenth century sayings, today we are up against a very simple choice: we will either *live* with the Communists of our world, or most certainly we will *die* with them.

Mr. Fish has told you—without offering one iota of proof for his statement—that college athletes are poor students, because the various sports take so much time that the athletes can't keep up with their studies. But let's look at the facts in the matter, instead of accepting the gentleman's unsupported opinion. The University of Minnesota places a good deal of stress on athletics; and players must give a great deal of time to practice. But in a recent study at that school, it was discovered that the football men who devoted the *most* time to practice did better work in their classes than those who practiced least. And may I quote Mr. Howe, who tells us, in his *Education of the Modern Boy,* "It has been my observation that during the autumn and spring terms in school when sports are at their highest, a quite parallel apex is reached in scholastic attainment." The evidence seems to show that, contrary to Mr. Fish's statement, athletics do not interfere with the player's studies.

Note the organization used in the two examples given. First, there is an introduction, in which the point to be attacked is stated. Second, there is the rebuttal proper, with evidence offered to support an opposite conclusion. And third, there is a statement of a conclusion opposing the one attacked.

In both the samples used, the rebuttal followed the *building-up* method. Since the points under attack were merely statements, with no evidence offered to support them, attack on the *proof* used it obviously not possible. The building-up method of rebuttal is the only one which can be used in attacking separate statements.

Attacking evidence. A second type of minor point rebuttal is that in which you attack some item of *evidence* which your opponent has advanced. Sometimes the point which the evidence supports is included in the attack; sometimes only the evidence itself is mentioned. In either case, the attack is made against the evidence used, rather than the contention it supports. And as a rule, the *tearing-down* process is the method used.

The gentlemen have cited several authorities who say that intercollegiate athletics benefit the student. They have quoted Professor Williams, a member of the athletic department at Columbia University, and John L. Griffith, commissioner of athletics for the Big Ten conference. Of course these men believe that athletics are valuable. If athletics were abolished, they'd lose their jobs. But can Mr. Brown give us similar statements as to the value of athletics from registrars of our colleges and universities—the men who know what grades the athletes make? Can he offer similar statements from *any* unprejudiced authorities? I suggest that he give us some *good* authorities on this point.

The gentleman from Oxford has compared our presidential system of elections to an alarm clock that wakes us up just once in four years. Well, as far as I am concerned, I would rather have an alarm clock that would ring at the time for which I have set it, than one that might sound its alarm every fifteen minutes during the night, or that might not ring at all. That's the situation you find in countries that have the parliamentary system of government; a parliament may be dissolved and the country thrown into the turmoil and confusion of an election every two or three weeks.

We've been asked to use some Main Street logic. I don't know what kind of logic goes on in Main Street in your town, but it isn't the kind that we should use on a debate platform; I'm sure of that. And I'm afraid it *is* the kind that the affirmative have been guilty of this evening. For instance, they have argued a need for Federal World Government because we have power alliances throughout the world. And they seem to reason with "Main Street logic" that Federal World Government would remove these power alliances—but would it? Wouldn't the capitalistic nations of the world still be able to rule because they are in the majority? Wouldn't that be a power alliance? Wouldn't Russia and her satellites be forced into a power alliance because they are in the minority—assuming, of course, that they joined at all? And if Russia didn't join, wouldn't we have a similar power alliance with our "world government" on one side and Russia's friends on the other? How, I ask the affirmative, can a world government remove power alliances? Give us something better than Main Street logic to show that it can.

Exposing assertions. A third type of minor point attack is that of *exposing unsupported assertions* in your opponent's arguments. While it is a rule of debate that every contention must be proved, nearly every debate speech will contain a number of statements—some of them very important—for which no proof has been offered. By listening carefully to your opponents' arguments, you usually can find several such statements. And the prestige of your opponents can be weakened with the audience by calling attention to the lack of proof for three or four such statements.

In presenting her argument this evening Miss Krekel has been guilty of several serious omissions. She has made a number of statements, some of them vital to her case, without giving us the slightest evidence to support them. She has told us, without proof, that Russia's propaganda machine is functioning smoothly in Latin America. She has stated, without proof, that there are thousands of Reds holding key government offices in *our* country. She has told us, again without proof, that Russia intends to attack this country with atomic bombs. Now these are serious charges; if they are true, we want to know it. But until Miss Krekel gives us evidence in support of these statements, we cannot accept either the statements themselves or the conclusions which she has drawn from them, as having the slightest bearing on our debate tonight.

Exposing misrepresentation. Still another effective method of weakening the prestige of your opponents is to call attention to distortions of evidence of which they may be guilty. Of course, in most debates, this method cannot be used; most debaters are extremely careful in their selection and use of evidence. But if your opponent misquotes an authority or omits some significant part of the authority's statement, if he gives misleading statistics, or if he misrepresents a statement made by some member of your team, call the listeners' attention to the error. Usually your opponent has simply been careless in distorting the material he quotes; but even carelessness in handling facts will weaken his standing with the audience.

In attacking errors of this kind, be very careful of the language you use. Never accuse an opponent of deliberately misrepresenting facts; suggest simply that he has been *careless,* or that he has *misunderstood* the statement he tried to repeat. A charge that your opponent has been untruthful will damage *you* in the estimation of your listeners, as much as it will your opponents.

> I was surprised to hear Mr. Sandra quote Chairman Minow of the FCC as believing that nothing is better than television. It is true that Mr. Minow said that (and I quote him), *"When television is good, nothing is better."* However, Mr. Sandra must have stopped reading Mr. Minow's speech at this point. For in the very next paragraph Chairman Minow went on to say:
>
> > But when television is bad, nothing is worse. I invite you to sit down in front of your television set . . . stay there all day . . . and keep your eyes glued to that set until the station signs off. I assure you that you will observe a vast wasteland.
>
> In fact, the entire tenor of Mr. Minow's speech was that the TV industry needs to clean up its programing and its commercials, with veiled threats that failure to do so would force the federal government to do it. Now that is quite different from the inference Mr. Sandra drew about Mr. Minow's conception of American television. I hope Mr. Sandra has been more careful in quoting from the other authorities he has named.

> You will remember that my colleague, Mr. Frank, outlined our plan for federal aid to education very carefully, and asked the negative to pay special attention to what we proposed. He pointed out that we proposed that federal government grant funds *directly to the states,* not to individual school districts, and that the *states* distribute these funds as need dictated. Apparently Mr. Arbuthnot of the negative did not hear Mr. Frank. For Mr. Arbuthnot has spent much of his time attacking federal aid by attacking *federal control* of education. Of course, attacks on federal control have nothing to do with the debate

tonight. The plan we propose specifically eliminates any possibility of federal control, leaving distribution to state officials and spending to local school boards. We have argued throughout that local boards and state officials can be trusted to provide equal educational opportunity to sons and daughters *if they have sufficient funds to do so.* Our proposal is for federal aid in providing funds, without federal control of education in any form. I ask Mr. Arbuthnot to confine his attacks to the plan we propose, rather than to something he expected us to propose before the debate began.

Exposing contradictions. Contradictions in the statements of your opponents will of course weaken the confidence of the audience in their arguments. If a striking contradiction can be discovered in the arguments your opponents present, call it to the attention of your listeners. In general, the most effective method is to use one of the statements to overthrow the other, as indicated in the examples below:

There is one point which the first speaker of the negative brought up which I am not quite clear about, and which I think needs some clarification in the next speech, for he told us two opposite things. First, Mr. Yawitz stated that there is no cooperation between the United States and Russia as they exist today. But a little later he said there is no need for a change in the United Nations, that it is fulfilling what it was set up to do. Now, surely he cannot mean both of these statements—surely he does not believe the United Nations was set up with the idea of keeping the United States and Russia from cooperating with each other. Mr. Yawitz must have misspoken himself on one or the other of these points, and I'd like to know which he believes. I hope he will clear up this inconsistency in his next speech.

———

We see also that there is a basic inconsistency in the affirmative case. First, they show you how important economic conditions are to world peace, yet the affirmative wants to limit the Federal World Government to power only in the control of weapons. How do they resolve this very, very illogical inconsistency?

If economic control is necessary and they are not going to give it to the World Government, how do they expect to keep peace—the only need they established in favor of a world government? We, like you in the audience, will await with interest the affirmative attempts to get out of this inconsistency of their own making.

Exposing evasion. If your opponent refuses to meet an argument squarely, he practically admits that it is too strong to be attacked. Sometimes, however, he may avoid the issue so skillfully that his evasion is not noticed by the audience. Whenever your opponent refuses to meet an argument, call that fact to the listeners' attention; make the listeners realize that your opponent is evading the issue.

I am forced to admire the very skillful way in which Mr. Starbuck has side-stepped one of the most important issues in this debate. You will recall that early in the discussion I pointed out that the Soviet Union would never join the World Federal Government if joining meant giving up the veto power that Russia has so consistently refused to give up in the United Nations. And you will remember, too, that I asked Mr. Starbuck to tell us *why* he believes Russia would give up this veto power and join the World Federal Government.

Apparently, Mr. Starbuck decided it wise not to try to answer this question. Therefore, he substituted a question of his own, explaining "why the Soviet Union would have no veto power in World Federal Government." He told you that no federal government grants veto power to a member state, so the Soviet Union would have no veto power to give up. And he apparently hoped you would not notice the substitution of his own question for the one we asked.

I congratulate Mr. Starbuck on the skill he used in evading the issue, but I insist that he explain to us *why* he believes Russia *would join* a World Federal Government since the Soviets would have no veto power there. Remember, Mr. Starbuck, that Russia refused to join the United Nations until this veto power was granted. I again ask the negative, directly, "In your very next speech please explain why you think the Soviet Union would join your World Federal Government without the veto power being granted—why would they join?"

Other methods of attacking prestige are sometimes used; but they usually are dangerous for beginning debaters. In one debate in which both affirmative speakers were unusually young, their more mature opponents made repeated reference to the *youth* of the affirmative, using such expressions as "our young friends of the affirmative," "my youthful oponent," and "the young men from Kansas."

In another contest before an audience of farmers, an affirmative speaker upholding farm price-fixing referred rather pointedly to the fact that both negative speakers had been raised in large cities and could have but little appreciation of the problems faced by farmers. In both these debates the attack on prestige was launched against the opposing speakers as individuals—not against their arguments as presented in the debate. In a debate between the state universities of Minnesota and Wisconsin a similar personal-prestige attack was made; following is the minor point rebuttal given to that attack:

Now, Mr. Schur has implied that Mr. Burnstein and I are nothing more than idealists, that we refuse to face reality. . . . If we are idealists, and if we do live in a world of fantasy, then Mr. Burnstein and I are in rather distinguished company, for with us, among those who believe that a Federal World Government is the only means by which we can achieve world peace, are some of the most hardheaded politicians that the world has ever known. If we are idealists, then so are Prime Minister Mackenzie King of Canada, as well as Pandit Nehru of India, Wellington Koo of China, and Winston Churchill, as well as Foreign Minister Ernest Bevin of England. . . . And if we are idealists, Gentlemen, then so is a gentleman named Harold Stassen, whom the voters of your own state of Wisconsin seem to think would make a pretty good President. If the majority of people of this great state are idealists, then we don't mind being called idealists, too.

While such personal attacks are both common and effective in political debates, and in other debates in practical life situations, they are not recommended to the beginner in college or high school debate. Direct your attacks against the *arguments* advanced by your opponents, and not against your opponents as individuals.

Meeting attacks on prestige. It is difficult to meet an attack on prestige, particularly when that attack is directed against some conspicuous weakness in your argument. The only safe method is to prevent such attacks by leaving no openings for your opponents. A careful debater wil not make assertions without proof, and he certainly will not misrepresent facts. Nor will he make statements that contradict those made by his colleague.

However, if your opponents do find weaknesses in your arguments and use them for attacks on prestige, some method of defense must be used. If minor statements or minor items of evidence are attacked, refute the rebuttal arguments your opponents have built in making the attack; present evidence to support your original statement, or to reinforce the item of evidence attacked. If they call attention to unsupported assertions in your case, you sometimes can insist that the statements attacked are so obviously true that no evidence is needed—then, if necessary, select *one* of the assertions mentioned and support it with adequate evidence. A second method is to use the *"you, too"* technique; admit that the statements were not properly proved, offer the excuse that time did not permit you to prove them— and call attention to two or three similar unsupported assertions in your opponents' arguments.

If your opponents accuse you of misrepresentation, your defense will depend on whether you really are guilty of the fault charged against you. If you actually have distorted a statement, your only course is to admit the fault and express your regrets for the error. Of course, if the charge is unfounded you have only to show that your original statement was correct. The same two possible courses are open to you to defend yourself against charges of evasion or of contradicting the statement of a colleague.

The examples below will illustrate several of the methods which may be used in meeting attacks on prestige:

Mr. Stevens has taken exception to our giving you the opinions of Professor Williams and Commissioner Griffith as to the advantages of college athletics, and has asked us to give you the names of some *good* authorities who believe that athletics benefit the student. Well, both Professor Williams and Commissioner Griffith are good authorities on this point; they certainly know the field from firsthand observation. But since Mr. Stevens wants me to name some other authorities who agree with them, I'll be glad to oblige him. I suggest the names of Professor White, registrar of your own college; of Dr. Elias Herron, of your department of history; of Professor James Tromley, head of your department of mathematics; and of Dr. James Barr Young, the president of your own college. Every one of these men has stated that the athletes here in your own school make grades that compare favorably with those earned by non-athletes. Mr. Stevens can find their statements in the minutes of your Athletic Council for February 16 of last year.

———————

The gentleman who just left the floor has charged me with making several statements in my constructive argument, for which I offered no proof. I did not catch all of the assertions I supposedly made, but I do recall that one was that a great many Reds hold offices in our own federal government. Well, I did make that statement; and it's true! And I cheerfully admit that I gave you no specific proof to support it. It wasn't necessary; every person in this audience knows that what I said was true, and I believed there was no need to waste your time by citing a long list of authorities who verify it. I think that most of you read the newspapers, and know what the Un-American Activities Committee has discovered. You also know what J. Edgar Hoover and his FBI have uncovered.

I think that Mr. Fellows knows quite well that in the limited time allowed us in debate, we simply can't cite proof for every statement— particularly those which are known to all. I would guess that Mr. Fellows wants me to waste time so I will have less to say about other arguments he knows are against him. But I shall continue to ignore this trap; when facts are well known, I won't take time in reciting them.

———————

Mr. Booster charged me in his constructive speech with misleading you as to Chairman of the FCC Minow's attitude towards TV programing, when I quoted that gentleman as saying that when TV is good it is better than magazines or newspapers. Actually, you will remember, I was quoting Mr. Minow as evidence that *some of our TV programs are excellent*, not that Mr. Minow or anyone else believes that all are as good as they might be. And remember that Mr. Minow said that the good programs on TV are better than the best magazines or radio, he recognized that television industry is in its infancy, wheareas we have had magazines and newspapers for more than 150 years. I did not ask you to believe that Mr. Minow thinks all programs are excellent. Everyone knows that everything in the world can be bettered. The point is that Mr. Minow, as Chairman of the FCC, was doing his job in urging the industry to make a special effort to increase the number of outstanding programs. May I remind Mr. Booster that when the Chairman of the FCC admits (and I quote him) "I could list many more programs that I am sure everyone here felt enriched his own life and that of his family"—when a government official charged with policing television makes such an admission, and when we realize that the industry is only fifteen years old, then we must conclude that TV has gone further in a shorter time than any other medium of communication. Mr. Minow's admission makes it obvious that there is no need for federal pressures on the TV industry.

MEETING USE OF STRATEGY

The second general type of minor point rebuttal includes the replies you give to the use of *strategic devices* by your opponents. Perhaps they have used some device which centers attention on an especially effective argument, or presented a time-wasting demand, or asked a dilemma question. If any of these devices has been used, some sort of reply will be necessary. But to prevent the point involved from assuming importance to your listeners, handle it simply as a minor point in your opponents' argument. Keep your reply as short as possible, and put it in the opening sentences of your speech.

Meeting time-wasting strategy. If your opponents ask questions concerning trivial details of your plan, or present a burden of proof, their purpose is probably to get you to waste your time in discussion of unimportant things. Call attention to the purpose behind their questions, and refuse to take up your listeners' time in discussing trivialities. If possible, pick out some one of the details about which your opponents have inquired, and show how little it means in the debate. The use of this method is suggested in the example below:

The speaker who preceded me asked thirteen detailed questions he wanted me to answer before the negative would fully understand the plan we advocate for medical care of the aged through Social Security. If these questions were of the slightest importance to the principle we are debating tonight, I would be glad to answer them. But looking over the list I find all referring to details of operation, rather than to the principal issue before us. Some are downright absurd. For example, he asks, "Suppose two or more of the aged asked for the same doctor at the same time. Who would get the doctor and what would the other aged do?" The same question could be asked about our present system of private medicine, I suppose. But because a doctor cannot be two places at once is no argument against Social Security medicare for the aged.

It would seem that these thirteen trivial questions were asked for one purpose—so that I would waste my time on them, rather than spend it answering his attacks on more vital issues. But, Mr. Johnson, I refuse to be led into a discussion of trivia. The things you asked about can be worked out when the legislation is drawn. And I ask you and Mr. Arnold to forget trivialities, and meet us squarely on the issues that are important in this debate.

Meeting strategy of emphasis. When your opponents present a point on which they have a marked advantage, and *challenge* you to meet them on that issue, the effect is to place a great deal of emphasis on that point with the listener. Consequently, you cannot afford to ignore the challenge; sooner or later you must meet your opponents on the point in question. But when you do attack the point, do it in the way which gives your opponents the least advantage possible To begin with, take up the point at the *earliest possible opportunity;* if possible, at the beginning of the next speech for your side. An early reply gives your listeners a chance to forget the matter before the end of the debate. Furthermore, when you answer the challenge, take care to make the matter seem as unimportant as possible. Accuse your opponents of exaggerating the importance of the issue involved, and of trying to make a trivial matter seem vital. Then, make a very short attack on the point he has presented.

Mr. Dunning has just given you an argument which he seems to think is extremely important. He has told you that under a system of state-supported medicine, the quality of medical service would be lowered. He has spent quite a bit of time stressing the importance of this point, and has challenged me to meet him on the issue.

Now, I don't believe that this is really the most vital issue in this debate. After all, the question is not primarily whether the people who would be aided by a system of tax-supported medicine get the highest quality of medical attention available to anyone— the real question is whether these people are to get any medical attention at all. As you know, most of them get no medical care whatever, today. But since Mr. Dunning wants me to discuss the contention he has advanced, I'm glad to accept his challenge.

I want to offer just one important fact. We already have a system of tax-supported medicine in operation, in the military service of the United States. And every medical authority in the United

States will agree that the average skill and average ability of the men in the medical corps of the United States Army is far above that of the private practitioners in the United States. They will also agree —and Mr. Dunning himself must admit—that the medical attention available at such tax-supported institutions as the Walter Reed Hospital in Washington, is infinitely superior to that in private hospitals in general. Consequently, the only experience this country has had with tax-supported medicine directly contradicts Mr. Dunning's belief that under a tax-supported system, the quality of medical service would be lowered.

Meeting the dilemma question. A dilemma question presented by your opponents should be handled in much the same manner as a challenge. Take up the question in the very first sentences of your speech—the first one following that in which the question was asked; make the issue presented in the question seem as unimportant as possible; then give your answer to the question. But in answering a dilemma question, try to give a *qualified* answer which offers little opportunity for attack. You will find it much safer not to answer with an unqualified "yes" or "no"; make your answer one beginning with "yes, provided that . . ." or "no, unless . . . ."

Mr. Snyder has asked me a question. He seems to think it very important; in fact, he spent quite a little time in telling you what an important question it is. He wants to know why we believe Russia would join the World Federal Government without keeping the right of veto power. Now, really, Ladies and Gentlemen, what two debaters from Kansas or two from Maryland believe this nation or that nation will or will not do is of little importance. Russia is not going to join or refuse to join because debaters say she will or will not. After all, we are debating the *wisdom* of Federal World Government, not the question of whether this nation or that would instantly join.

But, since Mr. Snyder is so vitally interested in our views on Russia's joining, I'm going to answer his question. I'm going to answer it definitely and directly. Yes, Mr. Snyder, I firmly believe Russia will join the World Federal Government if such government is set up with proper checks and balances.

But Mr. Snyder objected that Russia insisted on the veto power in the UN. Of course; and so did the United States. Remember that the United Nations was set up as a single body, *without* checks and balances other than the veto. Remember, too, the history of our own federal government. Before a federal government was possible, a UN-like Confederation of American States was set up in 1774. Even though it contained two types of veto—the two-thirds requirement and finances depending on the willingness of *each* state—your own state of Maryland took seven long years in joining. But from this feeble beginning, fifteen years later all of the states unhesitatingly joined the federal government of the United States with its system of checks and balances. It seems obvious to us that history is repeating itself. It took World War II and the dropping of atomic bombs to get nations to set up the present-day federation called the United Nations. Fear of the untried prompted the veto power as it did in 1774. However, atomic danger is a thousand times greater than it was in 1945. If a World Federal Government were to be set up with proper checks and balances, there is no doubt that the nations of the world would join it.

Occasionally you may find that the challenge or the dilemma question centers about an issue on which your position is unexpectedly strong. Possibly you know that you can handle the point in such a way as to gain a definite advantage. If that is the case, withhold your reply until late in the rebuttal speeches. Give your opponents every opportunity to build up the importance of the point; let them make the issue stand out as one really vital to the debate. Then, in a rebuttal speech, agree with them that the issue is vital, and spend *several minutes* if necessary, building up proof on your side of the issue. But never take the risk of using this method unless you are *positive* that your position on the issue is strong enought to win you the final advantage.

PREPARING FOR REBUTTAL

The constructive argument that you use in a debate may be worked out weeks in advance. Rebuttal, on the other hand, must fit the specific arguments presented by your opponents, and consequently, it must be worked out during the course of the debate. But this does not mean that you cannot prepare for rebuttal before the actual contest. Preparation not only is possible; it is extremely essential. If your study of the subject has been thorough, most of the major arguments your opponents may use can be discovered long before the debate takes place. And if you know in advance which arguments are possible, you can work out methods of attacking those arguments as a part of your preparation for debate.

Discovering possible arguments. In preparing for rebuttal, the first step of course is to find out what arguments your opponents are likely to use. Turn back to the section on selecting main points. Use the methods suggested there of finding possible arguments—not those upholding your side of the case, but those which might be used to support the side your opponents propose. Check these possible arguments against the list you made in your preliminary study of the subjects. Then, from the two lists, select all of the arguments that your opponents might reasonably be expected to use—all those which are strong enough to include in any opposing argument. This final list will usually include most, if not all, of the contentions which your opponents will use as the main points in their case.

Next, review the arguments in your own case. As well as you are able, list the possible *attacks* which might be made against your own main points, or against important sub-points. These possible attacks that you expect, combined with the contentions your opponents might use as main points, will give you a fairly extensive list of points that you must be prepared to refute.

To this list, material of another type may be added. During your reading on the subject for debate, you probably discovered a number of important items of evidence favoring your opponent's side of the question. If any of these items are strong enough so that you feel that your opponents are likely to use them, add them to the list of materials to be considered in preparing for rebuttal.

Planning your attacks. The next step, of course, is to plan the general type of attack to be used against each point. Naturally, any plans that you make must be very general. You may be able to foresee the arguments your opponents will use, but you cannot know the specific methods they will use in presenting or proving those arguments. As a result, the *tearing-down* portion of each of your rebuttal arguments must be worked out on the platform, after you discover what proof materials your opponents have used. But, knowing what general arguments to expect, you can work out in advance the *building-up* phase of your attack on each opposing point.

Many debaters use the method of preparing a *platform card* for each point likely to come up in rebuttal. For instance, a separate card would be prepared for each point likely to be used as main point or important sub-point in the opposing case, and a similar card for each major point in the debater's own constructive case. Each card lists evidence supporting a single point—the five or six strongest items which can be found relating to that point. If the point is one used in the debater's own case, the evidence listed on the card must of course not be the same as that used in the constructive argument. Cards about five by eight inches in size are most frequently used; they must be large enough to hold five or six different items of evidence relating to the point at issue. Figure 3, on page 242, illustrates the way in which material is arranged on the card.

Federal Government Already in Medicine

John L. Gleason, *VA Administrator, Washington, D.C.*
Reports—in 1961 the Veterans Administration operated 170 hospitals, plus financing many beds in non-VA hospitals. 22,403,000 veterans eligible under priority system: 1) All with disabilities or diseases incurred or made worse by service served first. 2) Any veteran with any illness or disease, if he is unable to pay for private medicine.
—*World Almanac,* 1962, p 738.

Government also provides hospitalization and total medicine and dental care for 821,000 servicemen and their families.
—*World Almanac,* 1962, p 725-6.

U.S. Dept. of Health, Education, & Welfare *(Publ. 969)*
In 1962 federal government spent $857 million on medical & health-related research, which was 35% more than government spent on all other types of research, excluding defense and space travel research.
—*Resources for Medical Research,* 1962-3, p 4.

The Kerr-Mills Law *(Public Law 86-778)*
Law provides federal grants of from 60 to 80% of total medical costs (providing state pays remainder) for aged persons not getting old-age assistance, and who lack funds for private medicine. Pays all costs: drugs, doctors, hospital, nursing care & nursing home; but really applies only to the aged on relief.
—*Reference Shelf*, v 34, no 4. p 123.

Conclusion—Social Security medicare for aged is next logical step:
Hubert H. Humphrey, *Senator from Minnesota*
"I believe that the Social Security method of prepaid health care insurance for our senior citizens is the better way. . . . The machinery is set up, and has worked well for 25 years. . . . It is the next step to take."
—NBC-TV debate, *The Nation's Future,* Ja. 14, 1961

Figure 3. Specimen Platform Card

The use of platform cards of this sort is a decided help in rebuttal. They permit the debater to find almost immediately the strongest evidence that is available in proof of any point. By using as many of the items listed as may be needed, he has before him the evidence he needs for the *building-up* phase of his attack on an opposing contention, or for supporting one of his own points which his opponents have attacked. By arranging the different items of evidence in order of their strength—the strongest items placed at the bottom of the card—he can use two or three items, or one, or all that are given on the card, as the need of the occasion demands.

Sometimes similar cards may be used for rebuttal of single items of evidence used by the opposing speakers, if the items are strong enough to justify special attention. In preparing such a card, check over the evidence to be attacked carefully. See what attacks can most effectively be made against it—see whether the information is the most recent available, or whether the evidence comes from a prejudiced authority, or whether representative years are covered in statistics offered. If you discover any weakness, note that weakness at the top your card, so that it suggests a method of attack to be used on the platform. And on the remainder of the card, list several items of evidence which contradict what you are attacking—examples, statistics, or opinions of authorities.

Whether you plan to use platform cards or not in the actual debate, use the method suggested in preparing for your rebuttal. Even if cards are not to be used, familiarity with the evidence which can be used in attacking each possible point will greatly increase the strength of your rebuttal.

REBUTTAL PRACTICE

When you present rebuttal arguments in debate, the language you use must be extemporaneous. You can't write out rebuttal in advance, and memorize it. Your rebuttal arguments must fit the situation; they must fit the specific reasoning and the specific evidence your opponents have used to support their points. So to be effective in rebuttal, *practice* is essential. The more practice you get, and the more varied the situations you face in practice, the more effective your rebuttal is likely to be.

The following list gives five different methods which may be recommended for practice in rebuttal:

1. Refutation of single arguments
2. Meeting attacks on single arguments in your constructive case
3. Refuting a hypothetical opposing case
4. Mock debates with the instructor
5. Complete practice debates

Refuting single arguments. Prepare a list of all of the possible arguments which your opponents might use in establishing their case. Then, from this list, select one argument; make the strongest attack you can on that argument. Have your instructor or some experienced debater listen to your argument, and criticize you after you are through, with special attention to organization, to the amount of time you use, and to your effectiveness in using the *tearing-down* process. After hearing his criticisms, attack the point again and see if you can improve your work. Then take another point on the list, and repeat the procedure. Continue until you have gone through the entire list over and over again. Use this method of practicing at meetings of your squad, or in individual meetings with your instructor— or use it alone, in your own home. The more practice you get, the more effective your attacks are likely to be.

Meeting opponents' attacks. When you have attained some fluency in speaking and are able to attack opposing points with a fair degree of effectiveness, try your hand at meeting attacks on your own constructive case. Have another debater outline an attack on some point used on your side; practice meeting his attack. Use the same routine suggested for practice in attacking opposing points; make an attack, let someone criticize, and make the attack a second time. As you gain in confidence, give more and more attention to the time you require; try to make your arguments short and compact, with the greatest possible strength in the shortest possible time.

Occasionally, see what you can do in handling minor points. See how effectively—and in how short a time—you can make an attack on the prestige of an opponent, or meet an attack on your own prestige. And see how well you can handle arguments used to meet time-wasting strategy, or the use of challenges or dilemma questions. Make your practice cover every situation likely to arise in a debate.

Refuting a complete case. When you are able to handle single points effectively, your rebuttal practice may be carried further. Ask your instructor, or some team mate, to outline an entire case, indicating the main points to be used and the major methods used to support each point. Then take ten or fifteen minutes to study that outline, and plan your rebuttal. At the end of that time, give a complete rebuttal of the entire opposing case. As before, ask for criticisms; find out your weaknesses, and see what you can do to correct them. After you have had three or four experiences with a skeleton case of this kind, arrange to have the outline prepared in greater detail. Have the debater who prepares it list the separate sub-points, and the items of evidence used to support each one. And follow the usual routine of planning your attack, making a refutation of the entire case, and getting criticisms.

Later, a variation of this method can be used. Have the outline that is given you list the rebuttal arguments an opponent might use against your own constructive case. Rearrange the arguments; list each one under the constructive point it attacks; plan the method to be used in attacking each argument; and give an organized *counter-rebuttal* in which you meet each major attack on your case.

In handling either type of rebuttal argument, give more and more attention to the element of time. At first, no time limits should be imposed; but after practice has given you some experience in organizing your arguments, limit yourself to a five-minute speech, whether you are attacking an opposing case or meeting attacks on your own constructive case. That is the time usually allowed you in actual debate; accustom yourself to staying within that time limit.

Mock debates. After you have become accustomed to meeting a case already outlined for you, the next step suggested is that of participating in a mock debate, usually with your instructor or with some older debater. In this stage of your practice, you follow the procedure used in a complete debate—the only modification is that a single speaker presents all of the opposing argument, and that to save time, he may offer his arguments in abbreviated form. This time, you are forced to take down the arguments that are presented, and to prepare your rebuttal to those arguments as you listen. And rebuttal will be inserted in your constructive speech, as well as being given in a separate rebuttal argument.

When presenting an argument in mock debate, your instructor may offer a very conventional case until the method has been used two or three times. But when you have gained some experience in selecting arguments to attack and meeting them as a regular part of your practice, the case he gives can go to greater extremes. Unusual interpretations of the question may be introduced; unusual arguments may be used; cases may follow the *shot-gun* pattern or that of agreement. Every possible situation that you may need to face in debate should be presented—the more experience you are able to gain in meeting such situations in practice, the better able you will be to meet them in actual debate.

Practice debates. When your rebuttal practice has passed through the four stages suggested, you are ready to engage in practice debates with other members of your debate squad. Arrange as many practice debates as you can with teams supporting the other side of the question. Use the customary time limitations, and follow the rules of debate. This will give you practice under regular debate conditions—except, of course, that you have no audience.

Don't neglect this most important phase of preparation for rebuttal. Get practice; get as much practice as you can; get experience under as many different conditions as possible. The amount of practice you get will in great degree determine your effectiveness in rebuttal.

ANALYSIS FOR REBUTTAL

The work you do in preparing for rebuttal is important; naturally you will be able to make more effective attacks on arguments for which you are prepared. But even more important is the work you do *on the platform,* during the actual debate. Not until your opponents are actually speaking can you decide what points must be attacked and the best methods to use in attacking them. In the few minutes available after the debate has begun, you must analyze your opponents' arguments and pick out the points to be attacked; you must decide on type of attack to be used for each argument; you must plan and organize your rebuttal speeches so that your arguments are a unified whole. And then, of course, your attacks must be presented to your listeners.

Your first concern on the platform is to pick out the right points to attack. You cannot tear down your opponents' case if you ignore the really important arguments they present. On the other hand, valuable time will be wasted if you try to refute every minor point. Selection of the proper points to attack is the first requirement of good rebuttal.

The points which should be attacked fall under four main heads. First, you must tear down *the main points in your opponents' constructive case.* Every major contention they offer must be *considered,* at least; if you are unwilling to admit it, it must be attacked. Second, you must meet *the important attacks made on your own vital arguments.* Attacks that are weak, or those made against arguments of little real importance, may safely be ignored; but every attack that weakens a *vital* part of your case must be attacked. These two classes of opposing arguments *must* be met; the attacks you make on them are the vital portion of your rebuttal.

In addition, certain other points *may* be attacked. Short rebuttal arguments may be directed against *minor points* in your opponents' case, especially when these points may be refuted in a way that will *injure your opponents' prestige.* These attacks on minor points constitute the third of the four classes of rebuttal arguments. The final class will include your consideration of *strategic devices,* either developing the devices used by your colleagues or meeting those used by opponents.

To select the points to attack in rebuttal, make a careful analysis of your opponents' argument as it is presented. Note down the points they advance. List the attacks they make on your own major arguments. And jot down the minor points which may be effectively attacked, and the strategic devices used by either side.

Analysis cards. An effective way to list these materials is to use a set of three *analysis cards,* on which your opponents' arguments are noted as they are given. Use cards uniform in size with the *platform cards* recommended—cards about five by eight inches are probably most convenient. The first of these cards will be used in planning your direct rebuttal. On this card, make an *outline* of your opponents' constructive case as it is developed. List the *main points* presented and the *sub-points* supporting each, just as you made the case outline for your own side. Under each point, make brief notations of the evidence which has been given. Your outline should take the general form suggested in Figure 4 (page 250).

If an outline of this kind is prepared, you will have little difficulty in choosing the points to be handled in *direct* rebuttal—in your attacks on your opponents' constructive case.

Perhaps not all the points you list will be attacked in your rebuttal; your selection of the points which *must be* attacked will be discussed later in this section. But the list you have made includes every point that *might be* attacked in your rebuttal of your opponents' case.

Give particular attention to the sub-points used to support each main point; be sure that each sub-point is noted down

Figure 4. ANALYSIS CARD ON OPPOSING CASE

OUTLINE OF OPPONENTS' CASE

	Rebuttal Method
First Speaker: Mr. Brown	
1. Present system of international relations cannot keep peace	
A. Is based on philosophy "will we win next war?" (no evidence)	No evidence
B. League of Nations was powerless—failed (cited examples of failure)	Agree
C. United Nations has no power—will fail to keep peace (calls attention to veto power; no police)	Is slowly getting cooperation 10 new related agencies for cooperation
D. It is unrealistic to rely on system of power alliances (cited Admiral Zacharias, Dr. Einstein)	Read card, 10 successes Zacharias misquoted Einstein not political scientist
2. World Government & law best way to peace	
A. Law is only answer to all types of conflict (cited and compared examples of civilian law, states in our Union, and World Government)	Carry on analogy to show necessary loss of freedom
B. Law is only answer to non-conflict disputes (cited civilian law)	Ignore
C. Dr. Hutchins' committee to draft world const. says this is true (quoted on refusal to give up atomic bombs, and bombs are "race suicide")	Poor authority biased Quote: Khrushchev Kennedy
D. Therefore must have World Government (no evidence showing we can get it)	HOW can it be gotten?

ANALYSIS CARD—*Continued*	
Second Speaker: Mr. White	
3. UN should be developed into Federal World Gov.	
A. Would operate like our own federal government (example of trouble between Spain & Portugal)	Ridicule, ask about Russia vs China
B. Would give it teeth—a world army (says "Aggression quelled by world army")	This means war Suppose U.S. ordered to give Alaska to Russia
C. Details of plan unimportant—work out later	Read list of MAJOR questions, ask if these are mere details
D. Representation on population, economics and education	OK for U.S., but Russia & Africa would not agree
4. It can be put into force	
A. Any 2/3 of nations and 7 members of Security Council can call amendment to charter, no veto	Haven't over-ridden veto because it would mean war with Russia NOW!

correctly. In nearly every case, your attack will be made not on the main point directly, but on the sub-points by which it is proved. Occasionally, some main point in your opponents' arguments does not give a really valid reason for accepting their proposal; in such an instance, the most effective attack will be that of showing that the main point does not support the proposition. But as a rule, you try to show that the statement in the main point is not *true* by attacking the *reasons* given for accepting it—in other words, the sub-points.

Figure 5. ANALYSIS CARD LISTING ATTACKS
ON OWN ARGUMENTS

OUTLINE: ATTACKS ON OWN CASE	
	Rebuttal
I. United Nations not a failure:	Methods
A. Is big improvement over the League of Nations	
1. Attack—same faulty structure of no power; can only recommend (White)	Power means war
2. Attack—failed same as League in China (White)	Cite 10 cases of UN success
B. Charter has Russia and U.S. behind it	
1. Attack—but both insist on veto (White)	Link with aff. case
C. Is a growing organization—53 new members	
1. Attack—none made—was ignored	Restate
D. Already agreed on 60 rules of procedure	
1. Attack—but failed on Russia in Hungary & Poland (Brown)	Russia in Iran South Africa
E. Economic & Social Council is working	
1. Attack—no attack—was ignored	Restate
II. Impossible to form a Federal World Government	
A. Nations won't give up sovereignty necessary	
1. Attack—if not, they should (White)	But WON'T
2. Attack—must or suicide (no evidence—White)	No evidence— UN
B. Nations will not agree on representation	
1. Attack—pop., economics, and education (White)	OK for U.S. not rest of world

ANALYSIS CARD—*Continued*

C. Nations won't agree on free immigration	
1. Attack—no need of free immigration (Brown)	Show need
D. Nations won't agree on free trade	
1. Attack—no need of free trade (no evidence) (Brown)	Restate **need,** show no evidence given
III. Is better to perfect United Nations	
A. Is already established and supported	
1. Veto power makes success impossible (Brown)	Link aff. case & war
B. Russian attitude in World Government means war	
1. Attack—Russia would fear to fight, quoted U.S. military men (White)	In 1939 said Japan wouldn't fight
C. Russian already threatened to fight to keep veto	
1. Attack—but UN has no army to fear (Brown)	Ignore
D. UN success will convince Russia we mean peace	
1. Attack—none	Restate

As your outline of the opposing case develops, choose the method you will use in attacking each point listed. Write a word or two that will suggest that method, in the right-hand margin of the analysis card, opposite the sub-point to be attacked. The general form to be used is suggested in Figure 4.

The second of your analysis cards will be used to outline the *attacks made by your opponents* on your own constructive case—points which you will meet in *counter-rebuttal*. These attacks should not be listed in the order in which they are presented by your opponents; the basis of listing should be their

Figure 6. ANALYSIS CARD FOR MINOR POINTS

MINOR POINTS	Rebuttal Methods
Brown: Used picture analogy of United Nations with long white nightgown	Carry analogy on
Contradiction: Brown: "Russia's attitude endangers world" White: "Russia will cooperate because of her fear of world might"	Stress contradiction
Brown: Quoted President Hutchins on politics	Ridicule "Professor"
Comparison: World Government & U.S. federal gov.	Carry analogy on to show loss of sovereignty
Unsupported Assertions: Brown—Present system can't keep peace —Russia will attack unless have World Gov. —Russia would fear army of a World Gov. —Peoples of the world want World Gov. White—Russia would join a World Gov. —Representation formula can be worked out	Cite lack of proof and ask for it
White—United Nations is flat broke; can't collect from Communists	Easier to get $ than sovereignty

---

ANALYSIS CARD—*Continued*

AFFIRMATIVE STRATEGY

White asked dilemma: "Would we rather take chance of war in a World Government, if war comes, or would we rather chance fighting it alone?"	Believe UN will work in time—but rather fight own battles with allies than expect world army to do it for us after we've lost sovereignty

---

relationship to main points in your own constructive case. Before the debate begins, write down on the card a statement of each of your major contentions. List them in the order in which they are to be presented, and leave plenty of space following each statement. Then, during the debate, as attacks are made by your opponent, jot down each important attack *in the space below the main point at which it is aimed.* Note under each attack a short summary of the evidence used in presenting it; and enter in parentheses the name of the speaker making the attack and the speech in which it was made. Then, as on the first analysis card, note in the margin the methods you will use to meet the various attacks. Figure 5 suggests the form which may be used.

Now we come to analysis card number three. On this card, list the *minor points* which may be effectively attacked, and notes on the *use of strategy* by your opponents. Divide the card into two parts; list minor points which may be attacked in the upper portion of the card, and strategic devices used in the lower.

Remember that no effort should be made to list *every* minor point in your opponents' argument. Minor point rebuttal should serve a definite purpose. So list only those minor points which you can attack *in such a striking manner* that the *prestige* of your opponents will be weakened. Under the head of strategy, however, list every strategic device which your opponents use, and the replies they have made to strategy used by your colleague. In many debates, this part of the card will be left completely blank; few teams make effective use of strategy in presenting their arguments. But if any device *is* used, list it on your card.

As minor points are listed, study each one to see what method of attack will be the best to use. Then note in the right hand margin of the card the same sort of suggestions as to methods of rebuttal that are used on analysis cards one and two. The form of the minor point analysis card is indicated in Figure 6.

Selecting points to attack. If your analysis cards are carefully prepared, they will list all of the points which *might* be attacked in rebuttal. But in most debates, you should not try to refute *all* of the points on your list; the time available for rebuttal is too limited. So you are faced with the problem of picking out the points which *must* be attacked or those which can be attacked most profitably.

Consider, first, the important points in your opponents' constructive case. Usually they have presented four or five main points. In nine cases out of ten, every one of those points should be attacked. Sometimes, however, one of the main points is one with which you can safely agree, or one of such little importance that you can ignore it entirely. Sometimes, too, you may be using the *eggs-in-one-basket* type of case, and in line with that case, you center your attack on the one or two main points which directly oppose your own contention. But cases of this kind are rare. The general rule is to attack *every* main point your opponents have advanced, with the possible exception of points which relate to need for a change.

In the matter of attacking sub-points, however, a different situation exists. Frequently your opponent has used four or even five sub-points supporting a single main point. If that is the case, do not attempt to attack every single one of the sub-points he has advanced—you simply do not have time to attack each one effectively. Pick out the *two* sub-points supporting each point which seem to be most effective, and center your attack on those two arguments. The rest may be safely ignored.

Next, look over the list of attacks that have been directed against your own main points. Usually a dozen or more such attacks will be included in your list. If you try to reply to all that have been made, you probably will not have time to meet any of them effectively. So pick out the attacks which are most important—those which apparently have had the most weight with your listeners. If you meet the strongest attack or the two strongest attacks made against each of the main points in your case, and meet those attacks effectively, your listeners will ask no more. They probably will feel that with more time at your disposal, you could have handled the remaining attacks equally well—if they remember the attacks you have ignored, at all.

Minor points should give you very little difficulty. You probably will attack one or two minor points to open each of your speeches in the debate—minor point attack makes a very effective form of speech introduction. That means that probably five or six minor points are all you will have occasion to attack during the debate. From the list on your minor point analysis card, pick out the one or two points which make possible the most effective attacks, and use them in the minor point rebuttal opening your speech. When your colleague is ready to speak, he can make a choice among those which are left—the list will probably be increased during the speech of your opponent who follows you. If points relating to strategy have been stressed, use them in your minor point rebuttal. Otherwise, make your selection from the points which give you the best opportunity of attacking your opponents' prestige.

Position of rebuttal. Not all of the points you select for attack will be held for refutation in the rebuttal speeches. The rebuttal speeches are usually short; in most debates you are limited to five or six minutes for each speech. Consequently, part of your rebuttal arguments must be given during the constructive part of the debate. The amount to be used in your constructive speeches will depend in part on the way your case has been planned, in part on the situation which develops in the debate.

Some debaters plan their constructive arguments in such a way as to leave only a minute or two free for rebuttal in each constructive speech. Others, particularly those who uphold the negative, arrange to have from three to as much as five minutes available for rebuttal in each main speech. If the time reserved in your speech is only a minute or two, use it for attacks on minor points; and hold your refutation of important points for the rebuttal speeches. But if as much as three or four minutes can be used for rebuttal, use a minute or so for minor point attacks, and the rest for consideration of one of the main points in your opponents' case. If you can dispose of a part of your opponents' arguments in your constructive speech, you can give more time to each of the remaining points in your rebuttal.

Frequently the situation which arises in the debate will force you to take a major rebuttal point during your constructive speech, even if the argument on one of your constructive points must be shortened by two or three minutes to provide the time for rebuttal. If your opponents use an unexpected interpretation of the question, for example, any attack you make on their interpretation must be given at the first opportunity. Take whatever time is needed to meet their interpretation at the very beginning of the first negative speech. Or sometimes the argument your opponents present will weaken the force of some constructive point you plan to offer before the point is given. Naturally, their argument must be attacked before your own point is presented. Place your attack immediately before the point affected is introduced, or make it a part of your development of the point.

With the exceptions indicated, most attacks on the main points in your opponents' case, and most of the rebuttal arguments in which you meet your opponents' attacks, will be presented during the rebuttal speeches. Unless you have an unusual amount of time free for rebuttal in your constructive speech, only minor point attacks will be given in that speech.

THE REBUTTAL SPEECHES

A very noticeable weakness of nearly all beginning debaters is their failure to organize their rebuttal speeches on any definite plan. While their constructive arguments are carefully planned, the arguments in their rebuttal speeches are presented in hit-or-miss fashion. Perhaps you feel that lack of rebuttal organization should have little effect on the beliefs of your listeners. In reality, it is extremely important; very often it is the deciding factor in debate.

Remember that in every debate, the final attitude of the listener is a result of all the different impressions he receives. On one point, the affirmative has an advantage; on the next, the listener favors the negative position. But the final attitude of the listener toward the question is not made up like the score in a basketball game. Listeners do not add up points as the debate progresses, and agree with the team that runs up the larger score. While striking points may be remembered individually, it is the effect of *the whole discussion* on the listener that determines his final belief. And for *the whole of your argument* to have the greatest effect, it must be presented in a way which makes *logical relationships* between separate arguments clear.

To use a simple comparison, suppose that two men are counting. One starts at the beginning and counts in order from one to ten; the other counts, "2, 9, 5, 1, 10, 7, 3, 8, 4, 6." As a listener, you find it very much easier to follow the first man's count; and likewise it is easier to be certain that he has mentioned all of the numbers. Your mind follows orderly progressions without difficulty; but when logical order is not followed, you find it hard to remember what has gone before. This same principle holds true in debate. Your listener will be much more certain that you have brought up every important argument if your arguments are carefully organized and presented in logical order. And in rebuttal, he is certain you have attacked all of the important points only if you follow the same orderly method in your rebuttal speeches.

Contents of rebuttal speeches. If you plan to use some method of organization in your rebuttal speeches, your first step is to decide what materials must be included. Considering the two rebuttals for your side as a unit, the rebuttal speeches should include five elements:

1. Minor-point rebuttal used as speech introductions
2. Final arguments on all points of strategy
3. Rebuttal of main points in your opponents' case
4. Counter-rebuttal to meet attacks on your own case
5. Conclusion to the rebuttal speeches

For convenience in discussing the use of these elements, the two rebuttal speeches which you and your colleague present will be referred to as *the rebuttal unit*. And since relatively little of your time may be given to minor point attacks or speech conclusions, the third and fourth elements listed above make up the major part of the rebuttal unit.

Now, let us consider these five elements, and the way they are used in your rebuttal. Plan your rebuttal unit so that it takes up each of the five, in the order listed above.

1. First, your rebuttal speeches should include the use of some minor point attack, as introduction. Refer to the analysis card on which minor points are listed. Pick out the *one* minor point which offers opportunity for the strongest attack—of course, it must be one not previously attacked in your arguments—and place a Roman numeral "I" before that point on the card, to indicate that the attack on this point is to be the first element in your rebuttal unit. If you have spent considerable time on rebuttal in the constructive argument and as a result need less time than usual for steps 3 and 4, you may wish to attack two minor points, rather than one. Use the same method with the

second point; place a Roman numeral "I" before each of the minor points to be attacked.

2. The second element in the rebuttal will be your final consideration of *strategy* used in the debate. Refer again to the same minor point analysis card. If you feel that further consideration is needed of any strategic device that is listed, put a Roman numeral "II" before the reference to that device on the card. That will indicate that the point referred to must be taken up as the second element in your rebuttal speech, immediately after you have introduced your argument with a minor point attack. In most debates, any consideration of strategy will have been taken care of during the constructive argument; none will be needed in the rebuttal speeches. If no discussion of strategy is to be included, write the word "NONE" in the strategy section of the analysis card, and place the numeral "II" before that word.

3. Next we come to the third element in the rebuttal unit— rebuttal directed against the *main points* in your opponents' case. Refer to the analysis card on which you outlined the opposing case. At the top of that card, place the Roman numeral "III." On that card, you have listed all the important points included in your opponents' argument; and opposite each point a suggestion of the method of attack to be used. In this third step in your rebuttal, attack each of the main points listed, in order, following the outline given on the card.

Introduce this section of your rebuttal by telling your listeners that you wish to consider your opponents' constructive case, and to take up every major argument they have advanced, "point by point, as they were given." Then proceed with your attacks on the various points. If one of the arguments listed was attacked during your constructive speeches, take up that argument in its proper place in the outline, and mention the fact that you have already attacked it. Usually it is best to add some very short additional argument on the point—of course, if your opponents have replied to your attack, you will have to meet their reply. If you *agree* with your opponents on any of the main points in the outline don't simply omit that point—mention it, and tell your listeners that you agree with your opponents on the statement they have made.

4. The fourth element in the rebuttal consists of your replies to the attacks your opponents have made on your own main points. Refer to the analysis card on which these points have been listed; and mark that card "IV." Here again, it will pay you to take up the points in the order in which you have entered them on the card. And here, too, an *introduction* to this phase of your rebuttal will be of definite help. Use some such phrasing as, "Now let us consider the attacks which our friends have made on our own constructive arguments. Our first main point, as you will remember, was that present conditions demand some sort of change. The negative has attacked this in two important ways. First, Mr. Brown has argued that . . ." etc.

In the same way, introduce other main points in your argument, and consider in connection with each one, the one or two attacks made by your opponents on that point. If more than two have been made, pick out those which are *most important,* and introduce them by telling your listeners that "the only *important* attacks our opponents have made on this argument," etc. If your opponents have not attacked some main point at all, do not omit that point from your outline; call attention to it, in its regular position, and emphasize the fact that your opponents have not taken issue with you on the subject.

This fourth step in your rebuttal unit should include your reply to every important attack your opponents have made against any main point in your argument. But for clarity of organization, take the attacks up in the order they are listed on your analysis card; in other words, consider each attack in relation to the point against which it was aimed.

5. The fifth and final element in the rebuttal will be your conclusion to the rebuttal, and to the debate. Coming at the very end of your argument, the concluding material you use has the *position of greatest importance* in the debate. That which comes last is remembered longest. Use as your conclusion some

sort of material which will strongly impress the listener, and give him a final reason for favoring your proposal. A striking statement by an authority, a compelling but brief presentation of statistics, a reference to an effective comparison or illustration already introduced in the debate, or a striking comparison used for the first time—any of these may be used effectively to conclude your case. At times, the entire discussion may be reduced to a single vital issue, and two or three minutes devoted to a final effective argument on that issue. But whatever type of conclusion you use, it should be one which brings your argument to an effective close.

If you are the closing rebuttal speaker, decide upon the type of final conclusion you will use, and jot down a reference to it at the bottom of the card you have marked "IV," or if need be on an additional card, and mark your reference "V" in the left-hand margin.

By numbering the various elements in the manner suggested, you have provided yourself with an outline for a well-organized rebuttal unit. All that is necessary for a well-organized rebuttal is to follow the outline you have prepared, of course using whatever introductory materials may be needed for the different steps in your rebuttal argument.

Division into speeches. In considering the rebuttals as a unit, no provision has been made for the division of arguments between the opening and closing rebuttal speeches. But that should cause little difficulty. If you are the opening speaker, begin with point I in your outline, and carry the rebuttal as far along as you are able in the time allotted to you. As a rule, try to finish the third step in the outline—the attacks on the main points in your opponents' case. If you are unable to go that far, try to complete the attacks, in this step in your outline, on all but the *last* of your opponents' main points. Time your arguments in such a way that you end your speech by concluding the attack on a main point—it is difficult to carry the attention of your listeners for one main point, across an intervening opposing speech. No separate conclusion for your rebuttal speech is necessary; end the speech with the conclusion of the point.

If you are presenting the final rebuttal speech for your side, begin where your colleague left off in the outline you have prepared. If plenty of time is available to handle the important arguments remaining, you can, if you wish, use a minor point attack by way of introduction. But a separate introduction is not important for this speech. The important part of your discussion will begin with a brief mention of what your colleague has considered—"Mr. Smith has considered, point by point, the main points in the affirmative case," or "Mr. Smith has considered the first three points advanced by the affirmative." After using this method of linking your argument to that which has gone before, proceed with the rebuttal, starting at the place in your outline where your colleague ended his speech. Then follow the outline, until your rebuttal is concluded at the end of step V, with the rebuttal conclusion.

Listed below are examples of well-organized rebuttal speeches. Study them carefully; note the methods that have been used to introduce various rebuttal points. For your convenience, the various steps in the rebuttal unit have been numbered with Roman numerals such as you have written on your rebuttal cards. Since the opening speaker did not complete the third step, that part was carried over into the closing rebuttal speech, where the attack on the final main point in the opposing argument follows a minor point attack. The arguments follow the outline of points built from the analysis cards used as illustrations in the preceding section.

FIRST NEGATIVE REBUTTAL

(I) Ladies and Gentlemen, Mr. Brown has drawn a very clear analogy between the federal government of the United States and the Federal World Government he wants. Very well, let us examine this comparison further and see what Mr. Brown is asking the United States to do in joining his World Government. As you know, the states in the Union are no longer sovereign states; they have very little real power. Would you be willing to see the United States reduced in world power to the position held by Oklahoma or Utah or New Jersey? Take the Senate, for example; it contains two representatives from each state, regardless of size. In the World Senate, we suppose, the United States would have equal power with Mexico, Japan, Bolivia, Iran or Luxembourg. Suppose the question of minimum wages, income tax, old-age pensions, or universal draft came up. Would you trust such a government as we are able to trust the federal government of our own people? Of course you wouldn't. And that is what Mr. Brown wants when he says his World Government will work like that of the federal government of the United States. We are glad he used this comparison, for it proves the major argument we have been making all evening—the United States does not dare join a World Federal Government; to do so would cause loss of our sovereignty. I only wish Mr. Brown could understand this point.

(II) And with this same lack of understanding, Mr. White posed his dilemma: Would we rather fight alone in case of war, or chance fighting with the other nations of the world under a World Government? Well, we've answered his question already in one way. We have pointed out that we believe the United Nations will keep the world from war. But, suppose war comes, asks Mr. White—what then? The answer is easy. *Every* good American would rather fight by the side of his allies in the army of the United States—with the United States exercising her full sovereignty—I repeat, every good American would rather fight in a U.S. army than have to depend on some questionable world army to do our fighting for us. But Mr. Brown forgets that this world army might not be on our side; it might fight against us. Suppose the World Government decided our immigration laws should be abolished, our gold reserve should be divided up, our tariffs wiped out, and our wealth passed around the world? Well, Mr. Brown, in that case, too, we would rather fight in the United States army for our sovereign rights than bow to the dictates of such a World Government.

(III) But why do the gentlemen believe we are in danger—why do they believe we should have a Federal World Government? Let us examine each of the arguments they have made, point by point in the order presented, and see why the gentlemen are wrong.

The first argument they used was that our present system of international relations, based on power alliances within the United Nations, cannot keep the peace. To prove this point Mr. Brown claimed the present system is based on a philosophy of "who will win the next war?" He offered no evidence at all; he merely made the claim. But everyone knows that was not the basis for the establishment of the United Nations; everyone knows the United Nations was established in the hope of avoiding future wars. So this statement does not prove Mr. Brown's point that war under the UN is inevitable. Mr. Brown went on to call attention to the veto power and lack of enforcement machinery in the present United Nations setup. These proved, he said, that war is inevitable. But he completely ignored the ten major successes of the UN cited by my colleague; he ignores the sixty cases of world-wide agreement in setting up the UN procedures; he ignores the nine outstanding successes of the Economic and Social Council of the United Nations; and he ignores the successes of the Security Council in settling British-Russian trouble in Iran, Indonesia, and Greece. Ignoring all of the successes of this new organization, during nearly twenty years of peace, he points to 91 vetoes and decides war is inevitable—the UN is bound to fail. Had he been debating the Federal Constitution in 1787, he would have prophesied failure of the United States. And the only other reason he cited for failure was a quotation from Admiral Zacharias and another from Dr. Einstein. But these men did not prophesy war as Mr. Brown concluded—instead, they both argued that there will be no winner if atomic war comes. Now these are the only ways in which the affirmative tried to prove their first main contention that war is inevitable under the United Nations. Until they can offer better reasons than these, we urge you not to be stampeded through fear into accepting this first argument.

The second main argument of the affirmative had even less evidence in support. You will remember they argued that World Government and law offer the best hope of peace. In proof they offered the analogy of the federal government of the United States which I have already answered, and a single quotation from Dr. Hutchins' committee appointed to draft a world constitution. Now I admire Dr. Hutchins a great deal; he is a great educator. But like the other authority the affirmative quoted, Dr. Einstein, a scientist, President Hutchins is hardly the man we'd pick as an expert in political science. An excellent university president, we understand, but by no stretch of the imagination has he proved himself capable of drawing up a world constitution. The world has long been amused at impractical statements of college professors who get out of the field for which they were trained. Most certainly we cannot accept the quotation of Dr. Hutchins alone as proof that World Government is the best way. On the other hand we have quoted such well-known statesmen as Tom Connally, Herschel Johnson, Sir Alexander Cadogan of the United Kingdom, Edgar P. Bell, Reinhold Niebuhr, Russia's Molotov, N. A. Pelcovits and others who disagree with Professor Hutchins. And all of you heard Mr. Khrushchev and also President Kennedy on television—both arguing for disarmament rather than World Government, disagreeing so far only on the details of disarmament. Until the gentlemen of the affirmative can offer you a great deal more evidence in support, they cannot expect you to agree with this second main argument—that World Government offers the best chance of peace.

Finally, the only other argument offered by the affirmative in its constructive case tonight was that World Government is possible. Mr. White showed us that the Charter of the United Nations permits amendment by two thirds of the nations plus seven of the twelve members of the Security Council. Therefore, he argues, the nations can get together without Russia's consent—World Government is possible, says he. Now, Ladies and Gentlemen, two things strike you at once about this argument. First, if this be true, the very fact that two thirds plus seven have not done so to date—or even threatened to do so after nearly 20 years and 91 vetoes—is rather good proof that Mr. White is wrong in telling us that the nations of the world are willing to establish a Federal World Government. Second, it is perfectly obvious that such action without Russia's backing would mean war—nuclear war—not peace.

(V) Ladies and Gentlemen, time will not permit me to go further with this argument, but my colleague will carry it on at his first opportunity. So far, I have brought up each of the three basic arguments of the affirmative team and have analyzed for you the evidence offered in support of those arguments. Until our opponents give you better reasons and more evidence in support, you certainly cannot agree that we should have a World Federal Government.

Second Negative Rebuttal

(I) Ladies and Gentlemen, I am sure you noticed one very serious inconsistency in the affirmative argument. You will remember that Mr. Brown told us "Russia's dogmatic and stubborn attitude is endangering world peace." But a few moments later his colleague, Mr. White, told us—and I quote him—"Russia will cooperate with the other nations because of her fear of world might." We wish the gentlemen would get together in their argument—is Russia stubbornly leading to war, or is she cooperating because she fears world war? Until the affirmative clears up this contradiction, we cannot accept either of the arguments in this debate.

(III) But let us turn to the arguments on which they agree. You will remember that my colleague, Mr. Smith, took up every constructive argument the gentlemen gave to show a need for World Government and that World Government will work. Time interrupted his refutation of the third point—that World Government can be established because the nations have the power and the willingness to establish it. Let us examine this argument a bit further.

It is true the United Nations Charter gives it this power on paper. But the affirmative, themselves, have continually told you that the United Nations has no real power—it can only recommend, not enforce. Mr. Brown and Mr. White seem to hold that the United Nations Charter is powerless to keep Russia from going to war over some inevitable and unknown issue of the near future —but that this same Charter has plenty of power to force Russia to join a World Government, give up her sovereignty without a fight. Now, which do the gentlemen believe? Is the UN powerless, or does the United Nations have great power? Listen carefully for the affirmative answer to that question, Ladies and Gentlemen —Mr. Smith and I do not get the floor again.

But let us go on with this argument that World Government is possible. Mr. White told us it is possible because he would give it "teeth"—and a world army to enforce its decisions. Of course, he didn't tell us *what* decisions. But, let us look at one of the very first decisions this imaginary World Government would have to make. Your daily papers have recently told you that Russia claims the Czar had no right to sell Alaska to the United States —that Russia does not consider that sale binding. Russia says she rightfully owns Alaska; the United States is just as certain it is hers. Very well, suppose this World Government decides Alaska should go back to Russia. Is *this* the decision which will be enforced by the world army? Or look at other questions which are certain to come before this World Government to which Mr. White wants us to surrender our sovereignty. The question of free immigration, the question of free trade, the question of rich nations dividing wealth through taxes—all of these questions came before our federal United States Government—we have free immigration, free trade, and rich states aiding education in poor states through taxation. That is all very well within our own country and among our own people. But how will the World Government decide these issues on a world scale? Obviously, it would force free immigration and free trade—American economy would be ruined overnight. And if we refused the World Government's order—Mr. White has given it a world army. Knowing Americans as I do—my, oh my, what a war!

Certainly, Mr. White has not proved that World Government is needed; he has not proved that it will keep world peace; and he has not established that it is possible to get such an organization accepted—even by the United States, let alone Russia. Yet those were the only three arguments in the affirmative case. There remains but one thing to be done by the negative in this debate— examine the attacks our friends have made on the arguments we have given against World Government.

(IV) The first negative contention was that we have no need of a World Government because the United Nations is succeeding. We showed that it has all world powers behind it, that it is a growing organization, that perfect agreement was reached on sixty separate issues of organization, that it has settled ten major disputes, and that the Economic and Social Council is working efficiently. To all of this evidence the affirmative made only three minor replies: first, they cited the failure to stop civil war in China; second, failure to aid the revolters in Poland and in Hungary in 1956 against communism, and third, failure to talk Russia out of using its veto power. Now, the veto examples do not show failure, since the Charter gives Russia that right. Use of a right included in an organization's charter cannot be held against the organization. You might as well condemn the United States Government as a failure because newspapers cannot be stopped from attacking our government, since the Constitution guarantees freedom of speech and press. The only real failures mentioned were those of stopping civil war in China and revolts in Poland and Hungary. But at least the UN members kept out of those wars, maintaining world peace. In the face of all the major successes named by the negative—successes nearly every year for the past eighteen years—the affirmative could find but three small failures, two of them involving civil war within nations, and the Charter does not permit the United Nations to settle internal disputes. The case of Hungary was in reality its only failure. If any baseball player had a batting average as high as the UN's, he would hold a record that would never be equaled. We maintain that this success is astonishing, and is proof that there is no need of loss of national sovereignty through Federal World Government.

Next, we argued it impossible to form a Federal World Government because nations would not give up sovereignty, could not agree on representation techniques, could not agree on the issues of free immigration and free trade. The affirmative seemed to agree that the nations might not give up sovereignty—but argued that the nations "should" to escape suicide. We have only their unsupported statement on that point. Next, they suggested representation on a basis of combined population, economic production and education, and assumed the nations of the world would love this. Of course, it would be fine for the United States—but would Russia or India or Mexico or England agree? Of course not. Finally, the affirmative said there would be no need of free immigration and free trade under World Government. Throughout the debate, however, they held up the United States as the ideal after which to pattern—without these two items, the United States could not exist as a unit. Surely, it is obvious that our point is valid—the nations of the world can never agree on the basic ingredients of World Government. It cannot be formed.

Finally, we argued that the best plan is to perfect the United Nations because it has established world support, its success will prove to Russia that we mean peace, and because Russia has already threatened to fight against loss of her UN veto power. On this the affirmative made two attacks; first they quoted some United States military men who claim that Russia would fear to fight a world organization—men who told us in 1939 that Japan would never dare attack the United States. Second, they again argued that the United Nations cannot succeed so long as Russia keeps the veto. Ladies and Gentlemen, time will not permit me to remind the affirmative again of the long list of UN successes *in spite* of this veto. Surely you will agree that our best chance of peace lies with the United Nations, and not with a Federal World Government.

(V) Ladies and Gentlemen, we have examined every argument our opponents have offered; we have met the attacks they made on our own case; and have shown you why we object to a Federal World Government. We have shown you that there is no need for the nations of the world to give up sovereignty to a World Government, that the United Nations is slowly bringing the nations nearer together. We have shown you that a World Government could not possibly be formed at this time. And we have shown you that an attempt to form it would bring immediate war. In view of the evidence brought out in this debate, you must agree that the nations of the world should not at this time try to form a Federal World Government.

PART VII—PRESENTING THE DEBATE

DELIVERY

If the members of the debate audience were going to read your arguments, this book might properly end here. However, the people who make up your audience do not read the discussion; they listen. And consequently, the way in which you present your arguments is of vital importance. Weak, hesitating delivery will destroy the effectiveness of the strongest argument, while a forceful speaker can often make a weak contention seem strong. Good delivery is a basic requirement of debate.

The memorized-extempore style. From the standpoint of preparation, your style of speaking will range between two extremes. The speech may be *memorized* and given word for word as it was written, or it may be given *extempore* in language chosen at the moment of delivery.

Extempore delivery is the ideal style for debate. It allows greater flexibility in speaking, and permits you to fit your language to the situation just as you would do in conversation. But the extempore method has its difficulties, especially for beginning debaters. Unless you have a great deal of experience on the platform, your language is apt to be vague and inconclusive if the extempore method is used, and your speech organization is almost sure to suffer.

Until you have a considerable amount of experience on the platform, the most effective style of speaking for you to use in your constructive argument, at least, will be that made possible by memorizing the greater part of the speech. But do not memorize simply the *words* you plan to use—make sure, first of all, that the *ideas* to be presented are firmly fixed in your mind. Give careful attention, too, to the exact language used in the *organization* parts of your speech—the introductions to new arguments presented, the conclusions to various points, the transitional phrases or sentences which lead from one argument to another. The language used in presenting the arguments themselves is less important; it may be memorized or not as you see fit.

Then, *practice* giving your speech, over and over again. Present it in practice debates with other members of the squad; go over it by yourself, alone. Talk to your reflection in a mirror in your own home. In these practice sessions, don't permit yourself to give your arguments word for word as you wrote them. Use the language you memorized for your organization materials, if you wish—but cultivate the habit of using "spur-of-the-moment" language for the actual arguments you present. The more you can train yourself to use an extempore style, the more at home you will feel and the more effective you will be in the actual debate.

After all, in every debate, the rebuttal portions of your argument *must* be extemporized. So must the materials you insert in adapting your constructive speech. So from the very beginning, in practice debates, try to phrase each argument in the words which come to you on the platform. Memorizing the organization materials will help give you confidence, but even the language you use in introducing arguments may have to be changed in an actual contest debate. So try to train yourself to the use of the extempore method.

This should not be understood to mean that the constructive argument should not be *written*, while you are preparing for any debate. Even experienced debaters should follow the practice of writing out their constructive arguments in full, so that they can fit their materials to the time allotted, and give each argument the relative amount of space it deserves. Writing permits you to test the strength of organization of your argument, and particularly to check for the presence of adequate interest materials. But if you are an experienced debater, memorizing any part of the speech should not be necessary. Once the argument has been checked for time and clarity of organization, and once you are sure that sufficient interest materials have been used, lay the speech aside, and go back to the outline from which it was written. Practice building an *extempore* speech upon that outline,

talking to an imaginary group of listeners and trying to make the
ideas presented forceful and interesting to them. In going over
the same ideas again and again in repeated practice sessions, you
no doubt will find that you express certain arguments in almost
the same language, time after time. Possibly you may use that
same phrasing when you get to the actual debate platform. But
you are not bound down to any definite way of expressing your
ideas, as you are when the memorized style is used; you have
from the beginning all of the freedom and flexibility of a completely extempore argument.

So far as rebuttal arguments are concerned, you will *have* to
use the extempore style, regardless of the extent of your experience. Even if you have a fairly definite idea of certain points
your opponents will use, a *memorized* argument attacking those
points or even a single one of them will never fit the exact situation. This portion of the debate must be delivered extempore,
from the very beginning.

Good debate delivery. The statement in the Declaration of
Independence that "all men are created equal" does not apply to
speaking ability. Some speakers enjoy certain natural advantages
over their fellows; one speaker may have the advantage of a com-
manding appearance, or another may have an unusually pleasing
voice. But every speaker can use the speaking abilities he has to
best advantage, and every debater should work to make his delivery as effective as possible. And after all, effectiveness in delivery is not merely a matter of voice or of personal appearance.
The three basic requirements for good delivery are *sincerity,
animation*, and a *sense of communication*—and these qualities
may be cultivated by any speaker.

The first requirement of good delivery is a *sense of communication*—a realization that you are *talking to* people. When you
are presenting an argument, keep in mind the fact that your purpose is to *convey some definite idea to your listeners*, and to make
them believe the way you want them to believe with respect to
the subject. So when you are giving a debate speech, *talk*; don't
give an oration. Speak clearly and distinctly, using enough car-

rying power in your voice to be heard by all of your listeners—
but *talk to* them, exactly as you'd talk to a single person in ordinary conversation. Talk slowly enough so that your listeners can
understand you, and follow your line of thought. Don't rush
things; it isn't the number of words you are able to get out of
your system, but the number of ideas your listeners accept, that
counts in debate.

Second, be *sincere.* Say what you believe, and make your
listeners realize that you believe what you say. If you can make
them understand that you really believe every argument you offer,
your very sincerity will help convince them. But perhaps you
may ask, "How can I be sincere about what I say, when I don't
know which side really is right?" Well, so far as the final decision is concerned, "right" is a relative term—it's impossible to say
which side is right. But with respect to the arguments that may
be given for the proposal or opposing it, truth lies on *both* sides.
No matter what subject may be discussed, you can find plenty of
good, sound arguments favoring the course which is advocated—
arguments which you know to be valid and true—and an equal
number of valid arguments against that course. Use the arguments on your side of the discussion that you personally know
are sound and worthy of belief. And make your listeners realize
that you yourself are *convinced* that they are sound. Confidence
inspires confidence.

Third, be *animated* in your speaking. Or in other words,
put some *life* into your delivery. It isn't enough simply to *talk*
to your listeners, even though you are entirely sincere in what
you say. If you want to win belief, you have to capture the *attention* and *interest* of your listeners, and impress your ideas upon
them. A monotonous, lifeless recitation of arguments certainly
isn't effective. A lively, sparkling style is needed, one that is
forceful and animated. You don't need to shout, and you need
not pound the table to be forceful. You can be forceful in a
whisper. But get plenty of variety into your way of speaking;
use variation in force and rate of speaking to mark the importance of your ideas. And don't be afraid to introduce *action.*
Let your face reflect what you are thinking; move about the plat-

form. An alert, animated speaker—one who shows plenty of life and enthusiasm—is the speaker who has the best chance of convincing listeners.

Personal qualities. Your effectiveness as a speaker will depend in great measure, too, upon the listener's attitude toward you as an individual. Every listener is more willing to believe something told him by a person whom he likes, than by one he dislikes. So if you can make the listener *like* you, and win his friendship and respect, he will be inclined to accept your views without much hesitation. By winning his confidence you create for yourself a certain *prestige* with the listener that makes him willing to accept your arguments.

The degree of prestige that you establish will depend in part upon the things you say; you cannot inspire respect or confidence by making inaccurate statements. But equally important is the way you conduct yourself on the platform. Certain personal qualities that you show help you build up prestige; other qualities tend to weaken the listener's respect for you.

The *confidence* that you show, and the *sincerity* you feel for your own argument will do much, of course, to increase the confidence of the listener in you. These qualities have been mentioned before. But further than that, the listener will be favorably impressed by an attitude marked by *fairness*. No one admires trickery or lack of sportsmanship; no one respects a speaker who is dishonest. Be scrupulously fair to your opponents. Be fair in stating their position on different phases of the question. Quote them accurately; attack the arguments they really have made. Don't do things which distract the attention of your listeners from an opponent who is speaking; don't move about excitedly at your table when a point is advanced, or engage in audible conversation with your colleague. And don't take advantage by minor violations of the rules of debate. When your time expires, finish the sentence you have started, and sit down. Don't add anything else, no matter how much you want to say it. Throughout the debate, be scrupulously fair.

Again, your conduct in the debate should be characterized by *friendliness* and *good humor*. Never lose your temper or act in a surly, ill-natured manner. Never permit yourself to be sarcastic or bitter. Regardless of the conventions of debate, good breeding would demand a different attitude on your part. After all, debate is not a matter of life and death. It's simply a friendly discussion. Be good natured about it. Have a good time while you are on the platform. Think of your opponents as friends, and treat them that way. Tear down their arguments if you can, but don't be waspish about it. You can even ridicule the arguments they use, if you do it in a good-natured way. Friendliness toward listeners and opponents, and an air of unfailing good humor will win you the respect of your listeners. Sarcasm, ill nature and bad temper will be resented by the listener. Keep your sense of proportion, and be friendly.

Specific suggestions for delivery. In addition to the general discussion of the requirements of good delivery given in the preceding paragraphs, a few specific suggestions as to conduct on the platform may be helpful to the beginning debater.

Beginning the speech. During the debate, the debaters usually sit at tables on the platform, facing the audience. When it is your turn to speak, remain in your chair until the chairman introduces you; then rise and address the chairman. Wait until he recognizes you, either with a nod or by repeating your name, before moving out on the platform. When you do leave your table, don't be in too great a hurry; come forward deliberately to the center of the platform. Take time for a breath or two before you begin. Then start your speech easily and conversationally; your first task is to win the friendship of the audience, and starting with a rush will not help in that respect.

Position. Stand erectly, with your shoulders fairly well back; keep your weight on both feet. Don't slump or slouch on the platform. An unattractive droop in the way you stand will hardly make the audience respect you. If there is a speaker's stand, stand slightly behind it and a little to one side, so that you can use notes placed upon it. Don't lean on the table; don't put the smallest part of your weight upon it. Leaning against a table or stand isn't an evidence of confidence. Whether there is a speaker's stand or not, don't take root in one place. Move about accasionally—it will help mark transitions in your speech. But when you move, move with purpose. Aimless wandering about and constant shifting of your feet will divert the attention of your listeners from your thought.

Eye contact. Keep your eyes constantly on the *faces* of your listeners. Do not look up at the ceiling or down at the floor; remember that you're talking to *people*, not to the building. Watch the expressions on your listeners' faces. See whether they're hearing you and understanding what you are saying, and whether they are agreeing with the ideas you present. You can read a great deal in the faces of your listeners. Pick out some individual in one part of the room and talk directly to him for a sentence or two; then switch to a man in another part of the audience. Make these individuals believe what you say; talk to them just as you would to a friend, in earnest conversation.

Centering. When you talk to one of your friends, your voice doesn't hold to the same level of emphasis all of the time. Whenever you say something important, you naturally increase the emphasis, or the force in your voice. Even in a single sentence, you make important words stand out. That's exactly the method that should be followed on the platform. If a sentence carries an important idea, give that sentence emphasis; make it stand out above the material around it. And within each sentence, give added force to each important word, just as you do in conversation. You need not always use more force in your voice to give emphasis to the important words or sentences. That is one method, of course; but you can get the same effect by changing the rate of speaking, or by using a pause before or after the important word. To make a very important idea stand out, some speakers cut the rate of speaking to not more than half the normal speed, and "frame" each word, by pausing slightly both before and after it is spoken. But no matter what method you use, center attention upon the important ideas.

Transitions. Usually a change in emphasis is desirable to mark a transition in your speech—a change from one idea to another. Whenever a new section of the speech is introduced, let your voice fall a bit, to a normal conversational level. As your development of the new idea progresses, your voice probably will rise somewhat in pitch, and your rate of speaking will be increased until the climax of the section is reached. Then, after concluding that point, pause a moment to mark the break in thought; then let your voice drop to its normal level to make your transition to your next point.

Gestures. Gestures are an important aid to speaking. They help make some ideas clear, they emphasize important points, and they supply an element of life and interest. Gestures are made with the head and body as well as with the arms; even facial expression is a form of gesture. When you are on the platform, don't hold yourself stiff and rigid. You don't stand that way in ordinary conversation. When you are arguing with a friend, your face reflects every thought; your head moves in emphasis; your hands are busy helping you make your meaning clear. *Let yourself* make the same sort of gestures on the platform. Don't try to memorize gestures as you would a part of your speech: don't try to decide in advance that you're going to "use a gesture" at some particular point. Never *force* a gesture at any time. Gesture should not be a matter of forcing the body or arms into motion; it is simply a matter of letting yourself go. If you are sincere and enthusiastic about your beliefs, and determined to make your listeners accept them, gestures usually will come without your thinking about them. And gestures of that kind are the only ones that are effective.

Notes. Many debaters use notes in presenting their arguments. If you plan to use notes, place them on cards of uniform size. Don't bring large sheets of paper to the platform when you speak; they divert the attention of the listener from your ideas. Use cards of reasonable size, neither overlarge nor extremely small. Hold them in one hand, and let that hand hang at your side when you are not using the notes or using the hand in gesture. Never hold your notes pressed tightly against your chest or stomach when they aren't in use, and don't put them behind your back. And don't try to read the notes on a card held at the level of your waist; when you wish to glance at a card, hold it chest high and at least a foot away from your body, so that you can see the card without shifting your eyes far from the faces of your listeners.

Charts. On certain questions, the use of charts may help you make your ideas clear to your listeners. If charts are to be used, make them large enough for listeners in the back of the room to see them. Mount them on an easel or stand which will hold them firmly; sheets of paper that are constantly falling to the floor make it difficult to keep your listener's attention on your ideas. In using material that is presented in chart form, explain its meaning to your listeners—don't simply tell them the information is on the chart and go on to a different point. If you do, they'll miss your argument on the new point entirely; their efforts to understand the figures on your chart will take all of their attention. At the close of your speech, move the easel which holds the charts to an inconspicuous position at the side of the platform, and see that none of your charts is left uncovered, where listeners can see it. If you do not cover the charts, you are unfairly diverting attention from the argument of the opposing speaker who follows you. But don't place the charts where your opponents do not have access to them, when they have the floor. Charts once presented as evidence are no longer your private possession; if your opponents wish to use them to attack the conclusions you have drawn in your argument, they have every right to use the charts in the same way you have used them.

Mannerisms. Many debaters have mannerisms in speaking which detract very greatly from the effectiveness of their delivery. Don't permit yourself to have such mannerisms. Don't keep your hands in your pockets while you speak; your listeners expect a reasonable degree of dignity from a speaker. Don't twist at buttons, or pull at the edge of your coat or adjust your collar or tie. Don't pull at a knuckle, or play with a pencil or a watch fob. If you are using notes, don't twist or bend the cards. Such mannerisms irritate your listeners and take attention from the ideas you are trying to present. Keep your hands free, except for notes; and let them hang at your sides except when you use them for gestures.

Concluding the speech. The conclusion of your speech is a place of importance in your argument. Make it as effective as possible, and by all means avoid doing things which divert attention from your ideas. If a timekeeper gives you a warning signal a minute or two before the expiration of your time, don't call attention to it by nodding or smiling, or by thanking him audibly. When the final time signal is given, don't ignore it, or try to evade by stretching your sentence by an extra fifty or a hundred words. Finish that one sentence, and stop. Don't make your listeners divide their attention by gathering up notes or sorting and arranging cards during the last half-minute or so of your speech. Wait until you have concluded; the chairman will give you time to get your materials together after your speech is finished. Take your seat quietly; don't create a disturbance that may interfere with the attention given your opponent.

Practicing for delivery. You cannot expect to present your speech effectively unless you devote plenty of time to practice. As soon as your constructive speech is outlined, practice speaking it aloud from the outline. Follow the organization you have planned; present the ideas as strikingly as you can. Keep up the practice after the speech is written. Language will probably come more easily, and greater attention can be given to details of delivery. If possible, practice giving the speech to a friend; try to make him agree with your ideas. If you cannot find a listener, talk to your reflection in a mirror.

As your preparation is carried further, try to fit your speech to possible conditions of debate. Work in some rebuttal in your constructive speech; adapt your arguments to meet different interpretations of the question or unexpected admission of points in your case by an opponent. Work out hypothetical situations with your teammates; let them outline the conditions you must meet, and practice fitting your speech to these conditions.

Don't limit your practice to presenting your constructive argument. Remember the importance of rebuttal in debate. Try your hand at meeting possible cases which your opponents may present. Have your teammates outline specimen cases on the other side of the question; and practice refuting the arguments they suggest. Have them attack the main arguments in the case to be used by your side, and practice meeting the attacks they make. In the early stages of your rebuttal practice, pay no attention to time; take ten or fifteen minutes, if you need it, to present your rebuttal speech. But as you gain ability to speak more easily, include the time limitation in your practice speeches.

Practice and still more practice is the only road to effective delivery. Don't slight this highly important part of your preparation for debate.

ADAPTING THE ARGUMENT

Except for the opening argument for the affirmative, no constructive speech in a debate can be given in exactly the way you plan it. Some adjustments will always be necessary, to meet the actual conditions in the debate. The process of changing your arguments to meet the needs of the occasion is known as *adaptation*.

Adaptation may take a number of different forms, some of the more important of which are listed below:

1. Meeting unusual interpretation
2. Meeting the use of admission
3. Clearing the way for argument
4. Expanding and contracting arguments
5. Linking up with opposing speeches

These various forms of adaptation are considered briefly in the following pages.

Meeting unusual interpretation. When your opponents have used an unexpected interpretation of the question, some adaptation of your argument is always required. One or two courses may be followed.

First, you may accept the unusual interpretation the affrmative has given. In such a case, no mention will be made of the interpretation in the introduction of the first negative speech, but your arguments will have to be changed materially to meet the unusual affirmative interpretation.

Second, if the interpretation is so extreme that there is a chance that your listeners will not accept it, you can challenge the interpretation. Make your attack on the affirmative interpretation in the opening of the first negative speech; insist that it is not a reasonable interpretation, and show why it is unreasonable. Then adapt your arguments, just the same, to conform to the affirmative interpretation. Audiences never enjoy debates that resolve into mere quibbles over the meaning of the question.

Meeting the use of admission. If your opponents agree with you on a point you have already presented, no changes in the later speeches for your side are required. But occasionally, they may admit some point you have planned to advance, *before* you have had a chance to present it. Their admission cannot simply be ignored; your speech must be adapted to meet the new situation. Two possibilities are open to you.

If you have planned to give only two or three minutes to the development of the point, the best way to deal with the situation is to omit your prepared proof entirely. Introduce the admitted point in its regular place in your speech, but instead of offering proof to support it, simply call attention to the fact that your opponents have admitted it. Then you can proceed to your next point.

On the other hand, if the point is one to which you had expected to give a great amount of time, the use of this method might place you in a difficult position. You might have six or eight minutes of time to be used, and nothing important to talk about. To avoid that difficulty, a second method of handling the admission should be used. Bring up your point as originally planned. Refer to the fact that your opponent has admitted it. Then make the charge that he knew that the point was so damaging to his case that he did not dare allow it to be given any importance in the discussion. Say that his action in admitting the point was an effort to cause the point to go unnoticed. Then, after insisting that you refuse to allow him to succeed with his strategy, go ahead with the proof you had originally planned. Frequently this method will make the admitted point the center of attention of the whole debate; your opponent's admission of a seemingly harmless point may be made extremely damaging to his case.

Clearing the way for argument. Most of your attacks on vital opposing arguments will be withheld until the rebuttal speeches, where they may be made with more lasting effect. Sometimes, however, an opposing point must be dealt with during your constructive speech, to make one of your own arguments effective. An opposing argument which indirectly contradicts a main point in your speech would kill all the force of your argument if allowed to go unchallenged; it must be attacked before you attempt to present your own argument on the point.

This gives us a third possible form of adaptation—the rebuttal of main points or sub-points advanced by your opponents, to *clear the way* for a point of your own. Rebuttal of this kind should be inserted in your speech immediately before the proof for your own point is offered.

Expanding and contracting. Whenever extra arguments of this kind are inserted in your speech, or whenever a part of your argument is for any reason omitted, every part of your speech is affected. Time limits remain the same; they do not change to correspond to your need for time. The rest of your arguments must be changed to meet the situation; either *contracted* so that they require less time, or *expanded* to fill up time which is unexpectedly available.

Adjustment in the length of arguments is made, for the most part, by dropping or adding items of evidence used to support your sub-points. A speech may be made longer by adding an extra item of evidence or two for each sub-point in your argument. Or, your development of a point may be shortened by dropping the weakest bits of evidence, or possibly by dropping one sub-point entirely. In extreme cases, drop sub-points; where the time needed is small, drop items of evidence.

Expansion of any argument demands some planning in advance. To make possible the expansion of your argument, an abundance of evidence should be at hand to support each point in your speech—enough to fill up twice the time you plan to give to that point. Then, on the platform, items of evidence may be added as required, bringing the development of the point to whatever length is necessary. On the other hand, to permit the contracting of your argument, the proof you use for each point should be checked carefully before the debate, to discover which items of evidence or which entire sub-points might best be dropped without seriously weakening your case.

Linking up with opponents. The final form of adaptation is less difficult than those which have been suggested, but is important from the standpoint of interest in the debate. Its purpose is to give the effect of a continuous clash between your arguments and those of your opponents. To secure this effect, work in frequent *references to opposing speakers* or to their arguments, at every point in your speech where such a reference is possible. Phrases of the following types are used: "As the gentlemen themselves admit," "as Mr. Harris has told you," "no doubt our friends of the affirmative would have you believe that," or "and the gentlemen have not dared to deny it." The more references of this kind you can work into your speech, the greater is the effect of *clash* produced, and the more interesting your speech becomes to the listener.

EFFECTIVE DEBATING

In the various sections of this book, we have outlined the methods of preparing and presenting a debate argument, in some detail. If you study the suggestions that have been made, and put them into practice, you can be sure at least of making a good *start* toward your goal of becoming an effective debater. But as a beginner in debate, you still will lack one of the things which is required for effectiveness—experience. An inexperienced debater can hardly hope to do the same effective work that he could do after a year or two of debate experience. So get as much experience as you can; crowd it into the weeks of preparation for each debate contest by engaging in as many practice debates as you can with other members of your own debate group. The greater the number of debates in which you engage, whether actual contests or mere practice affairs, the better debating you will be able to do.

While you are gaining experience, try to apply the suggestions which are given in this section. Some of them have been mentioned in earlier sections; others are presented here for the first time. But all of them are important; if you apply them consistently, you will increase the strength of your argument.

1. Make your argument direct and informal; don't follow rules to the extent of being formal and stiff.

For the beginning debater, definite rules are necessary. Without them he has little idea of the methods of preparing and presenting his arguments. But as you gain experience in debate, do not hesitate to disregard rules, if ignoring them will make your argument more effective. Do not stick to the same fixed, formal pattern in every argument. Try to find better ways of presenting your ideas. Think of debate formalities as a point of departure—something to be left behind as rapidly as you feel able to do without them. Like the steps on a railroad car, they are useful while getting on board, but you aren't supposed to ride on them after the train picks up speed. Informal discussion which persuades the listener and brings him to your point of view is the ideal debate style; make your discussion direct and informal.

2. Never attempt to prove more than is necessary.

Study the debate resolution thoroughly before you plan your argument. See how *little* you really are *forced* to prove to support your side. Most questions involve a change; if you have the affirmative, make the change as moderate as the statement of the question will permit. There is no reason to try to carry your listeners a mile if carrying them ten feet will do. The less you undertake to prove, the greater will be your chances of establishing your case. Never try to prove more than you are forced to prove by the statement of the question.

3. Fit your arguments to the beliefs already held by your listeners.

Men readily believe new things or accept new ideas that harmonize with the *things they already believe.* They refuse to accept new ideas that contradict the fixed beliefs already held. Plan your debate points or contentions to conform to the things your listeners believe to be true. Avoid using any contention which opposes a basic belief of your listeners. Cite instances and examples about which the listener already knows; use opinions of authorities whom he will recognize and accept; give illustrations or comparisons that show how your idea parallels his own experience. The more completely your arguments agree with the *existing knowldege and beliefs* of your listeners, the easier it is to prove your contentions.

4. Make every effort to hold the interest of your audience.

The strength of your argument means nothing if your listeners figuratively go to sleep while you are talking. At all costs, keep them awake. Use every possible method of holding your listeners' interest. Make your talk specific and concrete; use plenty of illustrations and comparisons. Be direct in argument; show how your plan will affect the listener's way of living or his well-being. Make use of humor; there is little chance that you can use too much for your audience, and a humorous illustration or comparison strengthens your point and makes it remembered. Keep up a continuous clash between your arguments and those of your opponents; audiences are interested in anything that resembles a fight. Use material that is novel and unusual, and keep in mind the need for variety. Be animated and alive in your delivery; use action and gestures to emphasize your points. An interested, attentive listener is usually a believing listener.

5. Make every effort to win the friendship and confidence of your listeners.

The personality of the debater determines in large part his ability to win the belief of his hearers. If you can make your listeners like you and trust you, the battle for belief is half won. Cultivate a pleasing manner on the platform. Don't be afraid to smile; if you can't smile, grin. Act as though you are enjoying yourself; as though you really like your opponents; as though you appreciate the attention of your listeners. Cultivate the qualities which win the respect of your listeners. Have confidence in yourself and your arguments; be scrupulously fair; show that you are sincere. Never be guilty of discourtesy to your opponents or your listeners, and never show signs of irritation or ill humor. You know the traits you like and admire in other people; cultivate the same traits in yourself.

6. Use every fair method to weaken your opponents' prestige.

The strength of your opponents' arguments depends in considerable degree upon the *prestige* that your opponents have as individuals. If you can weaken the confidence of your listeners in your opponents, their arguments are correspondingly weakened. So, use every fair method of attacking prestige. Call attention to errors your opponents make, or to contradictions in their arguments. Point out errors in reasoning, and stress inadequacy of evidence given to support opposing contentions. But be sure that your attacks on prestige are made in a friendly, good-natured way. Never accuse your opponents of being dishonest, or of deliberately distorting facts—simply charge them with carelessness. Above all, don't be sarcastic or bitter in your attacks; your attitude should be one of friendly good humor and courtesy. Otherwise, you damage your own prestige far more than that of your opponents.

7. Keep the position of offense in the argument.

A defensive battle is seldom a winning battle. Take the offensive in debate; keep your opponents on the defensive. Make your attacks strong enough to keep your opponents in constant difficulty. Hammer away at their weaknesses. Use the unexpected when it will help your case; agree with your opponents, when you can safely do so, on points they have spent eight or ten minutes to prove; use types of case organization that will give your arguments greatest strength and put your opponents at a disadvantage. Be so thoroughly prepared on the question that you have an advantage in evidence even on the issues your opponents present. The stronger your attacks and the more completely your opponents are kept in a position of defense, the greater your chances of bringing your listeners to the belief you uphold.

8. Follow up your advantages.

Throughout the debate, be quick to seize every advantage that offers. Listen carefully to your opponents' arguments; see if they make any statements or admissions that you can use to support your own contentions. Watch for contradictory statements; if any are found, use the weaker statement to attack the stronger, and let your listeners know that your opponents themselves have supplied the material to tear down their own contentions. Look for minor points which give opportunity for striking attacks. While your colleague is speaking, watch your

opponents closely. Usually you can tell which arguments worry
them. If they show that a given argument is causing them
difficulty, build that point up until it becomes the vital issue
at stake in the debate. Center your attention on the points upon
which your opponents are weak; the more this is done, the
greater will be your advantage in the debate.

9. Center your attention upon the vital issues.

Every debate really turns on two or three points upon which
the two sides disagree. Watch for the points that seem to be
most important. Disregard the minor arguments in your opponents' case; give your time and attention to the issues that
are vital. A fraction of an ounce of powder will drive a single
bullet through a two-inch board, but birdshot propelled by the
same initial force will hardly penetrate the surface. Center on
points that are vital; don't waste your time with the unimportant
things.

10. Practice giving your arguments.

The final suggestion—perhaps the suggestion of most importance—is that you practice giving your arguments. Practice the
delivery of your constructive speech; practice adapting it to meet
every possible situation; practice giving rebuttal arguments, and
organizing them into an effective rebuttal speech. Do your practicing before an audience, if possible; get a friend to listen to
you and talk to him. Ask him for criticisms; frequently his suggestions will be of considerable help. Arrange for practice debates
with other members of your group; hold such a debate every
day if you can. Try out new constructive arguments in these
practice debates; see what use you can make of different methods
of attack on opposing arguments. Of course, the best experience
comes from taking part in actual contests; but a practice debate
is the next best thing.

To increase the strength of your delivery, to improve the
phrasing of your arguments, to gain skill in rebuttal, to increase
your ability in every other phase of debating, the most essential
factor is practice. Time given to practice is always well spent.

APPENDICES

LOGICAL FORMS

Little conscious attention is given to logical forms in constructing or presenting an actual debate argument. However, for those who are interested, a brief outline of the more important forms is given below.

Reasoning processes. Reasoning is divided into two general classes, inductive and deductive. *Deductive reasoning* is that in which a conclusion is drawn from a general principle or universally accepted truth; *inductive reasoning* is the form in which a conclusion is drawn from a consideration of specific instances. Deductive reasoning proceeds from the *general* to the *specific;* inductive from the *specific* to the *general.*

The syllogism. The *syllogism* is the logical form in which deductive arguments are given formal statement. Every syllogism consists of three steps or parts: a *major premise,* a *minor premise,* and a *conclusion.* It will also include three *terms:* a *major or general term,* a *minor* or *specific* term, and a common term stating a characteristic. The major premise states that all members of a class have a common characteristic; the minor premise places some individual case within that general class; and the conclusion states that the individual case considered likewise has the common characteristic. A commonly used syllogism is given below:

Major Premise: All cows eat grass.
Minor Premise: That animal is a cow.
Conclusion: That animal will eat grass.

In the illustration, the three terms are (a) cow or cows, as a collective term; (b) that animal; and (c) eats grass. The first is the major term; the second, the minor term; the third, the common term.

Stated differently, the *major premise,* in a deductive syllogism, contains the *general* or entire assumption or accepted truth. The *minor premise* states the *specific* assumption or accepted truth and connects itself with the *major* premise. The *conclusion* connects the *major* and *minor* premises and draws a *specific instance* or *truth* from the two preceding assumptions.

> *Major Premise:* Anything that will raise the general standard of living should be supported by public opinion.
> *Minor Premise:* Economic planning will raise the general standard of living.
> *Conclusion:* Economic planning should be supported by public opinion.

It will be noted that the deductive form presented in the syllogism is the method of proof discussed on pages 31 to 38 as *proof by classifying.* In every syllogism, the minor premise is a *classifying statement,* placing the minor term within the general class covered by the major term. The deductive method is the form commonly used to show relationship between the proposition and supporting major contentions, and between major contentions and minor contentions. In each case the major premise of the syllogism is something which is already believed by the members of the audience; the minor premise is the point which must be proved.

The enthymeme. The word *enthymeme* is derived from two words meaning "in mind." An enthymeme, or a syllogism in enthymeme, is one of which some part is held in mind, but not expressed. Since the major premise of a syllogism is usually a truism or statement generally accepted as true by the listener, the deductive form of reasoning is most commonly stated as an enthymeme, with the major premise not expressed. For instance, the syllogism given as the first illustration would probably be expressed in actual argument as follows:

> That animal is a cow; consequently, it will eat grass.

Sometimes the unstated part of the syllogism is the minor premise, rather than the major premise. The minor premise, however, is left unstated only when it is obviously true, requiring no proof. Using for illustration the same syllogism as before, omission of the minor premise gives the following enthymeme:

All cows eat grass; therefore, that cow will eat grass.

In nearly every case where the word *therefore* or *consequently* or *because* or *for* is found connecting two statements, the two statements are an enthymeme. The two statements will include all three terms necessary to a syllogism, so construction of the complete syllogism will not be difficult.

Chain of reasoning. A series of syllogisms, with the conclusion of one used as a premise of another, is known as a *chain of reasoning*. In a chain of reasoning, the syllogisms are usually expressed in enthymeme; so that the chain is usually found in some form such as the following:

Government-owned railroads would be operated for service of the public instead of for profit; consequently, they would give better service at lower cost. So government ownership would be advantageous to the general public.

Broken down into separate syllogisms, the argument would be as follows:

FIRST SYLLOGISM

Major Premise: Anything operated for service instead of profit would give better service at lower cost.

Minor Premise: Government-owned railroads would be operated for service instead of profit.

Conclusion: Government-owned railroads would give better service at lower cost.

SECOND SYLLOGISM

(*With conclusion to the first syllogism as minor premise*)

Major Premise: Any system of ownership giving better service at lower cost would be advantageous to the general public.

Minor Premise: Government-owned railroads would give better service at lower cost.

Conclusion: Government-owned railroads would be advantageous to the general public.

Inductive reasoning. The enthymeme and the chain of reasoning, expressing one or more syllogisms in incomplete form, are the deductive forms most commonly found in argument. The common inductive forms, drawing a conclusion from specific cases, are the *generalization,* the argument from *analogy,* argument from *cause to effect,* and argument from *effect to cause.*

The generalization. The inductive method is found in its most perfect form in *generalization.* In the generalization, a principle or general conclusion is drawn from the examination of a number of specific instances. The method is given in the illustration below:

Instances:
Our cow eats grass.
Mr. Johnson's cow eats grass.
Mr. Smith's cow eats grass.
Mr. Brown's cow eats grass.
Conclusion:
All cows eat grass.

Every generalization proceeds from a group of specific, known facts to a general conclusion in which is stated a principle. Practically all of our stock of general knowledge has been derived by use of the method of generalization.

For accuracy in generalization, every instance observed should be one involving a member of a class; the number of cases should be sufficient to justify a conclusion; the cases observed should be typical; there should be no known exceptions; and the conclusion drawn should apply to members of the class as a whole. It will be noted that the method of generalization is the same as that used when supporting reasoning by the type of evidence called *examples* in the section beginning on page 46.

Argument from analogy. In this form of reasoning, two similar cases or instances are compared. After points of similarity have been stressed, the conclusion is drawn that a fact true in one case would probably be true in the other. In simple form, argument from analogy would be as illustrated in the following:

Similarities:

Detroit and Cleveland are cities similar in nearly every important respect. There is no great difference in size; both are industrial and manufacturing centers; both have the advantage of cheap transportation by water; the people living in both cities are of similiar type.

Conclusion:

Since municipally owned street railways have been successful in Cleveland, there is every reason to believe that they would be equally successful in Detroit.

As used in argument, analogy takes one of two forms. In *literal analogy,* comparison is made between two cases lying in the same field—between two states, or two cities, or two nations, or two individuals. In *figurative analogy,* the comparison made is between two cases lying in entirely different fields. (For examples of *figurative analogy,* see pages 63 to 69.) In each form, however, a fact *known* to be true in one case is *assumed* to be true in the other case.

Logically, the argument from analogy is exceedingly weak. In effect, it is a combination of generalization from a single case, and of applying the principle set forth in the generalization to a second case by use of the deductive process. And naturally, a generalization based upon a single instance is not to be considered as necessarily true. From the standpoint of its effect upon the audience, however, analogy is one of the strongest forms of proof.

It will be noted that argument from analogy is essentially the same as that used when supporting reasoning by the two types of evidence called *illustrations* and *comparisons* in the discussion beginning on page 63.

Effect-to-cause argument. The two remaining forms of inductive reasoning to be discussed are based upon the assumption of a *causal* relationship between two events or two factors. From the standpoint of pure theory, it is almost impossible to show that a causal relationship between two phenomena really exists; for purposes of argument, however, we assume such a relationship to exist in countless numbers of cases. In each case where causal argument is used, such a relationship is inferred between a *known* phenomenon, which has been observed, and an *unknown* or *hypothetical* phenomenon. In argument from *effect to cause,* we begin with a known fact which must be the result of some factor in the past, and assume or infer that another factor or event has been the cause.

Known effect:

Crime in general, and particularly crime committed by organized gangs, was far more common from 1920 to 1930 than ever before in the United States.

Assumed cause:

This was the result of national prohibition which became effective in 1919.

Cause-to-effect argument. The same sort of causal relationship is assumed to exist in *cause-to-effect* argument, which reverses the method used in argument from effect to cause and proceeds from a *known* causal factor to an assumed result in the future.

Known cause:

The adoption by the nations of the world of a policy of almost complete disarmament.

Assumed effect:

The result would be a great decrease in the number of wars between nations, and in the injury resulting from wars which might occur.

Neither form of causal argument is particularly sound. Each assumes a causal relationship to exist, in spite of the fact that such a relationship is impossible to establish with certainty. What is more important, each form rests on the assumption that every happening or circumstance is the result of a *single* major cause, although any intelligent person must realize that every phenomenon is the product of a combination of innumerable causes. The increase in crime between 1920 and 1930 was often attributed to prohibition, but it might have resulted in equal degree from the World War, from weather conditions, from a faulty immigration policy, or from a combination of hundreds of other factors. Similarly, the decrease in wars between nations predicted as the logical result of disarmament assumes that armaments are the one factor which produces war, though an examination of history would reveal dozens of other agencies which tend to cause war.

Although causal reasoning is far from sound from the standpoint of strict logic, it is widely used in argument. Benefits which will follow the adoption of a desired policy, or the evils which would result, are predicted on the basis of cause-to-effect reasoning; while the evils of the present system may be attributed to that system only by use of the effect-to-cause method.

Reasoning based on alternatives. Having given attention to the principal forms of inductive and deductive logic, we come finally to one logical method which, strictly speaking, is neither inductive nor deductive—the method based on the *principle of alternatives*. Every proposition may be reduced to a certain number of possibilities; railroads may be owned by the government, by private individuals, or by a combination of the two; our national policy concerning disarmament may be to continue the existing system, to increase our armed forces, to decrease them, or to eliminate them entirely. Having enumerated the possible alternatives, we next tear down the alternatives which are not true or not desirable, to lead to a desired conclusion.

Alternative reasoning is used in argument in two principal forms. First, it is the basis of the method of *residues*. When this method is used, alternatives are carefully enumerated; then each in turn is disposed of as impossible until but one remains, and the conclusion is drawn that since no other alternative is possible, the one remaining must be the correct method to follow. This is the method used in *proof by eliminating*, as discussed in the section beginning on page 38.

Analysis:

Our policy toward aggressor nations in other hemispheres must be one of the following: active official opposition, neutrality, unofficial opposition, or active official support and co-operation.

Elimination:

We cannot follow the first policy of officially opposing the aggressor because it might lead us to war; the American people oppose such a policy.

We cannot oppose unofficially; such a policy would be based on duplicity.

We must not offer active official support and cooperation to the aggressor; such action is contrary to the principles upon which our country is built.

Conclusion:

The only logical course to follow is to pursue a policy of strict neutrality toward aggressors in foreign hemispheres.

The second important form in which the principle of alternatives is used is the method known as the *dilemma*. In this, the various possibilities are enumerated; then each of the possibilities is eliminated in turn. The conclusion which logically follows is that the whole proposition involving these alternatives is impossible.

Analysis:

If we enter a League of American Nations, only two courses of action are possible: (a) we may agree to support every American nation in any disagreement with any non-American nation, or (b) we may agree with reservations and refuse to support other American nations in certain instances.

Elimination:

We cannot bind ourselves to support every nation in every instance of disagreement with non-American nations; to do so might force us to support the country in the wrong, and would embroil the United States in every grievance that occurred.

On the other hand, to enter the League of American Nations with reservations, agreeing to help only if we believed American nations in the right, would injure our own standing among the nations of the Western Hemisphere and cause the security of the Americas to suffer.

Conclusion:

Since neither alternative is possible, the logical course is to refuse to enter the League.

THE BRIEF

A debate *brief* is a complete analytic outline of the subject for debate, setting forth all of the contentions which might reasonably be advanced by either side and indicating the relationship of each contention to the rest of the argument. The preparation of a brief is a valuable aid in the analysis of the subject; briefing makes clear the relation between points and indicates which contentions are of major importance. However, the brief is not itself an outline from which a debate speech may be prepared; the debate argument actually presented will usually include only a few of the contentions included in the brief.

In the form most frequently used, the brief will include three main parts. First, there is an *introduction* in which background expository material is outlined; second, an *affirmative brief* in which all of the contentions supporting the affirmative of the question are presented; and finally, a *negative brief* in which possible negative contentions are set forth.

The introduction to the brief includes a concise outline of fact materials which will be admitted by both sides. Usually this material is arranged under four main heads:

I. The reasons for the importance of the question.
II. A brief outline of the history of the subject.
III. A statement of the definitions given any terms in the resolution as stated which call for definition.
IV. A statement of all points formally agreed to by both sides.

The introduction will include no statements for which proof is required. It merely presents an outline of general facts which both sides will accept as true. The two remaining sections, on the other hand, are distinctively argumentative. They present the contentions which may be advanced by the two sides, and subordinate to each major contention, sub-statements which give reasons for accepting that contention as true.

The argumentative sections of the brief should conform to the following rules:

1. Every statement in the brief must be in the form of a complete declarative sentence.
2. Each main contention must be an affirmative or a negative statement of one of the probable or possible issues of the debate, presenting a reason for accepting as true either the affirmative or the negative proposition.
3. Each sub-statement must help prove the truth of the statement to which it is subordinate.
4. Relation of statements and subordinate statements must be indicated by a system of indentation, and by use of symbols.

If these sections are correctly constructed, every statement may be connected with each statement subordinate to it by use of the word *because* or of the expression *for example.*

The system of indentation and symbols ordinarily used to show the relationship of points in argumentative sections of the brief is as follows:

I. .... (Main contention) ....
A. ...... (Supporting statement) ....
1. ... (Supporting statement of second rank) ......
a. (Supporting statement of third rank) ....

A specimen brief on the question of government-supported hospital care is provided below.

STATEMENT OF THE QUESTION: *Resolved: that the federal Social Security system should be extended to provide hospital insurance for all individuals covered by the system, and their families.*

INTRODUCTION TO THE BRIEF

I. The question of hospital insurance included as a part of the Social Security system was brought to public notice by the proposal, in 1962, that the system be extended to provide hospital care for the aged.

II. Hospital insurance is presently available to a large proportion of the people of the United States, on either a group basis or an individual basis.

    A. It is provided on a group basis for most employees of the federal government, including those in armed services.

    B. It is also provided on a group basis to employees of many industrial concerns, school systems, and the like.

    C. It is also available in most communities on an individual basis, but usually at rates substantially higher than those for group insurance, and with greater limitations on eligibility for insurance and on extent of hospital benefits provided.

        1. Most individual plans limit benefits to periods of not more than 60 days during each calendar year.

III. Terms in the resolution may be defined as follows:

    A. "Social Security" refers to the system of compulsory unemployment and old age insurance maintained by the federal government.

    B. "Be extended" implies that the same methods of administration and the same methods of taxation to provide funds for the program now used will also be used for the system of hospital insurance.

    C. "Hospital insurance" refers to insurance covering all or a major part of costs of hospitalization or of care in nursing homes, where required; it does not include medical or surgical services by medical practitioners or by surgeons.

    D. "Individuals covered" would include all eligible for unemployment insurance, or who by virtue of present or past employment will be eligible for old age retirement payments under Social Security.

    E. "Their families" refers only to members of immediate families: wives or husbands, children under 18 years of age living in the family home or attending school, actually living with the "covered" individual, or dependent entirely or primarily on him (or her) for support.

IV. The two sides have agreed on the following:

    A. The proposed plan will require no participation by state governments, as is required in some degree in the case of unemployment insurance.

    B. Payments will be made by the director of the program directly to hospitals on the basis of itemized statements submitted by authorized heads of hospitals, as with private insurance.

    C. All hospitals licensed or otherwise "officially" recognized by state authorities will be included in the system; there will be no certification or inspection by federal authorities included in the program.

    D. Beneficiaries may go to whatever hospitals they select or that are selected by their personal physicians, subject to availability of room; however, two provisos will apply: first, that the hospital or nursing home chosen be in or reasonably adjacent to their own home communities, and second, that in the case of individuals requiring hospital care for more than 21 days, arrangements may be made to move them to other but less crowded hospitals, with approval of their personal physicians.

AFFIRMATIVE BRIEF

I. A system of government-supported hospital insurance is needed.

    A. At present, large numbers of people are not covered by any type of hospital insurance.

        1. Group insurance is not available to all, covering hospitalization or nursing home care.

            a. Substantial numbers of industrial concerns have no group plan for hospital insurance.

            b. Group hospital insurance is not made available in most areas to those engaged in unusually hazardous occupations.

            c. Often, the group industrial plans that are available cover only the individual employee, and not members of his family.

            d. Industrial group plans do not cover employees who are on strike, or individuals in the process of changing from work with one company to work with another, or former employees who are presently unemployed, or who are permanently retired because of age or other disability.

        2. Although there are many insurance companies which provide health or hospital insurance on an individual rather than a group basis, not all applicants are considered insurable by such companies, and for those who would be accepted, costs are usually much higher than many of the uninsured can afford to pay.

    B. Even when individuals are covered by hospital insurance, whether on a group or an individual basis, the insurance provided in most cases does not cover prolonged illnesses requiring hospitalization or care in nursing homes.

II. A system of hospital insurance of the type proposed is sound in principle.
  A. Providing such insurance is a legitimate function of government.
    1. It is in general comparable to our system of universal public education, except, of course, that in the proposed hospital insurance system, costs would be borne by the federal government rather than by municipalities and states.
    2. It is analogous to the providing of government-supported institutions for care of the physically handicapped or mentally ill.
    3. It is an extension of the Social Security principle of providing insurance in cases of emergencies resulting from unemployment or for support of those who have reached retirement age.
  B. The system proposed is entirely just and equitable.
    1. It provides equal coverage and equal benefits to all citizens covered by Social Security, regardless of personal financial ability.
    2. It places the major burden of costs on those eligible to receive benefits.
      a. Somewhat increased Social Security taxes will be collected from all individuals "covered" under the Social Security system.
      b. Although a portion of Social Security taxes is paid by employers, even this is borne indirectly by the employees who benefit from the system.
    3. If costs of operating the system exceed amounts collected in special Social Security taxes and a portion of total costs must be paid out of general government revenues, this merely parallels such widely accepted policies of government as providing aid for dependent children, or for certain types of physically handicapped adults, or making special grants to individuals living in drought-stricken or flood-stricken areas.
  C. The system proposed would in no way interfere with existing doctor-patient relationships.
    1. The proposed plan does not cover costs of medical treatment or of surgery—only of ordinary hospital care.
    2. Under the plan, each individual would be left free to select his own physician or surgeon.
    3. Hospitals would be chosen as at the present time, on a basis of recommendation by the physician or surgeon selected by the individual requiring hospitalization.

D. There would be no control or "interference" with hospital operation by any agency of the federal government involved in the plan.
   1. All hospitals or nursing homes "approved" by individual states would automatically come under the plan.
   2. Standards for hospitals or nursing homes would continue to be set up and enforced by state medical agencies, not by the federal government.
E. A plan could be developed which would largely prevent abuses.
   1. As at present, no individual would be admitted to a hospital—other than in cases of emergency—except on the recommendation of a qualified and licensed medical practitioner.
   2. State health agencies and state and local medical societies could be notified in case any medical practitioner had an unusually high number of referrals, and could themselves take any action considered appropriate by them.
   3. Those eligible to receive hospital or nursing home care could be discouraged from making unnecessary use of hospital facilities by a provision in the plan that costs of hospitalization for the first three, four or five days of any one period of time spent in a hospital be paid by the individual, rather than by the government insurance agency.
   4. As at present, hospital authorities themselves could, in consultation with physicians of those receiving treatment, determine when continued hospitalization would no longer be needed, and when patients should be discharged.
   5. Although opportunities for abuses exist in present private hospital insurance plans, no less great than would be the case in a government system, most of the state or local Blue Cross insurance plans report that abuses are relatively infrequent.
F. Although a government system of hospital insurance would replace some existing non-government insurance plans, adoption of the system would not be productive of serious injury to those connected with such plans.
   1. Blue Cross plans, which might be largely displaced, are operated in any case on a non-profit basis, so their elimination would not produce economic injury.
   2. Other private hospital insurance companies might not be greatly injured.
      a. Hospital insurance is only a part of their total insurance business, and in most cases, a minor part.

    b. Since the government program would cover only basic costs, private companies should have a continued good business in providing insurance covering other important cost elements, such as extra costs of private rooms, or medical or surgical costs.

III. A system of government-operated hospital insurance in connection with the Social Security system would be entirely practical.

    A. The same principle involved has worked successfully in practice for other types of covered individuals.

        1. It has worked successfully in major tax-supported universities, which provide hospital insurance for students at a very low cost.

        2. It has worked successfully in providing hospital care for members of the Armed Forces, and their families.

           a. The quality of hospital care provided in Army and Navy hospitals compares favorably with the best available in private hospitals.

    B. The hospital service required could be provided at reasonable cost.

        1. At worst, it would be no greater than the cost of similar services provided under private hospital insurance plans.

        2. There is at least a good possibility that a government system could be provided at an annual cost per individual insured considerably lower than the amounts charged by private hospital insurance groups.

           a. As a part of Social Security, the government insurance plan would cover a tremendous number of insured individuals, with a possible resulting saving in overhead costs.

           b. All advertising and promotion costs could be eliminated, and these costs are substantial in many private insurance plans, along with costs of "selling" the service.

IV. A system of government hospital insurance covering practically the entire population would be productive of a number of major benefits.

    A. It would result in improvement in the general level of health of the American people.

        1. People with chronic ailments which can be corrected by surgery would be more likely, with such insurance coverage, to have the necessary surgery performed.

           a. They would be better able to pay the costs of having surgery, since in most cases costs of hospitalization preceding and following surgery are substantially greater than fees charged by the surgeons themselves.

B. The system would provide nursing home care for older men and women, or disabled younger men and women, who need such care.

C. It would permit more efficient use of hospitals than is possible today.
   1. Hospitals in recent years operate at between 80 and 85 per cent of capacity.
   2. Patients requiring long periods of hospitalization could be moved from overcrowded hospitals to those in areas in which facilities are less fully used.

Negative Brief

I. There is no real need for the adoption of a system of government hospital insurance of the type proposed.

A. Federal, state or local governmental agencies already provide hospital care for millions of people.
   1. The federal government provides complete medical care for the 2.5 million men in the armed services, for the 2.4 million civilian employees of the federal government; in most cases, families of employees are also given free medical care and hospitalization.
   2. Medical and hospital care is provided for all veterans by the Veterans Administration.
   3. Federal and state governments combine to provide substantial portions of costs of medical care for some 2.4 million men and women over 65 years of age, through one of the special "aid" provisions of the amended Social Security Act.
   4. An additional 3.5 million individuals receive aid from the federal government as being blind or disabled, or as dependent children.

B. A much greater number of individuals are covered by hospital insurance provided by private companies.
   1. More than 56 million individuals are enrolled in various Blue Cross plans, with coverage in most cases extending to members of family groups.
   2. Millions of others have hospital insurance in connection with health or accident insurance plans of various private companies.

C. Introduction of hospital insurance in connection with Social Security would not appreciably increase the number for whom such insurance is already provided, either through government agencies or through various private group or individual insurance plans.

II. The proposed system of compulsory hospital insurance in connection with the Social Security system is wrong in principle.
   A. It is another step in the direction of increased centralization in the federal government.
      1. Extent of existing centralization can be judged from the fact that nearly 5 million men are employed directly by the federal government, either in the armed forces or as civilian employees.
   B. It would result in a constantly increasing degree of control of hospitals by the federal government.
      1. The federal government would sooner or later set "standards" for approval of hospitals allowed to participate in the scheme.
      2. With private hospital insurance largely replaced by the government system, a hospital could hardly continue to operate without being a part of the government insurance scheme.
      3. Increased control by federal agencies supplying funds has characterized other activities of the federal government.
         a. Highway construction jointly supported by state and federal funds is increasingly controlled by the federal government.
         b. The federal government exercises a fairly high degree of control over instruction in agriculture given in land grant colleges.
         c. Industrial concerns having defense contracts with the federal government find themselves almost at the mercy of federal agencies, in their negotiations with organized labor groups.
   C. Government hospital insurance would be an entering wedge in the attempt to bring about a system of socialized medicine.
      1. With hospitals subject to government "approval," the government would also be able to determine what physicians would be permitted to use facilities of hospitals, and what physicians would be allowed to authorize hospitalization of government-insured patients.
      2. In hospitals maintained by the armed services or by the Veterans Administration, both hospitals and medical practitioners are under direct government control.
   D. Adoption of the system would drive most private hospital insurance concerns out of business.
      1. Blue Cross plans would be almost completely replaced, since the government system would be compulsory.
      2. Other private hospital insurance plans would lose so large a part of their total business that continued operation would become unprofitable.

III. The proposal for government hospital insurance through Social Security is not economically sound.
   A. It would greatly increase the total costs of providing hospital and nursing home care.
      1. With costs paid by the government, a much greater number of people would go to hospitals than is now the case.
         a. Minor ailments now treated at home would "justify" hospitalization, and "a few days' rest."
         b. Similarly, tremendous numbers of older people now living with their children would be placed in nursing homes.
      2. Time spent in the hospital by individuals admitted would similarly tend to increase.
         a. It would cost the patient nothing if he spent more time being waited on by hospital attendants.
         b. Doctors, who probably would not be too highly pleased with the adoption of a government insurance system, would be slower than now is the case in ending the period of hospital convalescence.
         c. Members or officials of labor organizations might exert strong political pressures to "keep in line" hospital authorities who attempted to shorten the time spent in hospital beds by patients.
      3. With the "government paying the bills," per-day costs would also tend to rise.
         a. Per-day costs of hospital care for dependents of men in military service who are treated at government expense are twice as high as the per-day costs for patients covered by Blue Cross plans.
   B. In addition, the plan would have to provide for construction of hundreds of additional hospitals and nursing homes.
      1. At present, the fewer than 7,000 hospitals in the United States are used to about 85 per cent of capacity.
      2. Any appreciable increase in total demands on hospital facilities would necessitate construction of additional hospitals.
      3. In a system in which costs of hospitalization are guaranteed by the government, private funds would not be likely to be available for new hospital construction, making it necessary for government-owned hospitals to be erected.
      4. Demands for increased facilities in the field of nursing homes would be even greater than for hospital facilities.
   C. The plan would also have to carry the costs of a continually growing administrative bureaucracy.
      1. In ten years from 1950 to 1960, administrative costs of the existing Social Security system increased from $70 million to $234 million a year.

2. The Department of Agriculture, since its creation, has expanded until it now has nearly 100,000 employees; the Veterans Administration has more than 170,000 full-time employees.

3. Total number of civilian employees of the federal government has increased from 600,000 in 1930 to approximately 2.4 million today.

D. Financing the plan would increase the amount of the Social Security tax to unbearable levels.

    1. Social Security taxes are already high.

        a. To provide a total Social Security tax income of $10 billion in the fiscal year 1960, a tax on wages totaling 6 per cent had to be levied, half of which was paid by employees, half by employers.

        b. To meet anticipated increases in the cost of the present Social Security system, provision has already been made to increase the tax on wages to 9 per cent, starting in the fiscal year of 1969.

    2. A further increase of from 6 to 9 per cent of wages in Social Security taxes would be required to meet the costs of government hospital insurance.

        a. Present total costs of hospitalization are estimated at from $13 billion to $15 billion a year, on the basis of 500 million total patient-days spent in hospitals, with average costs at from $25.00 to $30.00 a day.

        b. While the government hospital insurance plan would probably not pay all costs of care, nor apply to all patients, a reasonable and conservative estimate is that from the beginning, costs of providing hospital care would be at least $10 billion a year.

        c. This amount would later be increased by increased patient-load, and by the resulting necessity for construction of additional hospitals and nursing homes by the government.

        d. On the basis of the present requirement of a rate of 6 per cent of wages to produce revenues of $10 billion a year for the Social Security system, the amount of Social Security taxes would have to be increased by at least 6 per cent, and probably by even more, to provide the more than $10 billion a year required by the plan for government hospital insurance.

        e. Economists estimate that the present 9 per cent rate, to become effective in 1969, is all that can be borne without serious resulting injury to the economy.

ANALYSIS OF THE PROPOSITION

An analysis of the proposition: *Resolved, That the United
States and Canada Should Join in Forming a Common Market
Patterned After the European Common Market.*

THE PROBLEM

The idea of "economic union" or a "common market" between Canada and the United States is not new. Over fifty
years ago, in 1911, the U.S. Congress approved, and President
Taft signed, legislation providing for a "reciprocity" agreement
with Canada that would have largely ended the tariff barriers
between the two countries. However, the Canadian Parliament
failed to pass similar legislation. At that time Canada had a
population of 7.2 million people; the United States was a nation
of 92 million. Today, Canada is a nation of 18.5 million, and
the United States has grown to 185 million people. And tariff
barriers between the two neighbors remain relatively high.

The problems facing both nations today are very serious
ones, involving problems of national survival undreamed of fifty
years ago. In today's world an economically weak nation, such
as Canada, is unable to defend itself and must depend for protection on someone else. On the other hand, no single nation
regardless of strength can stand alone against the Communist
bloc. The United States must depend for survival on strengthening its friends and allies so that the combined strength of all
can deter aggression. The economic strength of Canada is of
primary concern to the United States. For example, communistic
Cuba causes vital concern in the United States, although the
nearest Cuban point is ninety miles across the ocean from the
tip of Florida. The four thousand miles of unprotected border

between the United States and a communistic Canada would be unthinkable.

Canada cannot become economically strong without improved capital for development of her vast and untapped resources, improved foreign trade, and increased production know-how. Without such improvement her raw material resources will remain undeveloped, her industries will continue to operate a part of the year because of lack of markets, and her development at best will remain static. If undeveloped she must continue to spend only $89 per capita on national defense, whereas the United States is able to spend over $230 per capita on such defense.

The problem becomes immediate and grave in the face of Canada's loss of much of her foreign trade because of the growing strength of the European Common Market. If Canada is to prosper, and in turn provide the United States with the potent northern ally the United States needs, something must be done. This is the problem.

THE PROPOSITION

Resolved: That the United States and Canada Should Join in Forming a Common Market Patterned After the European Common Market, is one of several solutions that might be advanced to solve the problem outlined above. An analysis of any proposal calls for a consideration of the various alternative proposals, and their evaluation in a comparative manner. The affirmative in the above proposition must attempt to establish a need for economic union between the two countries, show that such union will solve this need better than any other possible solution, and be ready to show that the affirmative solution will not cause problems more serious than those solved. Before any of these things can be done, however, it is essential that the terms of the proposition should be analyzed so that it is clearly understood exactly what is being proposed.

DEFINITIONS

United States and Canada: means the central governments of the two countries, acting as representatives of the people.

Should Form: means ought to agree to legislate and put into effect. The question is not *will* the two governments so act, but *should* they.

A Common Market: the words "common market" have come to be accepted as meaning "free trade" between the countries involved.

Patterned After: means essentially like in all basic or major respects.

European Common Market: is the layman's way of referring to economic agreements in effect among the nations comprising the European Economic Community. Basically, these agreements call for: free trade among the member nations, a tariff wall around the member nations against trade with non-member nations, a period of time over which the agreements were put into effect, unanimous agreement before new members are accepted, and an agreement to buy from each other rather than others so long as the items needed are available for sale in member countries.

ADMITTED MATTER

Admitted matter in a debate represents certain basic assumptions that are acceptable to both sides, or certain issues that can be agreed upon before the debate starts. For instance, the affirmative and negative debaters will readily agree that *political union* is not involved. They will agree that trade between the two countries is desirable. They will agree that both countries want to see Canada stay free of communism. And they will agree that present tariffs were not designed as revenue measures, but were designed as barriers to trade.

A more troublesome admission may be made by some negative teams and denied by others. If both sides should agree that there is desperate need to strengthen Canada economically, much time and argument might be saved. However, some negative teams may deny that a strong Canada is essential to defense of North America, or more likely argue that Canada and the United States collectively *are strong today,* and that the problem is not an urgent or vital one.

Irrelevant Matter

Admitted matter calls for the acceptance of certain concepts while irrelevant matter *excludes* from the debate contentions that may *appear* on the surface to be relevant. For example, the question of whether it is likely that the two governments *will* act is irrelevant to the debate. In every *policy* proposition where a change from the current practice is advocated, the arguments must center around the *advisability* of adopting the change. The question is always: *Should* the new policy be accepted? If the recommendations of the affirmative can be proved to be desirable and advisable, it is presumed that means can be found and used to put the plan into effect. In other words, the debate must be on the *merits* of the proposition. Likewise irrelevant in the above proposition is the question of whether other countries should be brought into the proposed economic union. Inclusion of other countries is provided for by mutual consent and in no way disproves the need for the proposed union. In a similar way the question of political union between the two countries is irrelevant because political union is a broader type of union which automatically includes economic union.

The Issues

So far in this analysis an attempt has been made to indicate the meaning of the essential terms and to point out the major admitted and irrelevant contentions. However, the real purpose of any analysis is to discover and outline the basic issues of the proposition. What, then, are the basic issues?

Issue Number One—Is There a Need?

The affirmative, because it is encumbered with the burden of proof, must present the usual stock issues of need and remedy. As in every debate the affirmative has the advantage of outlining the *need* which it believes the proposal will solve. So long as the *need* outlined is sufficient to warrant the change proposed, the *need* outlined by the affirmative is the only *need* relevant to the debate. As in every policy debate a great many different types of need *might* be advanced for the proposal.

For example, one type of need that might be advanced by the affirmative was outlined at the beginning of this discussion, i.e. the need for an economically strong Canadian ally. However, other *needs* might be argued for economic union between Canada and the United States. For example, Canada needs a market for her tremendous supply of raw materials, and the United States is in great need of most of those self-same raw materials. Canada needs to import manufactured articles, and the United States needs to export these articles. Canada needs capital in order to develop her raw materials and her industries, and the United States needs to expand the use of its capital abroad. Canada needs industrial "know-how" which the United States is eager to supply. In short, the affirmative might advance a purely economic need unrelated to national defense or national survival.

Generally speaking the *need* outlined by the affirmative will be the one most likely to be corrected by the proposal, large enough in scope to justify the change, but no larger in scope than necessary. The greater the need outlined by the affirmative, the more the affirmative is forced to prove the proposal will remedy. On the other hand a relatively minor *need* may not justify a change, even though the change would remedy the situation. When any change is made many things are affected. If the *need* declared by the affirmative is minor in nature, it may be easy for the negative to show that other effects of the remedy are worse than the problem outlined by the affirmative, and that the proposal should not be adopted. Further, if the affirmative can outline a really vital *need* the affirmative may have an advantage of an audience eager for a solution, and psychologically ready to give favorable consideration of the remedy the affirmative proposes.

In the case of the proposal under discussion, it would seem wise for the affirmative to develop the need of national defense, security and survival, rather than declaring the need to be merely one of economic gain.

In outline form, then, the affirmative *need* might be developed from the following points:

1. In today's dangerous world both the United States and Canada desperately need an economically strong Canada. With a 4,000-mile unguarded common border, both countries could suffer if Canada remains weak.
2. In order to be economically strong, Canada needs expanding markets for raw materials and manufactured products. It also needs capital for development and industrial "know-how" which the United States is eager to supply.
3. The United States on the other hand needs most of the raw materials Canada has for export, needs a friendly place for foreign investment, and needs a market for manufactured goods which Canada must import.
4. Present tariffs seriously hamper the flow of these needed materials between the two countries, cause suspicion between the two governments, and hold back Canada's economic development.

Issue Number Two—The Remedy

The Affirmative Remedy

The *affirmative remedy*, proposed to overcome or perhaps answer the above outlined need, is the common market between the United States and Canada patterned after the European Common Market. The basic elements of the *remedy* are:

(1) Free trade between Canada and the United States, developed over a five- or ten-year period to include all items of trade and finance.

(2) An agreement to purchase the items only from the other country so long as the item is available for sale.

(3) Relatively high tariffs applying to all other countries, on those items available within the two countries.

(4) Inclusion of additional nations into this common market only when Canada and the United States are in agreement on the proposed member.

(5) Each country will be solely responsible for any subsidies it finds necessary for industries adversely affected by the change.

In developing its proposal, no doubt the affirmative would point out the weakness in nationalistic isolation inherent in tariffs in a world in which most nations are forming into economic blocs. The affirmative would probably point out that economic union between the United States and Canada can be accomplished much more easily and with fewer problems than confronted any of the other economic unions established by other countries. For example, Canada and the United States complement each other phenomenally from the standpoint of trade. Each needs most of the things the other has for sale. Further, both countries are alike in many important ways. Basically, they have the same origin and history. They have the same language excepting for minorities speaking French in Canada and Spanish in the United States. Their business viewpoints are similar. They have no traditional national rivalries such as faced the nations in the European Common Market or even in Communist trade blocs. They lie side by side. The existence of freedom in each country depends on the continued freedom of the other country. Their money is nearly identical. Conditions of labor, products used, standards of living, and interests in world affairs are remarkably similar. Nearly all of Canada's population lies within one hundred miles of the United States border, as does 80 per cent of her manufacturing and two thirds of her retail trade. Nowhere in the world today are two countries so similar and yet separated by such high tariff barriers.

The Negative Position

Generally speaking, the negative may adopt one of several positions. It may, for instance, deny that tariff barriers between the two countries hold back the development of Canada, any more than they have held back the development of the United States. Instead, the negative may argue, Canada's relative lack of development has resulted from continued ties with the Commonwealth within which free trade has existed throughout history. Or the negative may deny that a strong economic Canada is necessary to the survival of the two countries. The negative may argue that under present conditions the two countries through mutual military agreements form the strong deterrent to aggression that the affirmative desires. In support the negative might point out that the Communists have never attempted to make inroads in Canada, even though closer to Russia and even though the 4,000 miles of undefended border would make the winning of Canada desirable. Instead, the Soviets entered Cuba and are attempting to enter South American countries. In other words, the negative would belittle the affirmative *need,* pointing out that the real need lies to the south.

Or the negative might choose to base the major portion of its attack upon the proposal itself, pointing out that resulting disaster to our trade with South America and other free countries of the world would create conditions much worse than exist under a relatively weak Canada. Under such an attack the negative might offer a *counter proposal,* recommending a common market with Latin American nations and excluding Canada.

Or the negative might agree that Canada's military defenses need strengthening, but propose that it is wiser and cheaper to give Canada the needed money than it is to disrupt the American economy by abolishing our traditional and proved system of tariffs.

In short, the negative has three basic methods of attack open to it, any one of which or any combination of which may provide its *case.*

(1) It can destroy the affirmative *need,* thus showing that the proposed change is not necessary.

(2) It can agree to the existence of *need,* but show that the affirmative proposal will not solve that need without causing conditions worse than those it corrects.

(3) It can agree that a *need* exists, but offer a *new solution* that will cost less than the affirmative proposal. However, should the negative suggest a *counter proposal* or *new solution,* the negative automatically shoulders a *burden of proof* that would not exist without the counter proposal.

SUMMARY ON COMPARATIVE EVALUATION

From the foregoing discussion, it would appear that any intelligent evaluation of this proposition must of necessity take into consideration the major remedies that might be proposed, and attempt to study the comparative merits and demerits of each plan. Such comparative studies must be made by both affirmative and negative teams, if each is to be adequately prepared for the debate. Should the affirmative neglect such a study, it may find itself facing a counter proposal by the negative that the affirmative is unprepared to refute or attack. If the negative neglects such a study, it may miss the strongest possible attack open to it.

Analysis of the proposition by both teams includes a careful analysis of all possible alternatives, in so far as such alternatives seem to be reasonable ones. Analysis of the merits and demerits of every alternative proposal, then, is an essential and basic part of the analysis of the proposition.

SPEECH DEVELOPMENT

To illustrate in detail the process of organizing and developing a constructive speech, the major steps taken in the preparation of an actual debate speech are outlined below. The subject for debate was stated: *Resolved, That the United States Should Provide Immediate and Complete Medical Care to the Aged Through the Social Security System.* The speech used as illustration is that of the first affirmative speaker in a radio debate.

After analyzing the question and studying it, the first step in preparation was to choose the main points to be advanced. Below are listed the possible main points which the affirmative team found in answer to four questions which every affirmative team should ask itself.

Why do we need to change our present system of medical care for the aged?

1. Medical care for the aged in the United States is unsatisfactory.
2. The problem is being complicated by increasing numbers of retired and by rapidly rising medical costs.
3. The aged require the most expensive types of medical care.
4. In the near future the problem will become hopeless unless corrected.

Why will our proposal improve conditions?

5. It will eliminate the need for self medication and dependence on quacks.
6. It will encourage those needing medical care to obtain it early, rather than wait until it is too late.
7. It will spread the cost of medical care after retirement over the productive life-span of all.
8. It will guarantee medical care to the growing numbers of aged, regardless of rising costs.

What other advantages will our proposal bring?

9. It will benefit the medical profession.
10. It will raise the quality of medical service available to the aged.
11. It will eliminate tragic burdens on relatives of the aged.
12. It will wipe out the necessity of proof of pauperism now demanded under the Kerr-Mills bill.
13. It will relieve younger generations from planning for unknown medical problems following retirement by placing medical care on a sound insurance basis.
14. It will make use of existing machinery, thus reducing the cost of medical care on a per-patient basis.

Why are our opponents wrong in attacking our proposal?

15. Such a plan is the legitimate function of government.
16. It is entirely just and equitable.
17. It is entirely practical.
18. The cost would not be prohibitive.
19. No other system would be adequate.

Obviously, time would not permit an affirmative team to develop all of the above points satisfactorily in any one debate. Therefore, the affirmative examined each of the possible main points listed above in terms of likely acceptance by the radio audience, and selected from that list those which are shown below as the points which would be strongest. In many instances the points listed above were believed to be sub-points of more general statements to be used as *main points*.

Affirmative Main Points

I. The problem of medical care for the aged is fast reaching crisis proportions.
II. Our proposal will avert this crisis.
III. Our proposal will benefit all concerned.

You will note that *main point* I is a more general statement of points 2, 3, and 4 of the above list, with point 1 in that list being ignored as not important to this debate on radio. Also, *main point* II is a more general statement of points 5 through 8, relegating each of these to the sub-point category. *Main point* III is a more general statement of points 9 through 14, relegating each of these to sub-points. And points 15 through 19 were left out of the affirmative constructive case, leaving them for rebuttal should the negative team in the radio debate use arguments calling for these points.

The next step in preparing the case was to discover the sub-points which best supported each of the three main points selected, and to choose from all possible sub-points those which would be most convincing to the radio audience. When the sub-points were chosen and listed under the main points, the following case outline was the result:

CASE OUTLINE

(*Without evidence*)

I. The problem of medical care for the aged is fast reaching crisis proportions.
   A. The numbers of persons living past retirement are rapidly increasing.
   B. The cost of medical care is rising rapidly.
   C. The aged require the most expensive types of medical care at a time when income is lowest.
   D. Most retired persons can't pay for the medical care needed.
   E. In the near future the problem will become hopeless unless corrected.

II. Our proposal will avert this crisis.
   A. It will spread the cost of medical care after retirement over the entire productive life-span of all.
   B. It will eliminate the need for self-medication and dependence on quacks.
   C. It will encourage those needing medical care to obtain it early, rather than waiting until it is too late.
   D. It will guarantee care to the growing numbers of aged, regardless of advancing costs.

III. Our proposal will be beneficial to all.
    A. It will benefit the medical profession.
    B. It will raise the quality and quantity of medical service available to the aged.
    C. It will eliminate the tragic burden on relatives of the aged.
    D. It will wipe out the Kerr-Mills "pauper's oath."
    E. It will benefit all by eliminating one of the major worries in growing old.

The next step in preparation was to select the evidence which supported the various sub-points chosen, and to arrange that evidence in the best possible order, considering the demands of emphasis and variety. Since the evidence cards thus selected and arranged were placed in piles, it is impossible to reproduce them here.

Next, the debaters determined how much time should be allowed to each of the sub-points, and how much time would be needed for the first affirmative introduction and conclusion. They decided that the first two *main points* deserved enough emphasis and evidence to occupy all of the time the first affirmative would have after his introduction. The third *main point* was therefore to be covered by the second affirmative speaker, plus refutation of any counter proposal which the negative team might advance. The division gave the first two *main points* to the first speaker, and the third *main point* and refutation to the second affirmative speaker.

From this point on we shall follow the efforts of the first speaker only. He now inserted in his part of the case outline the evidence he had selected, and indicated in the right-hand margin the amount of time he planned to allow to the development of each sub-point. His outline now looked like this:

FIRST AFFIRMATIVE OUTLINE

Introduction   (1½ minutes)
Body

  I. The problem of medical care for the aged is fast reaching crisis proportions.
    A. The numbers of persons living past retirement are rapidly increasing.   (¾ minute)
       (Statistics—Senate Sub-Committee on Prob. of Aged)
       (Testimony—David Lester)

B. The cost of medical care is rising rapidly.   (¾ minute)
(Statistics—U.S. Social Security Admin.)
(Report—American Hospital Association)
(Example—common knowledge)
(Example—home town)

C. The aged require the most expensive types of medical care at a time when income is lowest.   (1¼ minutes)
(Statistics—National Health Survey)
(Examples—common knowledge)
(Testimony—Donald P. Kent)

D. Most retired persons can't pay for the medical care that they need.   (1¼ minutes)
(Testimony—Donald P. Kent)
(Statistics—Economic Status of Aged Survey)
(Testimony—Senator Hubert H. Humphrey)

E. In the near future the problem will become hopeless unless corrected.   (1 minute)
(Testimony—Senate Sub-Committee on Prob. of Aged)

II. Our proposal will avert this crisis.

A. It will spread the cost of medical care after retirement over the entire productive life-span of all.   (1 minute)
(Basic elements of Social Security proposal)
(Example—common knowledge)

B. It will eliminate the need for self-medication and dependence on quacks.   (1 minute)
(Statistics—Drug Topics Magazine)
(Example—radio and TV advertising)
(Statistics—Sponsor Magazine)

C. It will encourage those needing medical care to obtain it early rather than waiting until it is too late.   (1 minute)
(Example—American Medical Association)

D. It will guarantee care to the growing numbers of aged, regardless of advancing costs.   (1 minute)
(Illustration—common knowledge)
(Illustration—fire engine analogy)

Conclusion   (1½ minutes)

After inserting references to evidence in his portion of the outline, and after allotting time to each sub-point, the first affirmative speaker next worked out his introduction. He decided to use the *striking statement* type of approach because he believed it best for a radio audience that might otherwise tune out the debate. He decided to introduce the problem and expand upon it through a comparison with sick pets. And he decided to end his introduction with an appeal for unprejudiced consideration by the audience. The outline of his introduction appeared as it does below:

Introduction:

1. (Approach) One of every five persons ever born is alive today.
2. (Introduction of problem) We will hire veterinary care for a sick pet dog, but we ignore the needs of our senior citizens.
3. (Statement of proposal) We propose that all costs of dental, medical and nursing care for senior citizens be borne by the government through the Social Security system.
4. (Appeal) We must lay aside our prejudices and look at the facts.

With the outline of his speech complete and the introduction planned, the first affirmative speaker next planned his conclusion. He decided to conclude with two comparisons, followed by a restatement of his proposal. The outline of his conclusion appeared as follows:

Conclusion:

1. Our problem is parallel to that of education 100 years ago.
2. Like use of a marvelous fire engine, we should provide use by all with payment through taxation.
3. Summary statement.

The next step in preparation was to write the first draft of the speech. In this draft primary attention was given to organization. Naturally, the speech demanded a considerable amount of revision and of polishing to put it into final form. Parts of it were rewritten as many as six times; the whole speech was revised twice. Language used to introduce and conclude the various sub-points was considerably altered, as was some of the wording of those points. Even some of the evidence used to support the points was changed because some proved to be weaker than anticipated, and stronger evidence was discovered. Finally, the speech was timed to be certain that it was exactly 12 minutes long, the time assigned to the first speaker.

In revising, particular effort was made to secure *directness, interestingness, variety,* and *striking comparisons.* Because the debate was to be presented over the radio, effort was also made to use a simple vocabulary and relatively short sentences. Further, wording was changed to include *commands* to suppose or think as well as the word "you."

The final speech as presented appears below. The various parts of the introduction and conclusion have been numbered as they were numbered in the outline above. The paragraphs devoted to the sub-points are indicated by the alphabetical letter in parentheses, corresponding to similar letters found in the first affirmative outline.

FIRST AFFIRMATIVE SPEECH

(1) Ladies and Gentlemen, according to the best estimates of historians, fewer than 15 billion people have been born since Adam and Eve—15 billions since the beginning of the human race. But the astonishing thing is that according to the Statistical Office of the United Nations, there are *three* billion people living in the world today. This means that, because of population explosion and because people are living longer, one out of every five persons ever born is still alive.

(2) I mention this to point up the serious problem we are debating today—a problem that is rapidly reaching crisis proportions in the United States. In a country where few families would refuse veterinary help for a sick pet dog, hundreds of senior citizens are unable to pay for the medical care they need.

(3) This is why Miss Glenn and I propose *that the United States should provide immediate and complete medical care to the aged through the Social Security system.*

(4) Now I realize that this proposal has become a political issue, with President Kennedy favoring it and some doctors opposing it. But when a problem affecting all of us is so vital, we must forget political prejudices and look at the facts as they exist. And if you will examine the facts, you will discover that America must act—and act now—or the situation will become hopeless in the very near future.

(I,A) Very well, let us look at the facts. In the first place, the number of retired senior citizens is increasing rapidly. The Senate Sub-Committee on Problems of the Aged reported that back in 1900 there were 3 million persons over 65 in the United States. By 1957 the number had increased more than five times to a 17 million total. By 1990 the number is expected to double again to a figure between 30 and 40 million. And of more importance, 13 million of these will be over *seventy-five* years of age. The reason for this dramatic increase is two-fold: 1) the population explosion, and 2) people are living longer than they used to live. The report estimates that by 1999 the average

American will be living *twice* as long as the average American lived back in 1900. So, you see that the number of senior citizens is growing rapidly.

(I,B) Second, the cost of medical care is rising rapidly, too. The United States Social Security Administration reported that back in 1940 Americans spent less than $4 billion on medical care. But by 1962 the cost was eight times as great, for a total of $31.3 billion. And the American Hospital Association in 1962 announced that the average cost of one patient for one day in the United States was only $9.39 back in 1946, but by 1960 was $23.23. And the cost is increasing at a rate of over 8 per cent per year. You are all familiar with costs of medical care in your own home town. Take hospitals alone. In my town the cost for a single room has risen from $10 a day in 1940 to $25 a day in 1963. But I need not belabor the point. You all know that the costs of medical care are rising rapidly.

(I,C) Not only are the numbers of aged and the cost of medical care rising, but our senior citizens require the most expensive types of medical care—at the very time income is lowest, after retirement. The National Health Survey reported that those over 65 years of age are twice as likely as younger persons to be disabled, and twice as likely to have total annual incomes under $2,000. And what is worse, they are *three* times as likely as younger persons to be disabled for periods of over 3 months of the year. The survey showed that those over 75 *years of age* are twice as likely as others to have trouble with teeth and with general physical ailments; they are 6 times as likely to be paralyzed; 8 times as likely to be deaf; and 15 times as likely to be blind. All of the most expensive types of medical care are required by senior citizens much more often than others—nursing care, hospitalization, cancer, mental illness, diabetes, senility, heart problems, arthritis, pernicious anemia, liver ailments. You know the list as well as I do. Donald P. Kent of the United States Department of Health, Education and Welfare sums it up nicely by saying, "Age brings greater health problems. Persons past the age of 65 consume $2\frac{1}{2}$ to 3 times more medical services than those below that age. They are forced to go to the hospital more frequently, and they must stay there longer."

(I,D) And of course, with income down and in some cases nonexistent, most of the aged can't afford to pay for the medical care they really need. In 1962 Mr. Kent reported, "The median annual income of aged couples is about $2,500 a year, and among single individuals two thirds of the women and one fourth of the men have annual incomes of less than $1,000." Such incomes are hardly enough to provide the bare essentials of life, and nothing is left over for expensive medical care. The Economic Status of the Aged Survey discovered that 30 per cent of couples over 65 and 40 per cent of the single persons over 65 received *no* medical service at all in 1957. Further, only one in eight of all our senior citizens owned health insurance policies, and only 6 per cent of the others got free medical aid through the Kerr-Mills or other charity plans.

Senator Hubert H. Humphrey in a televised debate in 1961 summed it up by saying, "We know that three fifths of all our citizens 65 years of age or older have an income of less than $1,000 per year. And four fifths of our senior citizens have incomes of under $2,000 a year. We also know that persons 65 years of age and over have about twice as many days in the hospital per year, even with this inadequate income, as the rest of the general community. Their medical and hospital bills are about 90 per cent more, almost double that of the average person."

(I,E) In the very near future the problem will become hopeless unless we correct it soon. Consider this for a moment—in the near future the average person reaching retirement will still be supporting older parents, and in the not too distant future the retired will even be supporting grandparents still alive. The Senate Sub-Committee on Problems of the Aged reported, "For more than 80 per cent of today's Americans who are now 40 to 44 years of age, there will be not only the problems of preparation and provision for their *own* retirement years, but also the challenge of responsibility for older relatives."

When you look forward to 35 million retired persons within a few years, a large portion of whom will have retired *parents* still living, and with medical costs soaring, and with the aged needing the most expensive types of care, it becomes obvious that the problem of medical care for the aged is rapidly becoming hopeless. We must do something to solve this problem, and we must do it in the very near future.

(II,A) This is why Miss Glenn and I strongly urge that the federal government provide immediate and full medical, dental, and nursing care to all persons over 65 years of age through the Social Security system. We propose that an increase in the Social Security tax be collected from all workers to pay for the medical care of the aged—so that the entire project is placed on a sound insurance basis.

If this is done, everyone concerned will benefit—the doctors, the aged, and the younger workers. First, the medical profession itself will benefit. No longer will it be asked to provide free service to older people unable to pay for it. No longer will doctors have uncollected bills from senior citizens. No longer will doctors find patients waiting until too late to seek medical care, because paying for that care will no longer be a problem. So first of all, it is obvious that the doctors will profit.

(II,B) Second, the aged will benefit through elimination of self-medication and dependence on quacks. The professional drug magazine, *Drug Topics,* tells us that civilians spend twice as much for non-prescribed drugs and health aids at our drug stores, as they do for drugs prescribed by doctors each year. And the pharmaceutical industry appeals to us daily over radio and TV to buy unprescribed drugs. *Sponsor Magazine* reports that between 1952 and 1960 drug companies increased TV advertising over twice as much as did any other industry. And all of this advertising is directed at the people to encourage self-medication.

When our proposal is adopted, the finest of medical care and advice will be available to the aged free of charge. It is obvious that the aged will no longer need to depend on self-medication or on quacks who promise cheap cure.

(II,C) Further, our proposal will encourage senior citizens to go to the doctor when illness first occurs, rather than waiting until it is too late because of fear of large medical bills. The American Medical Association yearly spends vast sums in urging people to see their doctor at the first sign of trouble, rather than wait. You hear their pleas on dentistry, cancer, heart disease, flu, and many other ailments. One of the biggest complaints of the medical profession has been that too many people put off going to the doctor or dentist until the situation is hopeless. Hundreds of thousands may be saved each year under our proposal because they will see their doctor earlier.

(II,D) Finally, our proposal will *guarantee* medical care to the growing numbers of aged, regardless of what individual cases may cost. Whether it's merely tranquilizers or whether it's a costly operation and nursing care, it will always be available without cost to the patient. Already we have recognized the wisdom of guaranteeing food and shelter for the aged by adopting the Social Security retirement plan. It is just as wise to provide for medical care after retirement. For sickness in old age is inevitable—one day it will come. The only way we can guarantee that medical care will be available to all, regardless of savings or income, is through some central and compulsory medical insurance plan that spreads the cost of old-age medication over all of the productive years of our lives. This will guarantee medical care to all senior citizens, regardless of what is needed or how much it costs.

(1) Ladies and Gentlemen, in conclusion let me point out that today we face the problem of medical care for the aged, exactly as our forefathers faced the problem of education of the young 100 years ago. They saw an expanding population. They saw fewer dying at birth. They saw that it would be impossible to expect adequate education for all under a system of private schools. Therefore, our forefathers established a system of *public* schools in which every child was guaranteed education through high school free of charge. Our forefathers were wise.

(2) Today we face the problem of adequate medical care for the aged. We cannot hope to solve it by expecting each to pay as he becomes sick. With the finest medical facilities and the finest doctors

in the world, we cannot hope to solve our problem on a pay-when-ill basis. Even in the case of fire protection that is infrequently needed, we long ago abolished the pay-as-used plan. The fire engine is on call to all, free of charge, and paid for by all through taxation. The same should be true of medical care for the aged. We should no longer expect these unemployed people to pay for medical service as they need it. It should be provided free of charge, and should be paid for by a compulsory tax spread over the entire productive period of every person's life.

(3) Therefore, Miss Glenn and I urge you to agree with us that the United States should provide immediate and complete medical care to the aged through the Social Security system.

APPENDIX 5

RULES IN DEBATE [18]

Although the regulations for formal interschool contest debates vary somewhat in the several states, the following are reasonably typical of the high school rules in debate.

Individual Eligibility Rules
For High Schools

The following rules apply to each student who represents his school in any interschool activity. Additional regulations that apply to students engaging in athletics, music, speech or other activities may be found in sections of the rules devoted exclusively to individual activities.

Bona Fide Student Rule—He shall be a bona fide undergraduate member of his high school in good standing.

Exception: Elementary students of the same school system, or of an elementary school that lies wholly within an organized high school district, may participate in bands, orchestras, choruses or glee clubs representing member high schools without affecting their eligibility after they become high school students. Grade school students are not eligible to represent a high school in any other type of activity.

Interpretations

1. An undergraduate student is one who has completed less than seventeen units of high school credit, or has not completed some course to which no exception is made, or has not been granted a diploma of graduation from his high school.

2. A student who is under penalty of suspension or whose character or conduct brings discredit to himself and his school is not in good standing.

3. A student who is enrolled in three or more subjects of the ninth grade or above, even though he may be carrying subjects of lower grade also, is classified as a high school student.

4. In determining subjects of unit weight, physical education, military drill or any extra-curricular activity shall not count; except that

[18] *The Kansas State High School Activities Association Handbook, 1962-1963*, Published by the Board of Directors, Topeka, Kansas, p 18-22 and 37-42. Reprinted by permission.

combination courses in health, hygiene and physical education that require at least half the classtime to be spent in academic classwork, may be considered subjects of unit weight, provided such courses are approved by the State Department of Public Instruction.

5. No make-up work is permitted after the close of the semester for the purpose of becoming eligible. A "condition" or an "incomplete" shall count as a failure.

Scholarship Rule—He shall have an average of passing grades in at least three subjects of unit weight from the beginning of the semester to the close of the week immediately preceding the activity in which he participates.

He shall have passed in at least three subjects of unit weight at the end of the previous semester, or the last semester of his attendance.

Interpretations

1. Any subject taken one full period daily, five times a week, for which one credit toward graduation is given each semester, is considered as one of the "three subjects of unit weight" required for eligibility. Subjects for which two units of credit are awarded toward graduation shall be counted as two subjects of unit weight toward eligibilty.

NOTE: a student's eligibilty does not depend upon his grades from day to day or week to week, but upon his average grades from the beginning of the semester to the close of the week prior to his participation.

2. If a student is eligible the closing day of one week he is entitled to be certified for all activities beginning Monday of the following week. If he is ineligible at the close of the week, he may not participate the following week. If he makes up work during the week, so that his grades are passing at the close of the week, he is not eligible until Monday of the following week.

3. If a student drops out of school four weeks or less before the close of the semester and has completed a sufficient amount of work to give him a semester's credit, without relying upon the work that is incomplete, he may be certified as eligible the following semester, as far as his grades are concerned.

Age Rule—Any student who reaches the age of nineteen on or before September 1, shall be ineligible for participation in interscholastic activities. Any student who reaches the age of nineteen after September 1, but on or before January 1, shall be eligible for interscholastic participation up to and including December 31, but shall be ineligible thereafter. Any student who reaches the age of nineteen after January 1, shall be eligible for the balance of the school year.

Enrollment Rule—He shall have been regularly enrolled and in attendance at some school not later than Monday of the fourth week of the semester in which he participates.

Interpretation

1. A student who attends one class after enrolling is considered in attendance. Attending a class the opening day of school which is called for the purpose of organization or class assignment, counts as attendance. If a student transfers to a new school, enrolls and attends one class, as indicated above, and then goes back to the school formerly attended, he may not become eligible until after he has attended eighteen weeks, in accordance with provisions of the transfer rule.

Eight-Semester Rule—He shall not be eligible if he has attended high school eight semesters. Attendance for fifteen days, or participation in an interschool activity, shall constitute a semester's attendance. The last two semesters of possible eligibility must be consecutive.

NOTE: Students in three-year schools shall be limited to six semesters and those in two-year schools to four. Under no circumstances shall a student be eligible for interschool activities more than eight semesters in the ninth, tenth, eleventh and twelfth grades.

Interpretations

1. Question—If a student attends school five days, is absent three days, attends another seven days and then drops out, is he charged with a semester's attendance?
Answer—Yes. The time is counted from the first day of his attendance until he ceases to attend school.

2. Protection under the provisions of the fifteen-day attendance rule applies only to those students who drop out of school altogether before attending fifteen days. It does not apply to students who transfer to another school and continue their attendance.

Transfer Rule—A student may not transfer from one secondary school to another and become eligible to participate in any interschool activities until after he has been in attendance eighteen weeks, unless his parents, or legal guardian in case neither parent is living, actually change their residence and move to the vicinity of the school to which the student transfers, where a bona fide and permanent home is established.

In transferring from one secondary school to another each student shall be required to present a certificate of transfer showing his scholastic standing, his length of school attendance, and a record of his participation in interschool activities.

The fundamental principle of the transfer rule requires attendance of eighteen weeks before a pupil may participate, the exception being that a pupil may continue to reside with his parents after they have moved and retain his eligibility.

Exceptions

a. Students who transfer to private boarding schools, ALL of whose students reside on the campus, may become eligible immediately upon enrolling; provided, they have not participated in that particular activity prior to changing schools, and provided further that a record of all transfer students is filed in advance with the K.S.H.S.A.A.

b. Students who complete the course of a high school that does not offer a full four-year course, may transfer to a secondary school where they may continue their education and become eligible immediately.

c. In cities having more than one public high school where the Board of Education has designated one to serve all students who enroll in a particular course such as vocational education, students from the entire city may enroll in the special course and be eligible immediately. The school must offer a complete schedule of subjects for the entire three years above the ninth grade. Students must enroll and enter school at the opening of the first semester following the completion of their junior high courses.

d. Any newly-married high school girl who changes schools in order to live with her husband shall become eligible immediately.

e. Any student transferring from a closed or discontinued school shall be eligible for participation in interschool activities immediately upon enrollment in another school, provided he attends a school in the vicinity of his home close enough so that he continues to reside at home. If difficulties are involved, the situation may be presented to the Executive Board, which shall render a decision based on the merits of the case.

f. Any student who transfers to another school because of an official change in school district boundaries shall be eligible upon enrollment, provided transfer is made to the school into which district his home has been annexed, and provided enrollment in such school is not later than the opening of the school year following the official change of school boundaries.

g. Any student who transfers from a non-accredited school to one accredited by the State Department of Public Instruction shall be eligible upon enrollment, provided he attends school in the vicinity of his home and is close enough so that he continues to reside at home. Such transfers must be made within ten days after his former school has been officially declared non-accredited, or at the opening of the next semester or school year. A student who transfers to another school because there is doubt that his school will be accredited, may not become eligible after enrolling in another school until his former school has been officially denied accreditation, or for eighteen weeks. If difficulties are involved, the situation may be presented to the Executive Board for a decision.

Interpretations

1. A graduate of a three-year junior high school located in a district in which there is also a senior high school may not transfer to a high school outside the district and become eligible until after attending eighteen weeks, unless there is an accompanying move on the part of his parents or legal guardian.

2. Guardianship while either parent is living is not recognized and only those appointed by the courts to a full personal and estate guardianship are recognized. Following the death of a student's last surviving parent, he may transfer immediately to the home of the legal guardian and become eligible. He may not transfer to another school and become eligible at once, unless the legal guardian also moves and establishes a permanent home.

The Executive Board may sanction the eligibility of students who move with families upon whom they have been continuously dependent and with whom they have made their homes. ("Families upon whom they have been continuously dependent," in general, are those with whom the students have made their homes for at least one year.)

3. If a student's parents move to the vicinity of a new school and he elects to remain at the school in which he has been enrolled, he may do so without affecting his eligibility.

If the parents move during the school year and the student wishes to transfer to the school in the vicinity of the new permanent residence of the parents, he may become eligible immediately, only under the following conditions:

a. If he transfers within ten days of the time his parents move he becomes eligible at once, as far as the transfer rule is concerned.

b. If he remains until the close of the current semester, or until the close of the school year, he may become eligible immediately upon enrolling and attending classes in the new school.

4. If a student attends school away from home and then transfers to his home school, he shall not become eligible until after he has attended one full semester, or eighteen weeks. However, if a student has lived and attended school away from home for at least one school year, he shall be eligible for interschool activities upon his return home, provided he meets all other general eligibility requirements. Questionable cases must be submitted to the Executive Board for a decision. (See exception for foreign exchange students in item 6)

5. If a student changes schools and his parents change their residence, it is necessary for him to attend the high school in the vicinity of the residence of his parents. If he attends some other high school he does not become eligible until after he has attended eighteen weeks. The term "vicinity" shall be interpreted by the Executive Board and any questionable case must be presented for a decision.

6. A student who transfers from one school to another before or without regard to a move by his parents, does not become eligible if the parents move later for the purpose of making him eligible. If the move was contemplated and the change in schools made for some justifiable reason such as to start a new semester, a student may be declared eligible as soon as the new family home has been established. Information on each individual case must be submitted to the Executive Board for a decision.

The Executive Board may waive provisions of the transfer rule in order to permit students from foreign countries and those returning to their home school from a foreign country to participate, provided they are sponsored by recognized agencies and applications are filed with the Executive Secretary before their participation.

7. Students who must attend a semester to gain eligibility may not participate in interschool activities until after they have attended classes in the new semester. Those who must attend eighteen weeks to become eligible may not participate until after they have attended classes in the nineteenth week.

8. A student who is "on his own" and not dependent upon his parents or guardian for a home, and who transfers from one school to another, is required to attend a full semester, or eighteen weeks before becoming eligible.

Undue Influence—The use of undue influence by any person or persons to secure or retain a student or to secure or retain one or both of the parents or guardians of a student as residents, shall cause the student to become ineligible for high school activities for a period subject to the determination of the Executive Board and shall jeopardize the standing of the high school in the Association.

Hardship Rule—A high school student who, because of unavoidable circumstances such as broken home conditions, death of parents or guardian, abandonment or other exceptional or emergency reasons, finds it necessary to change high schools in order to have a home, may be declared eligible by the Executive Board, provided the principal of each high school involved files a statement with the Executive Board that the change was necessary and that no undue influence was attached to the case in any way. If the transfer of any student from one school to another is approved by the Executive Board under the foregoing circumstances, he shall not be eligible for interscholastic activities until after he has been in attendance for a period of twenty school days.

NOTE: The hardship rule applies only to transfer students and does not apply to cases involving students who, because of illness or other emergency, are forced to drop out of school for a period of time.

To be declared eligible under the hardship rule, a student must meet all general eligibility requirements such as having passed in three subjects of unit weight, etc.

Anti-Fraternity Rule—He shall not be a member of any fraternity or other organization prohibited by law or by the rules of the Association.

A school fraternity is any organization composed wholly or in part of students which seeks to perpetuate itself by taking in additional members from the students enrolled in the school on the basis of the decision of its membership, rather than upon the free choice of any student who is qualified by the rules of the school to fill the special aims of the organization.

NOTE: Student organizations whose meetings are not open to attendance by faculty members do not meet the requirements of the Association.

Ineligibilty for violation of the rules against membership in a fraternity may be removed only by action of the Executive Board. . . .

Rules for Forensics and Dramatics
Individual Eligibility

The provisions of the Eligibility Rules shall apply to all pupils who participate in interschool debate and forensic activities. In addition the following rules shall also apply:

Students shall not attend any special summer sessions which provide training in debate based on the subject to be used in the Association debate tournaments.

Administration and Approval of Events

Section 1. All forensic activities, including debate, extempore speaking, one-act plays and such additional activities or festivals as may be subsequently approved by the Board of Directors, must be approved by the Executive Board.

Section 2. No school may be represented in any tournament or festival in debate, extempore speaking, drama, or other speech activities, whether in Kansas or outside the state, unless it has been approved by the Executive Board. There shall be no ranking for positions in a district or state speech festival.

Section 3. No member school shall be permitted to be represented in a national debate, speech or drama tournament or contest unless approved by the Executive Board.

Awards

The issuance of awards to students for participation in speech activities shall be governed by the same general regulations as those for participation in athletics. The Executive Board may sanction awards other than felt or chenille school letters, provided their cost does not exceed that of the school letters.

Debate Tournament Regulations

Section 1. For participation in district and state tournaments, all schools shall be divided into three classes, AA, A, and B. However, any school may elect to go into a class composed of schools of higher enrollments, but may not elect to enter a class of schools with smaller enrollments.

Section 2. Entry Fees: An annual participation fee for each school represented in debate activities shall be set by the Executive Board.

Section 3. Enrollment: Entry blanks for debate tournaments shall be mailed to all member schools before September 20. All schools desiring to enter debate activities shall return the entry blanks, accompanied by the fee, to the K.S.H.S.A.A. on or before October 1.

Section 4. The Executive Board shall arrange district debate tournaments to be held as qualifying meets for state championship tournaments in each class. The state championship tournaments shall be held according to regulations provided by the Executive Board.

Section 5. Calendar: The state debate tournaments shall be held at times and places designated by the Executive Board. All district tournaments shall be held between January 20 and the week of the state tournament, the exact time and place to be designated by the Executive Board.

Section 6. All managers shall send to Association headquarters a complete report of the results of the tournaments.

Section 7. Tournament Expenses: Local managers appointed by the K.S.H.S.A.A. shall conduct the district debate tournaments and arrange for judges and all other necessary services. Itemized statements of expenses shall be submited to the Executive Secretary, who shall issue checks upon the funds of the Association to cover the expenses of the judges and other items necessary for the administration of the tournaments.

Invitational Tournaments

Section 1. All invitational debate tournaments (including those out of state) and the dates on which they are to be held shall be submitted to the Executive Board for approval.

Section 2. No student may represent his high school in more than five tournaments, including league and out-of-state tournaments. Travel distance on tournaments outside the state shall not exceed 300 miles for the round trip. No student shall participate in more than one out-of-state tournament during a school year. No coach of a team entered in an invitational tournament may serve as a judge in more than forty per cent (40%) of the rounds.

Section 3. All tournament managers shall send to Association headquarters a complete report of the tournament results.

Debate Participation Regulations

Section 1. In the district and state tournaments each team shall consist of four debaters, two representing the affirmative and two the negative. Before the district or state tournaments begin, the coach of each team shall designate the two members of his four-speaker team to debate the affirmative, and the two to debate the negative. They shall not be changed during the tournament. In other words, they shall debate only that side of the question which their coach has designated. A maximum of two alternates may be carried on the squad but they may be used only as substitutes. A substitute may replace any member of the team between different rounds of the tournament, but not more than one substitute may be used in any one round. The alternates must always be used as substitutes and at least three of the four members of the originally designated team of four must participate in each round.

Section 2. At all contests the debaters shall be separated from the audience and shall receive no coaching while the debate is in progress.

Section 3. The time and order of speeches shall be as follows and no part of any one speaker's time shall be given to another:

Main	Rebuttal
Affirmative, 10 minutes	Negative, 5 minutes
Negative, 10 minutes	Affirmative, 5 minutes
Affirmative, 10 minutes	Negative, 5 minutes
Negative, 10 minutes	Affirmative, 5 minutes

Section 4. Speakers shall be entitled to such warning signals as they shall direct.

Section 5. The timekeeper shall be appointed by the tournament manager and the presiding officer shall strictly enforce time rules.

Section 6. There shall be no cheering while any debater is speaking. Time so consumed by a speaker's friends shall be deducted from the time allowed the speaker. The presiding officer shall make this announcement and strictly enforce it.

Section 7. In all district tournaments the round robin type of schedule shall be arranged, with each school meeting every other school in its class on both sides of the question. Judges shall be appointed by the local managers, with the approval of the Executive Board.

Section 8. In the state championship tournaments the round robin type of schedule shall be arranged, with each school meeting every other school in its class on both sides of the question. Semifinal and final rounds may be held in state championship tournaments.

Section 9. Instruction to Judges: A copy of the following instructions shall be given to each judge: The judges, who shall sit apart during the debate, shall judge the contest as a debate voting "Affirmative" or "Negative" without consultation, on the merits of the debate, irrespective of the merits of the question. In deciding which team has done the more effective debating, the judges shall take into consideration thought and delivery in both main and rebuttal speeches. Each judge shall sign and seal his vote and deliver it to a teller appointed by the tournament director. Rebuttal speeches shall be directed against the argument of the opposing speakers. If, in the opinion of the judges, the rebuttal speeches seem to be memorized and given without specific reference to the argument of the opponents, the judges shall discount the argument accordingly.

In all debates each judge, in addition to voting for either the affirmative or negative team, shall rank each of the speakers in order of merit, giving a rank of "one" to the speaker he considers best, and giving no two speakers the same rank.

Section 10. Decisions: In all tournaments conducted on the round robin plan, if two or more schools shall tie in the highest number of decisions won, the school receiving the votes of the greatest number of judges shall be declared the winner; and in case of a tie in judges' ballots for all rounds of the tournament, the school having the lowest total of speaker rankings for all its debaters shall be declared the winner. In any tournament in which a single judge is used for some debates and three judges for others, the total of judges' ballots shall not be considered, but the decision, in case of a tie between two or more schools, shall be determined on the basis of the lowest total rankings of the individual debaters.

If any school refuses to accept a decision rendered by the Executive Board, it automatically defaults and forfeits its privilege of continuing in either the district or state tournaments.

Section 11. Disqualification: Any pupil in a member high school shall be ineligible for participation in either the district or state tournament during the ensuing year if he attends a special summer session which provides training in debate based on the question to be used in the tournaments that year.

Section 12. Scouting: Audiences may attend all speech events. Spectators may follow their own teams, but scouting shall not be allowed. It is not permissible for anyone to attend a debate in which his school is not represented.

Section 13. Plagiarizing: It shall be considered dishonorable for any debater in any manner to plagiarize in his speech. When ample evidence has been presented to the district director of a violation of either of these points of etiquette, he may request the judges to make proper allowance for this when serving on any debate in which the offending student or students participate during the remainder of the tournament.

Section 14. Selection of Question: The question for debate shall be approved by the Executive Board and published in the *Activities Journal* not later than the May issue.

Speech and Drama Regulations

Section 1. The Executive Board shall have authority to sanction speech and drama festivals and tournaments and formulate regulations for their administration.

Section 2. In events where schools participate according to classes, the classification shall be the same as for debate.

Section 3. Participants in all district and state speech and drama events, with the exception of debate, shall be rated according to a four-point scale, those in the highest class of performers to receive First Division ratings. The others shall be given Second Division, Third Division, or Fourth Division ratings in keeping with the decisions of the judges.

Section 4. Each school shall be limited to a maximum number of entries in each individual event.

Section 5. Each pupil may represent his school in not more than two events, whether as an individual performer or as a member of a one-act play cast. No pupil may enter twice in the same event.

Section 6. The state shall be divided into a convenient number of districts and the Association shall sponsor speech and drama festivals in those districts, the time and place of each to be determined by the Executive Board.

Section 7. State speech and drama festivals shall be held at a time and place designated by the Executive Board. Only those participants receiving a First Division rating in the district festivals shall be eligible to enter.

Section 8. Uniform entry fees as set by the Executive Board shall be charged for each participant in both the district and state speech and drama festivals.

Extempore Speech

Section 1. In all the extempore speech events sponsored by the Association the following rules shall apply:

a. There shall be one subject for extempore speech, which shall be approved by the forensic committee and Executive Board.

b. Specific sub-topics approved by the Executive Board shall be prepared for the district and state festivals.

c. The extemporaneous speech topics shall be selected from a list of magazines dating from December 1 to the earliest March issues, the list of magazines to be published in the *Activities Journal* early in the fall.

d. A participant shall draw three sub-topics before he is scheduled to speak. After studying the topics, he shall select one and then return all topics for drawing by other speakers.

e. The speakers shall remain in one or more rooms under neutral supervision after they have drawn their topics. During this period they shall not be permitted to confer with anyone. They may consult both printed matter and prepared notes or manuscripts which they have brought with them.

f. During the speech, brief notes may be used, but they must be reduced to what can be written on a single three-by-five-inch card. The chairman is expected to enforce this rule, with the penalty of disqualification for the use of more copious notes.

g. Participants shall be disqualified for a First Division rating if they speak less than five minutes or more than seven minutes. A participant may complete his sentence after time is called.

Section 2. "The extemporaneous speech is a spontaneous, original oral expression of ideas on a given subject about which the speaker has had previous knowledge, preparation and planning. The speech is never memorized."

Informative Speech

Section 1. Students participating in the district or state informative speech contests shall select their own subjects.

a. Speeches shall not be more than seven minutes in length. Participants shall be disqualified for a First Division rating if they exceed the seven-minute time limit. A participant may complete his sentence after time is called.

b. Brief notes on a three-by-five-inch card are permissible. Charts, displays, maps, graphs, or any other materials which could be used for demonstration purposes are not permissible.

c. Informative speeches shall be the original work of the student.

Section 2. An informative speech is one which provides a learning experience for the listener by instructing or giving new information in an interesting manner.

One-Act Plays

Section 1. The Executive Board shall approve and publish criteria to be used in selecting plays for presentation at the district and state speech and drama festivals.

a. Plays which receive First Division ratings for two consecutive years in the state festivals shall not be presented for a period of one year.

b. One-act plays exceeding thirty minutes performance time shall be disqualified.

c. Fifteen minutes shall be allowed by district and state festival managers between each one-act play. This shall be interpreted to mean that the stage shall be cleared by one cast and set by the second cast within the fifteen-minute period.

d. All plays shall be presented before neutral drapes.

e. Participating schools shall be sent a list showing the stage properties and lighting effects which will be available at each festival center. If additional properties or lighting effects are desired, they shall be provided by the producing group in the time allotted.

Duet Acting

Section 1. Schools may choose duet acting in place of a one-act play or two individual readings. A school may have a maximum of three entries in duet acting, each to be presented in place of a one-act play or two individual readings.

Oratory

Section 1. Original orations shall not be more than ten minutes in length.

a. A participant shall be disqualified for a First Division rating if his oration exceeds ten minutes. He shall be allowed to complete his sentence after time is called.

Section 2. Original orations shall be memorized and given without notes.

Section 3. An original oration shall be defined as a memorized original persuasive speech with a unique approach to a universal theme, demonstrating outstanding qualities of logic, organization, language, and delivery, and rising above the commonplace in its impact.

Readings

Section 1. Reading selections shall not be classified, but may be either humorous or dramatic, and shall not be more than ten minutes in length.

a. Participants shall be disqualified for a First Division rating if their reading exceeds ten minutes. The participant shall be allowed to complete his sentence after time is called.

Section 2. Reading shall be memorized and given without notes.

Section 3. Stage properties or costumes shall be prohibited with the exception of a chair.

Oral Interpretation

Section 1. Oral Interpretation of Poetry:

a. A participant shall give a brief introduction to his selection or selections.

b. He shall read one or more selections of poetry from the printed manuscript.

c. Selections shall be made by the student and prepared before the festival.

d. The one or more poems chosen by the participant shall not exceed seven minutes. He may complete his sentence after time is called. A participant shall be disqualified for a First Division rating if he exceeds the time limit.

Section 2. Oral Interpretation of Prose:

a. Prose selections shall not be known to speech instructors or to participants.

b. Prose selections shall be taken from standard works of literature.

c. The participant shall draw two of the three prepared selections, and shall have four minutes to choose one of the manuscripts which he shall use for the festival.

d. The participant shall retire to an assigned room for twenty minutes and, without assistance, prepare the selection and an introduction.

(1) A dictionary shall be provided for each student.

e. Oral interpretation of prose shall be divided into three sections for each participant.

(1) He shall give a one-minute introduction of the selection without notes.

(2) He shall read for four minutes from the prepared selection, which he has studied.

(3) He shall be instructed to draw one selection from a set of two and to read immediately upon drawing for two minutes.

f. Timekeepers shall be provided for the oral interpretation of prose. A warning and final signal shall be given for the one-minute introduction; for the four-minute prepared selection; and for the two-minute impromptu reading.

INDEX